McDougal Littell
LITERATURE

InterActive
READER & WRITER
for Critical Analysis

Grade 6

McDougal Littell
EVANSTON, ILLINOIS · BOSTON · DALLAS

COVER

Detail of *Tree Goddess* (1994), Jerry N. Uelsmann. © Jerry N. Uelsmann.

ISBN 13: 978-0-618-92120-1   ISBN 10: 0-618-92120-6

Printed in the United States of America.

15–0982–15

4500527364

SENIOR PROGRAM CONSULTANTS

Janet Allen
Internationally-known Reading and Literacy Specialist

Arthur N. Applebee
Leading Professor, School of Education, University of Albany, State University of New York; Director of the Center on English Learning and Achievement

Jim Burke
Lecturer, Author, English Teacher, Burlingame, California

Douglas Carnine
Professor of Education, University of Oregon

Yvette Jackson
Executive Director, National Urban Alliance for Effective Education

Robert Jiménez
Professor of Language, Literacy, and Culture, Vanderbilt University

Judith A. Langer
Distinguished Professor, University of Albany, State University of New York; Director of the Center on English Learning and Achievement; Director of the Albany Institute for Research in Education

Robert J. Marzano
Senior Scholar, Mid-Continent Research for Education and Learning (McREL), Denver, Colorado

Donna M. Ogle
Professor of Reading and Language, National-Louis University, Chicago, Illinois; Past President, International Reading Association

Carol Booth Olson
Senior Lecturer, Department of Education, University of California , Irvine

Carol Ann Tomlinson
Professor of Educational Research, Foundations, and Policy, University of Virginia; Co-Director of the University's Institutes on Academic Diversity

ENGLISH LEARNER SPECIALISTS

Mary Lou McCloskey
Past President, TESOL; Director of Teacher Development and Curriculum Design for Educo, Atlanta, Georgia

Lydia Stack
Past President, TESOL; International ESL Consultant

CURRICULUM SPECIALIST

William L. McBride
Nationally-known Speaker, Educator, and Author

TABLE OF CONTENTS

The InterActive Reader & Writer

The InterActive Reader & Writer is a literature book to mark on, write in, and make your own. As you will see, this book helps you become an active reader. It also helps you become a better writer.

An Easy-to-Carry Literature Text

This book won't weigh you down. It fits as comfortably in your hand as it can in your backpack. Yet it is packed with great things to read and do:

- Important works of literature by leading authors
- A rich selection of nonfiction texts—Web pages, magazine articles, and more
- A variety of genres—such as short stories, biographies, speeches, poems, and myths
- Activities that will help you think more deeply about yourself and the world beyond

Becoming a Critical Reader

Most people get more out of a work of literature the second time they read it. To help you get the most out of the literature in *The InterActive Reader & Writer*, you'll read each core literary work two times.

- You'll read it once on your own, marking the text as you choose.
- You'll read it a second time, using the notes in the margins to help you think critically about the text.

BEFORE READING ACTIVITIES

Big Question The first activity in each unit gets you thinking about a real-life question that the literature addresses.

Learn the Terms A brief skill lesson helps you understand the most important features of the literature and teaches terms you will need in order to talk and write about the selection. Additional skills terms increase your ability to think critically about literature.

DURING READING ACTIVITIES

A wide variety of side column notes challenges you to dig deeply into each selection.

VOCABULARY SUPPORT

Words to Know Important words are underlined and boldfaced in blue. Their definitions appear nearby in the side column.

Specialized Vocabulary Vocabulary notes in nonfiction selections explain special words used in certain careers or fields of study.

TEST PREPARATION

No one likes tests, but everyone likes doing well on them. *The Interactive Reader & Writer* will help you become a better test-taker.

TestSmart TestSmart questions appear right next to the text you are reading. These give you an opportunity to practice answering multiple-choice questions about literature—without worrying about being scored!

Test Tips You'll be given helpful strategies to use when answering test questions.

Assessment Practice Multiple-choice test items help you focus on how well you've read the texts provided. They also help you prepare for real tests.

Written Responses Many tests ask you to write one or more paragraphs about a reading passage. This book gives you the opportunity to write about each selection you read. A **Test-Taker's Toolkit** shows you how to develop each written response, step-by-step.

NONFICTION READING

Each main literature selection in *The InterActive Reader & Writer* is paired with one or two nonfiction selections that are related in some way to the literature. You will learn many different strategies for getting the most out of the nonfiction you read. These strategies will help you on tests, in other classes, and in the world outside of school. For example, you will learn how to:

- Use text features to preview a text
- Identify main ideas and details
- Identify an author's purpose for writing
- Understand how ideas are organized

LINKS TO

McDougal Littell Literature

If you are using *McDougal Littell Literature,* you will find the *InterActive Reader & Writer* to be the perfect companion. *The InterActive Reader & Writer* helps you read certain core selections from *McDougal Littell Literature* more carefully and in greater depth.

Read on to learn more!

User's Guide

The InterActive Reader & Writer for Critical Analysis has an easy-to-follow organization, as shown by these sample pages from the short story "Nadia the Willful" by Sue Alexander.

1. Anchor Selection
Each unit is made up of a cluster of readings. The main literature selection is called the **anchor selection.** You will read this first.

2. Related Nonfiction
The titles in smaller type are the **Related Nonfiction** pieces. As you preview each unit, read the titles and think about how all the readings might be related.

UNIT 3
UNDERSTANDING THEME

Nadia the Willful **1**
BY SUE ALEXANDER

RELATED NONFICTION
Sahara

Bedouins: The Desert's **2**
Nomadic Hosts

48

Can MEMORIES ③
keep the past alive?

Memories are how we hold on to people we have known, places we have been, and things we have done. As time goes by, those memories can fade unless we find ways to keep them fresh. In "Nadia the Willful," a character takes action to protect precious memories.

SKETCH IT Think about a happy or important event you want to remember. It might be a birthday, a holiday, or a day spent with friends. In the notebook shown, plan a scrapbook entry for your memory. Be sure to label the items you plan to include, such as photos, postcards, or other souvenirs.

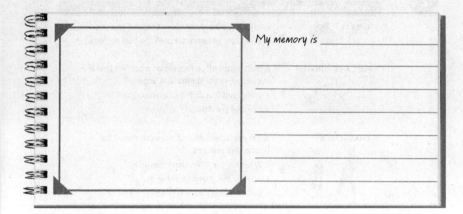

My memory is _____

ASSESSMENT GOALS ④

By the end of this lesson, you will be able to . . .
- analyze theme in a work of fiction
- apply critical thinking skills to analyze text
- identify main ideas and details in nonfiction texts
- analyze a writing prompt and plan a description

③ **Big Question**
Each unit begins with an activity that gets you thinking about a real-life question that the literature addresses. Sometimes you'll work in a group to complete this activity. After reading, you'll return to this question. Don't be surprised if you have a different perspective.

④ **Assessment Goals**
This box sums up the unit's main learning goals. The first goal names the unit's **literature skill.** The second goal is your overall **reading objective.** The third goal names the skill you'll be learning with the **nonfiction** selections. The last goal names the **writing activity** you'll complete at the end of the unit.

1 **Learn the Terms: Academic Vocabulary**
This page presents a brief, easy-to-understand lesson that introduces important terms and explains what to look for in the literature you read.

2 You will come back to these academic terms several times during the unit. For example, in Unit 3 you will come across the terms *theme, conflict, characters,* and others many times in the side notes of the main selection.

3 **Additional Terms for Critical Analysis**
Additional terms for critical analysis will challenge you to think and write about the literature even more deeply.

1

Theme

"Nadia the Willful" is a story about how one family faces a terrible loss. Like many stories, it has a THEME—a message about life or human nature that a writer wants you to understand. Use these tips to identify a story's theme:

- A story's theme can usually be expressed in a sentence, such as "Winning isn't everything" or "Be true to yourself."
- Sometimes the theme of a story is directly stated by the writer. However, most of the time, it is simply implied. You will have to discover the theme on your own.
- A story may have more than one theme.

As you read, you may find clues to the theme in the story's title, plot, characters, and setting. Use the chart below to help recognize these clues.

2

CLUES TO A STORY'S THEME	
TITLE	**A title may hint at the story's theme. Ask yourself** • What idea or character does the title emphasize?
PLOT AND CONFLICT	**A story's plot often focuses on a conflict that is important to the theme. Ask yourself** • What conflicts do the characters face? • How are the conflicts resolved?
CHARACTERS	**What characters do and learn can reveal the theme. Ask yourself** • What are the main characters like? • How do the characters change? • What lessons do the characters learn?
SETTING	**A setting can suggest a theme because of the conflicts it creates. Ask yourself** • What conflicts does the setting create? • How does the setting affect the characters?

3

ADDITIONAL TERM FOR CRITICAL ANALYSIS

Here's a term that will help you interpret the deeper meaning of Sue Alexander's story.

- A SYMBOL is a person, a place, an object, or an activity that stands for something beyond itself. For example, a white dove is a symbol of peace.

NADIA THE WILLFUL

SUE ALEXANDER

(4)

SECOND READ: CRITICAL ANALYSIS

(5)

(6)

BACKGROUND This story is about a Bedouin girl named Nadia. The Bedouin live in the deserts of North Africa and the Middle East. They are nomads, or wanderers, who move from place to place to find food for the animals they raise. In Bedouin culture, people try not to show strong emotions.

In the land of the drifting sands where the Bedouin move their tents to follow the fertile grasses, there lived a girl whose stubbornness and flashing temper caused her to be known throughout the desert as Nadia the Willful.

Nadia's father, the sheik[1] Tarik, whose kindness and graciousness caused his name to be praised in every tent, did not know what to do with his willful daughter.

Only Hamed, the eldest of Nadia's six brothers and Tarik's favorite son, could calm Nadia's temper when it flashed. "Oh, angry one," he would say, "shall we see how long you can stay that way?" And he would laugh and tease and pull at her dark hair until she laughed back. Then she would follow Hamed wherever he led.

One day before dawn, Hamed mounted his father's great white stallion and rode to the west to seek new grazing

---

1. **sheik** (shēk): a leader of an Arab family or village.

MARK & ANALYZE

Read this selection once on your own, marking the text in any way that is helpful to you.

Then read the story a second time, using the questions in the margins to help you analyze the literature. When you see this pencil (✎), you'll be asked to mark up the text.

graciousness (grā′shəs-nəs) *n.* the condition of being pleasant, courteous, and generous

(7)

ANALYZE
Underline details in the boxed text that help you understand why Tarik and Nadia were so deeply affected by Hamed's death. ✎

NADIA THE WILLFUL **51**

---

(4) SECOND READ: CRITICAL ANALYSIS
You'll read each selection once on your own, marking the text as you wish. Then you'll read it a second time, using the questions in the margins to provide a deeper understanding of the selection.

(5) ✎
The pencil symbol appears whenever you are being asked to circle, underline, or mark the text in other ways.

(6) BACKGROUND
This paragraph gives important information about the selection you are about to read. Always read this section before starting the main text.

(7) ▶
When you come to the arrow symbol, follow the arrow to the side column. Answer the question. Then read on.

Notice the blue underlined details, showing how one student responded to the side column note.

1 **TestSmart**

TestSmart questions will give you practice answering multiple-choice questions typically found on tests. Some **TestSmart** questions will ask about words found in the selection. The **TIP** that follows will help strengthen your word-attack skills in testing situations.

2 **Vocabulary**

Important vocabulary words are underlined and boldfaced in the text. A definition and a respelling appear in the side column.

3 **Footnotes**

Some selections in this book include definitions of special words and phrases. When you see a number in the text, look down at the bottom of the page for an explanation of the meaning.

---

1 **TestSmart**

VOCABULARY

What is the meaning of *bazaar* in line 25?

Ⓐ a marketplace
Ⓑ an oasis
Ⓒ a leader
Ⓓ a city

TIP A test question may ask you to identify the meaning of an unfamiliar word. To answer, look for **context clues** in the same sentence or in the sentences nearby. One context clue for *bazaar* is the word *merchants*, which appears in the same sentence. Use this and other clues to choose the best meaning.

2 **console** (kən-sōl′) *v.* to ease someone's sorrow; to comfort

clan (klăn) *n.* a family group; a group united by common interests or qualities

---

ground for the sheep. Nadia stood with her father at the edge of the oasis[2] and watched him go.

Hamed did not return.

20 Nadia rode behind her father as he traveled across the desert from oasis to oasis, seeking Hamed.

Shepherds told them of seeing a great white stallion fleeing before the pillars of wind that stirred the sand. And they said that the horse carried no rider.

Passing merchants, their camels laden with spices and sweets for the bazaar, told of the emptiness of the desert they had crossed.

Tribesmen, strangers, everyone whom Tarik asked, sighed and gazed into the desert, saying, "Such is the will of Allah."[3]

At last Tarik knew in his heart that his favorite son,
30 Hamed, had been claimed, as other Bedouin before him, by the drifting sands. And he told Nadia what he knew—that Hamed was dead.

Nadia screamed and wept and stamped the sand, crying, "Not even Allah will take Hamed from me!" until her father could bear no more and sternly bade her to silence.

Nadia's grief knew no bounds. She walked blindly through the oasis neither seeing nor hearing those who would **console** her. And Tarik was silent. For days he sat inside his tent, speaking not at all and barely tasting the meals set before him.
40 Then, on the seventh day, Tarik came out of his tent. He called all his people to him, and when they were assembled, he spoke. "From this day forward," he said, "let no one utter Hamed's name. Punishment shall be swift for those who would remind me of what I have lost."

Hamed's mother wept at the decree. The people of the **clan** looked at one another uneasily. All could see the hardness that

---

2. **oasis:** a fertile or green spot in a desert or wasteland, made so by the presence of water.
3. **Allah** (ăl′ə): the name for God in the Islamic religion.

52   UNIT 3: UNDERSTANDING THEME

---

had settled on the sheik's face and the coldness in his eyes, and so they said nothing. But they obeyed. ▶

Nadia, too, did as her father decreed, though each day
50 held something to remind her of Hamed. As she passed her brothers at play, she remembered games Hamed had taught her. As she walked by the women weaving patches for the tents and heard them talking and laughing, she remembered tales Hamed had told her and how they had made her laugh. And as she watched the shepherds with their flock, she remembered the little black lamb Hamed had loved.

Each memory brought Hamed's name to Nadia's lips, but she stilled the sound. And each time that she did so, her unhappiness grew until, finally, she could no longer
60 contain it. She wept and raged at anyone and anything that crossed her path. Soon everyone at the oasis fled at her approach. And she was more lonely than she had ever been before.

One day, as Nadia passed the place where her brothers were playing, she stopped to watch them. They were playing one of the games that Hamed had taught her. But they were playing it wrong.

Without thinking, Nadia called out to them. "That is not the way! Hamed said that first you jump this way and then
70 you jump back!"

Her brothers stopped their game and looked around in fear. Had Tarik heard Nadia say Hamed's name? But the sheik was nowhere to be seen.

"Teach us, Nadia, as our brother taught you," said her smallest brother.

And so she did. Then she told them of other games and how Hamed had taught her to play them. And as she spoke of Hamed, she felt an easing of the hurt within her.

So she went on speaking of him. ▶

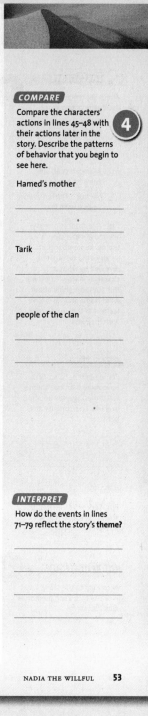

COMPARE
Compare the characters' actions in lines 45–48 with their actions later in the story. Describe the patterns of behavior that you begin to see here.

Hamed's mother

_____

_____

Tarik

_____

_____

people of the clan

_____

_____

INTERPRET
How do the events in lines 71–79 reflect the story's theme?

_____

_____

_____

_____

NADIA THE WILLFUL **53**

4 Challenging Questions
Questions such as this one ask you to use high-level critical thinking skills in order to achieve a deeper understanding of the selection.

The selection continues . . .

1 TestSmart

Here is another TestSmart question. Notice how the **TIP** gives you a useful strategy for figuring out the answer to a typical multiple choice test question.

2 Big Question

At the end of each main literature selection, you'll be asked to think again about the **Big Question** you discussed before reading.

---

1 TestSmart

Which sentence *best* states the theme of this story?

- (A) A sheik's eldest son has died.
- (B) Life in the desert can be harsh.
- (C) Memories can keep the past alive.
- (D) Silence is the best way to deal with loss.

TIP A test question may ask you about a story's **theme.** Remember that a story's theme is often **revealed by what a character learns.** To answer this question, think about what Nadia and Tarik have learned as they try to cope with their loss.

INTERPRET

Remember that a story can have more than one **theme.** What message can you find in Nadia's personality and behavior?

_____

_____

_____

Put stars by details in the story that support your interpretation.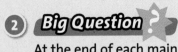

Big Question 2

According to the story, what is one way to keep memories alive? *CLARIFY*

_____

_____

And he wept.

150 Nadia's tone became gentle. "There is a way, honored father," she said. "Listen."

And she began to speak of Hamed. She told of walks she and Hamed had taken, and of talks they had had. She told how he had taught her games, told her tales, and calmed her when she was angry. She told many things that she remembered, some happy and some sad.

And when she was done with the telling, she said gently, "Can you not recall him now, Father? Can you not see his face? Can you not hear his voice?"

160 Tarik nodded through his tears, and for the first time since Hamed had been gone, he smiled.

"Now you see," Nadia said, her tone more gentle than the softest of the desert breezes, "there is a way that Hamed can be with us still." ◄

The sheik pondered what Nadia had said. After a long time, he spoke, and the sharpness was gone from his voice.

"Tell my people to come before me, Nadia," he said. "I have something to say to them."

When all were assembled, Tarik said, "From this day 170 forward, let my daughter Nadia be known not as Willful, but as Wise. And let her name be praised in every tent, for she has given me back my beloved son." ◄

And so it was. The shepherd returned to his flock, kindness and graciousness returned to the oasis, and Nadia's name was praised in every tent. And Hamed lived again—in the hearts of all who remembered him.

Reading Comprehension

Assessment Practice I

DIRECTIONS *Answer these questions about "Nadia the Willful" by filling in the correct ovals.*

1. Based on the title, what is one possible theme of the story?

   (A) It is reckless to disobey laws.

   (B) Being willful can lead to conflict.

   (C) It is important to think for yourself.

   (D) Those who are truly wise are obedient.

2. Which of the following is *not* an effect of Tarik's decree?

   (A) It causes conflict in the family.

   (B) It makes Nadia lonely and angry.

   (C) It makes members of the clan afraid.

   (D) It brings peace to the clan.

3. In this story, all of the following give you clues to the theme *except*

   (A) Nadia's response to Hamed's death

   (B) Tarik's response to Hamed's death

   (C) the main character's appearance

   (D) the conflicts caused by the decree

4. Why does Tarik change Nadia's name?

   (A) because she outsmarted everyone

   (B) because she taught him an important lesson

   (C) because she is now the leader of the clan

   (D) because she has changed her behavior

5. The black lamb is most likely a symbol of

   (A) Hamed's death

   (B) Bedouin culture

   (C) Hamed's memory

   (D) Nadia's willfulness

6. Why does Nadia stand up to her father?

   (A) She wants to protect the traditions of her people.

   (B) She decides that Tarik should take back his order.

   (C) She refuses to let him take Hamed's memory away from her.

   (D) She is upset because the shepherd has been banished.

7. Based on context clues, what is the meaning of the word *scimitar* in line 120?

   (A) a desert hawk

   (B) a sword

   (C) a sharp word

   (D) a harsh decree

8. Based on context clues, what is the meaning of the word *pondered* in line 165?

   (A) looked for

   (B) thought about

   (C) disagreed with

   (D) turned away from

GO ON ▶

---

③ Assessment Practice I: Reading Comprehension

After reading each main literature selection, you'll have an opportunity to practice your test-taking skills and strategies by answering questions about the selection. The direction line will tell you how to mark the answers.

④ Test Strategies

Certain test items will give you a chance to use the **TestSmart TIPs** from earlier in the lesson. Here, notice how the **TIP** on page 56 can help answer test items 1 and 3. The **TIP** on page 52 can help answer test items 7 and 8.

⑤ Literary Skills

Some of the test items, such as number 1 and 3, will ask questions that are related to the literary skills. You can review these skills by turning back to **Learn the Terms,** page 50.

⑥ Vocabulary

The last two test items focus on vocabulary. Remember to use the line numbers to help locate and reread the sentences in which the words appear.

1 **Responding in Writing**
After each main literature selection, you'll write a short response. This activity might ask you to use some of the literary terms you have learned.

2 **Test-Taker's Toolkit**
The **Test-Taker's Toolkit** helps you plan your response. Completing the graphic organizer will give you the ideas you'll use in your writing.

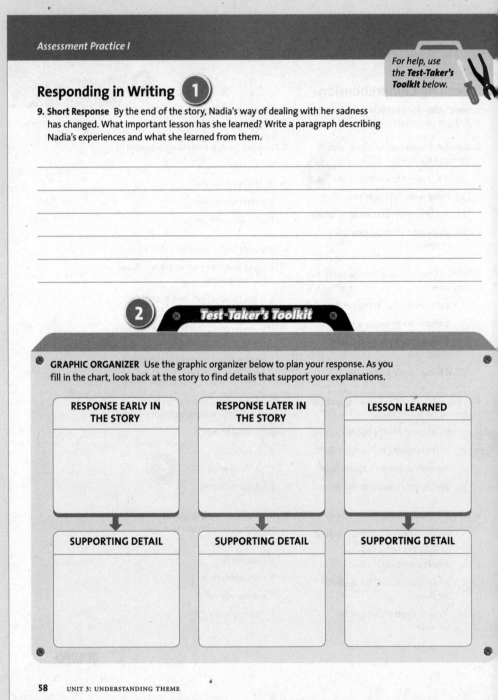

For help, use the *Test-Taker's Toolkit* below.

Responding in Writing **1**

9. Short Response By the end of the story, Nadia's way of dealing with her sadness has changed. What important lesson has she learned? Write a paragraph describing Nadia's experiences and what she learned from them.

_____

_____

_____

_____

_____

2 **Test-Taker's Toolkit**

GRAPHIC ORGANIZER Use the graphic organizer below to plan your response. As you fill in the chart, look back at the story to find details that support your explanations.

RESPONSE EARLY IN THE STORY	RESPONSE LATER IN THE STORY	LESSON LEARNED
↓	↓	↓
SUPPORTING DETAIL	SUPPORTING DETAIL	SUPPORTING DETAIL

What's the Connection?

Nadia and her family are Bedouins who live in the deserts of North Africa and the Middle East. The brochure "Sahara" describes the mix of traditional and modern ways of life in the desert. The magazine article "Bedouins: The Desert's Nomadic Hosts" describes Bedouin customs.

TEST YOURSELF If you visited the Sahara today, what do you think you would see? With a group, discuss each cultural detail listed below. Decide whether it is part of the past, the present, or both. Record your responses in the first column of the chart. After reading the selections, review your responses and note any changes in the last column.

LIFE IN THE SAHARA: THEN AND NOW		
Response Before Reading	Cultural Detail	Response After Reading
	camel caravans	
	salt traders	
	huge cities	
	goat herds	
	living in tents	
	long, flowing robes	

LEARN THE SKILL: IDENTIFY MAIN IDEAS AND DETAILS

The **main ideas** in a nonfiction text are the most important points the writer makes about a topic. **Supporting details,** such as facts or examples, give more information about a main idea. Recognizing the main ideas and understanding supporting details can help you remember the key points of any text you read.

You can use these text features to help identify main ideas:

- The **title** gives or suggests the topic of a nonfiction text.
- **Subheadings** tell the main idea in each section of the text. Often a sentence near the beginning of a section states its main idea.

As you read each section, look for supporting details that tell more about the main idea.

For more on main ideas and supporting details, see *Nonfiction Handbook* page R14.

Related Nonfiction

- *Sahara*
  BROCHURE
- *Bedouins: The Desert's Nomadic Hosts*
  MAGAZINE ARTICLE

Use with "Nadia the Willful," p. 48

---

3 Related Nonfiction

Once you've completed the literature section, you'll get ready to read the **Related Nonfiction.**

4 What's the Connection?

This activity gets you thinking and talking about the nonfiction selections you are about to read. It also explains how they connect to the literature selection.

5 Learn the Skill

Before you read the **Related Nonfiction,** you will learn a useful skill or strategy. You will encounter the boldfaced terms later as you are reading and as you complete the practice test.

① Set a Purpose

You will begin the **Related Nonfiction** by setting a purpose for reading. One student's purpose for reading appears on the lines provided. Yours may be different.

② Specialized Vocabulary

When a nonfiction selection contains a word that is unique to a certain area of study, a note is provided that will help you figure out the word's meaning.

CLOSE READ

SET A PURPOSE ①

My purpose for reading is to learn more about the Sahara and the Bedouin people.

SPECIALIZED Vocabulary ②

When you read about different cultures, you should expect to come across unfamiliar words. One example is the word caravans in line 10. Circle context clues in the text that can help you figure out the meaning of this word. One has been done for you. 👁

Sahara

The Sahara has amazed outsiders for centuries. It is the world's largest desert, and its size is difficult to imagine: 3.3 million square miles, or around 25 percent of Africa. Not surprisingly, the Sahara's name in Arabic means simply "desert."

10 Camel <u>caravans</u> looking for gold, ivory, grain, salt, and slaves made the Sahara the world's first gateway to Africa. These endless trains run by Tuaregs, Arabs, and others, gave rise to the legendary era of trans-Saharan trade— a phenomenon that still defines the Sahara to many outsiders.

20 Today, the Sahara still serves as a border between the continent's black African south and Arab-influenced north. Its scorching heat and size still influence the cycle of drought and rainfall in sub-Saharan Africa. With one

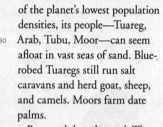

of the planet's lowest population densities, its people—Tuareg, Arab, Tubu, Moor—can seem afloat in vast seas of sand. Blue-robed Tuaregs still run salt caravans and herd goat, sheep, and camels. Moors farm date palms.

But much has changed. The Arabs have retreated to Saharan cities like Cairo; at roughly 10 million people, Africa's largest. Trucks are replacing camels in the salt trade. Tuaregs are acting as guides to Western adventure tourists, and oil and gas operations promise far greater riches than gold and ivory ever could. Political unrest has gripped the region. In the late 1990s, armed Tuareg rebel groups blazed across the desert. Nor has the Sahara escaped the Internet revolution. Rissani, Morocco, a tiny desert oasis, offers several Internet cafés, primarily for tourists about to begin their own exploration of the most famous of deserts.

TestSmart

Which sentence *best* states the main idea of the passage?

(A) More Arabs live in Cairo today.

(B) Trucks are replacing camels.

(C) Much has changed in the Sahara.

(D) Morocco has Internet cafes.

TIP A test question may ask you to identify the **main idea** of a passage. Remember that a main idea is a general statement, not a specific fact or example. To identify a main idea, **ask yourself what *most* of the sentences in the passage are about.** Use that information to choose your answer.

① Main Idea

These notes ask you to apply the skill or strategy you learned before reading.

① MAIN IDEAS AND DETAILS

Underline the main idea in lines 12–22. Circle the supporting details.

SPECIALIZED Vocabulary

Social studies articles will often use legal or political terms, such as <u>territorial rights</u> in line 25. This term is related to the word *territory*, which means "land." On the lines below, use this information to guess the meaning of *territorial rights*.

WORD ANALYSIS

_____

_____

Bedouins:
THE DESERT'S NOMADIC HOSTS

Lost and thirsty in the desert sands, a traveler in North Africa or the Middle East would be wise to seek shelter in a Bedouin tent. These desert people live in areas that cover the Sahara, Sinai, Negev, and Arabian deserts. Their tribes are used to finding resources in a challenging land. Because of this, they are some of the most famous hosts on earth.

A Herding Culture

A desert is a huge expanse of nearly
10 waterless land. It is barely able to support human and animal life.

But the Bedouin have adapted to the harsh climate. They herd animals like sheep and goats that need little water. They use camels or horses for travel. They are semi-nomadic, moving from place to place throughout the year. When they begin to run out of grass and water,
20 they move to a new area until the first has recovered enough for them to return to it.

Life in the desert has made the Bedouin protective of their resources and <u>territorial rights</u>. If a tribe or family's resources

The selection continues . . .

Reading Comprehension

DIRECTIONS *Answer these questions about the three selections in this lesson by filling in the correct ovals.*

3

1. Which sentence *best* states the main idea of lines 20–35 in "Sahara"?

   Ⓐ The Sahara is the border between northern and southern Africa.

   Ⓑ The Sahara affects the climate of sub-Saharan Africa.

   Ⓒ Population is very spread out in the Sahara.

   Ⓓ Many parts of life in the Sahara have changed little over time.

2. In the brochure, which details are used as examples of recent changes in the Sahara?

   Ⓐ camel caravans

   Ⓑ tourism and political unrest

   Ⓒ trade in ivory, gold, and salt

   Ⓓ the heat and size of the desert

3. What generalization can you make about the Bedouin people, based on details in "Bedouins"?

   Ⓐ They have separate areas for men and women.

   Ⓑ They do not welcome strangers.

   Ⓒ They do not enjoy life in the desert.

   Ⓓ They are no longer nomads.

4. According to the sidebar on page 65, what made some nomadic groups change their lifestyle?

   Ⓐ a terrible drought

   Ⓑ a population increase

   Ⓒ fighting in the region

   Ⓓ economic changes

5. Which detail from "Nadia the Willful" is *not* supported by facts in "Bedouins"?

   Ⓐ Bedouins move from place to place.

   Ⓑ Bedouins live in tents.

   Ⓒ Bedouins often banish people.

   Ⓓ Bedouins keep herds of sheep.

6. According to the articles, all of the following are threats to the nomadic lifestyle *except*

   4

   Ⓐ severe droughts

   Ⓑ modern transportation

   Ⓒ date farming

   Ⓓ the growth of nearby cities

7. Using your knowledge of the Latin root *sol,* you can guess that *solitude* in line 76 of "Bedouins" means

   Ⓐ a card game

   Ⓑ being alone

   Ⓒ a large group

   Ⓓ the height of a place

8. Based on context clues, what is the most likely meaning of the word *indicate* in line 42 of "Bedouins"?

   Ⓐ show

   Ⓑ maintain

   Ⓒ increase

   Ⓓ insure

2 **Assessment Practice II:**
Reading Comprehension
In this second practice test, you'll answer test items about all the selections you have read in the unit.

3 **Nonfiction Skill**
Some test items ask about the nonfiction skill or strategy you learned. Remember to use the line numbers to locate and reread the text you are being asked about before you choose an answer.

4 **Connecting Texts**
Test items such as number 6 ask you to connect information from more than one source. You can look back at the selections if you need to.

① Timed Writing Practice
This writing activity is an opportunity to practice responding to a prompt on a writing test—without the stress of test-taking!

② Budget Your Time
This feature helps you plan how much time to spend on each step. The blue text shows how one student budgeted her time.

③ Test-Taker's Toolkit
The **Test-Taker's Toolkit** shows you how to break the writing process into three easy steps. Fill in the graphic organizer provided. This will help you gather the information you'll need to write your full response. (You may want to copy the graphic organizer onto a larger sheet of paper.)

Timed Writing Practice ①

PROMPT

If you took a trip to the Sahara, what would you see? Write a description of this region. Include physical details about what it looks and feels like. Also include cultural details about how people live in the region. Make sure to choose details from all three selections.

② BUDGET YOUR TIME

You have 30 minutes to complete this assignment. Decide how much time to spend on each step.

Analyze _____5_____
Plan _____10_____
Write _____10_____
Review _____5_____

Test-Taker's Toolkit ③

1. ANALYZE THE PROMPT

A. **Read the prompt twice** to make sure you understand it.
B. **Circle key words** in each sentence. One phrase has been circled for you. These words tell you what you must include to get a good score.
C. **Write down a list** of the key elements you need to include.

2. PLAN YOUR RESPONSE

A. **Make notes** Use your list to create a chart that gives a detail or example for each main idea. Review your list to make sure you've included details from each selection.
B. **Organize your information** Use your notes to help organize your description. For this prompt you could begin by giving general facts about the Sahara's geography and climate. Then you could continue by showing how people have adapted to these conditions.

Geography & Climate
•
•
•
How People Live
•
•

3. WRITE AND REVIEW

A. A good description uses carefully chosen details that create vivid images in the reader's mind. Instead of saying "huge area," try saying "25 percent of Africa."
B. Be sure to leave time to read through your description to check your spelling and grammar.

Thinking Critically

The skills and strategies found in this book will help you tackle critical thinking questions you encounter in school—and on tests in particular. Critical thinking questions are often challenging because the answers are usually not directly stated in the text. But you will find that tackling these types of questions is worth the extra brain power it takes to answer them. That's because they help you get more out of the selections you read. Here is a list of the critical thinking skills and strategies you will encounter most often in this book:

Make Inferences
Make logical guesses based on details in the text and your own experiences.

- Keep track of important details in your reading.
- Ask: How can what I already know help me "read between the lines"?

Draw Conclusions
Decide what's happening based on evidence, experience, and reasoning.

- Start by making inferences as you read.
- Then combine your inferences to reach a logical conclusion.

Analyze
Break things down to gain a better understanding.

- Consider the experiences and feelings that make a character act a certain way.
- In nonfiction, look for details to help you learn how something works or is defined.

Interpret
Find deeper meaning in what you read.

- Think about what the author is trying to tell the reader.
- Consider the outcome of events and what they might mean.

Evaluate
Examine something to decide its value or worth.

- You can decide to evaluate the actions of a particular character, for example.
- You can also decide on the value of what you are reading.

Make Judgments
Form an opinion based on information given.

- Gather evidence from the text.
- Be ready to support your opinion.

continued on next page

Compare/Contrast
Identify similarities and differences in two or more subjects.

- Make a list of the qualities of each subject. In what ways are the lists the same? Different?
- Decide if the subjects are more alike or more different.

Synthesize
Combine information together to gain a better understanding.

- Think of what you already know about the subject.
- Add this to the facts, details, and ideas presented in your reading.

Make Generalizations
Form a broad statement about a subject.

- Gather evidence.
- Then decide what ideas are suggested by this evidence.

Classify
Decide how pieces of information might fit into categories.

- Look for common characteristics in the information provided.
- Cite evidence from your reading to show why you classified as you did.

Examine Perspectives
Think about the values and beliefs presented.

- Look for a writer's statements of opinion.
- Decide how perspective affects the information you get.

UNIT 1
PLOT, CONFLICT, AND SETTING

The School Play
BY GARY SOTO

RELATED NONFICTION
Through Children's Eyes

Trail Basics

What do you FEAR *most?*

Have you ever been terrified by a noise late at night? Have you jumped at the sight of a harmless bug? Or maybe you have waited in line to ride a roller coaster, only to change your mind at the last minute? The things that frighten people can be big or small, living or nonliving, seen or unseen. In "The School Play," a student struggles to overcome a fear that many people face.

SURVEY The chart below lists some of the most common fears people have. Rank the fears by writing a number between one and ten on each line. (Use one for the thing you are *most* afraid of.) Then survey the class to find out which answer most people chose as their number-one fear. Write the result of your survey on the last line of the chart.

SURVEY

WHAT SCARES YOU THE MOST?

____ **Heights**

____ **Spiders and Insects**

____ **Being in the Dark**

____ **Dentists**

____ **Thunder and Lightning**

____ **Failing a Test**

____ **Being Bullied**

____ **Airplane Rides**

____ **Public Speaking**

____ **Being in a Crowd**

The Most Common Fear: _____

ASSESSMENT GOALS

By the end of this lesson, you will be able to . . .

• analyze plot, conflict, and setting in a work of fiction

• use critical thinking skills to analyze text

• use text features to navigate nonfiction text

• analyze a writing prompt and plan a personal narrative

Plot, Conflict, and Setting

Good stories have the power to make us wonder what will happen next. For example, "The School Play" is a story about a young boy who struggles to face his fear. Will he succeed or fail? Knowing the following terms will help you understand how the parts of a story work together to capture and hold your attention.

- **SETTING** is the time and place of the action. The time can be a year, a season, or a time of day. The place might be a country, a neighborhood, or a room.

- **CONFLICT** is the struggle or problem that a character faces in a story. The struggle can be between characters, such as a fight between enemies. Conflict can also take place within a character, as he or she struggles with strong emotions.

- **PLOT** is what happens in a story. A story's plot usually includes five stages.

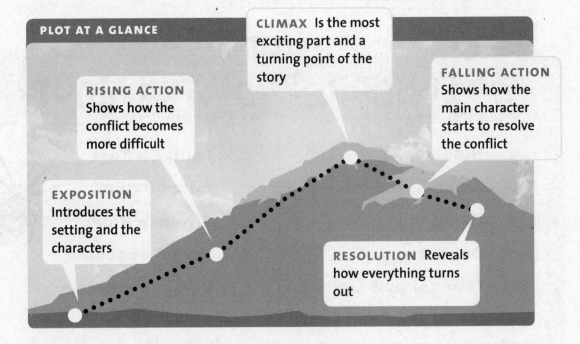

PLOT AT A GLANCE

CLIMAX Is the most exciting part and a turning point of the story

RISING ACTION Shows how the conflict becomes more difficult

FALLING ACTION Shows how the main character starts to resolve the conflict

EXPOSITION Introduces the setting and the characters

RESOLUTION Reveals how everything turns out

ADDITIONAL TERMS FOR CRITICAL ANALYSIS

Gary Soto uses these elements to create an exciting plot.

- **FORESHADOWING** is a writer's use of hints or clues to suggest events that will happen later in a story. Foreshadowing creates suspense. It makes readers eager to find out what will happen next.

- **SUSPENSE** is the excitement that readers feel as they wait to find out how a conflict will be resolved. The climax of a story is usually the most suspenseful part.

The School Play

Gary Soto

BACKGROUND In this story, the students perform a play about a group of settlers known as the Donner party. While trying to cross the Sierra Nevada mountain range in eastern California, the Donner party became trapped in a snowstorm. The travelers ran out of food and some died of starvation. In desperation, some group members ate the bodies of the dead.

MARK & ANALYZE
Read this selection once on your own, marking the text in any way that is helpful to you.

Then read the story a second time, using the questions in the margins to help you analyze the literature. When you see this pencil 🖉, you'll be asked to mark up the text.

In the school play at the end of his sixth-grade year, all Robert Suarez had to remember to say was, "Nothing's wrong. I can see," to a pioneer woman, who was really Belinda Lopez. Instead of a pioneer woman, Belinda was one of the toughest girls since the beginning of the world. She was known to slap boys and grind their faces into the grass so that they bit into chunks of wormy earth. More than once Robert had witnessed Belinda staring down the janitor's pit bull, who licked his frothing chops but didn't dare mess with her. ▶

10   The class rehearsed for three weeks, at first without costumes. Early one morning Mrs. Bunnin wobbled into the classroom lugging a large cardboard box. She wiped her brow and said, "Thanks for the help, Robert."

Robert was at his desk scribbling a ballpoint tattoo that spelled dude on the tops of his knuckles. He looked up and stared, blinking at his teacher. "Oh, did you need some help?" he asked.

EVALUATE
Underline the details that help you identify the **conflict** between Belinda and Robert. 🖉

In your opinion, is the story's **exposition** effective?

☐ yes
☐ no

Give reasons for your answer.

_____

_____

_____

_____

_____

She rolled her eyes at him and told him to stop writing on his skin. "You'll look like a criminal," she scolded.

20 Robert stuffed his hands into his pockets as he rose from his seat. "What's in the box?" he asked.

She muttered under her breath. She popped open the taped top and brought out skirts, hats, snowshoes, scarves, and vests. She tossed Robert a red beard, which he held up to his face, thinking it made him look handsome.

"I like it," Robert said. He sneezed and ran his hand across his moist nose.

His classmates were coming into the classroom and looked at Robert in awe. "That's bad," Ruben said. "What do I get?"

30 Mrs. Bunnin threw him a wrinkled shirt. Ruben raised it to his chest and said, "My dad could wear this. Can I give it to him after the play is done?"

Mrs. Bunnin turned away in silence. ◀

Most of the actors didn't have speaking parts. They just got cutout crepe-paper snowflakes to pin to their shirts or crepe-paper leaves to wear.

During the blizzard in which Robert delivered his line, Belinda asked, "Is there something wrong with your eyes?" Robert looked at the audience, which at the moment was
40 a classroom of empty chairs, a dented world globe that had been dropped by almost everyone, one limp flag, one wastebasket, and a picture of George Washington, whose eyes followed you around the room when you got up to sharpen your pencil. Robert answered, "Nothing's wrong. I can see."

Mrs. Bunnin, biting on the end of her pencil, said, "Louder, both of you."

Belinda stepped up, nostrils flaring so that the shadows on her nose quivered, and said louder, "Sucka, is there something
50 wrong with your eye-balls?"

"Nothing's wrong. I can see."

"Louder! Make sure the audience can hear you," Mrs. Bunnin directed. She tapped her pencil hard against the desk.

She scolded, "Robert, I'm not going to tell you again to quit fooling with the beard."

"It's itchy."

"We can't do anything about that. Actors need **props**. You're an actor. Now try again."

Robert and Belinda stood center stage as they waited
60 for Mrs. Bunnin to call "Action!" When she did, Belinda approached Robert slowly. "Sucka face, is there anything wrong with your mug?" Belinda asked. Her eyes were squinted in anger. For a moment Robert saw his head grinding into the playground grass. ▶

"Nothing's wrong. I can see."

Robert giggled behind his red beard. Belinda popped her gum and **smirked**. She stood with her hands on her hips.

"What? What did you say?" Mrs. Bunnin asked, pulling off her glasses. "Are you chewing gum, Belinda?"

70 "No, Mrs. Bunnin," Belinda lied. "I just forgot my lines."

Belinda turned to face the snowflake boys clumped together in the back. She rolled out her tongue, on which rested a ball of gray gum, depleted of sweetness under her **relentless** chomp. She whispered "sucka" and giggled so that her nose quivered dark shadows. ▶

The play, *The Last Stand,* was about the Donner party just before they got hungry and started eating each other. Everyone who scored at least twelve out of fifteen on their spelling tests got to say at least one line. Everyone else had to
80 stand and be trees or snowflakes.

Mrs. Bunnin wanted the play to be a success. She couldn't risk having kids with bad memories on stage. The nonspeaking trees and snowflakes stood humming snow flurries, blistering wind, and hail, which they produced by clacking their teeth.

Robert's mother was proud of him because he was living up to the legend of Robert De Niro, for whom he was named. Over dinner he said, "Nothing's wrong. I can see,"

prop (prŏp) *n.* an object an actor uses in a play

MAKE JUDGMENTS

Does the **conflict** between Robert and Belinda seem realistic to you?

☐ yes
☐ no

Explain your answer.

_____

_____

_____

smirk (smûrk) *v.* to smile in an insulting way

relentless (rĭ-lĕnt'lĭs) *adj.* refusing to stop or give up

DRAW CONCLUSIONS

Based on the story's **resolution,** do you think that Belinda is as tough as she acts? Use details from the entire story to support your answer.

_____

_____

_____

_____

COMPARE

Circle words in the boxed text that reveal the **setting** of this part of the story.

What aspects of the setting have changed since the story began?

_____

_____

_____

ANALYZE

List two ways that the school play affects Robert's life at home.

1. _____

_____

2. _____

_____

How does it help the story to show Robert in two different **settings**?

_____

_____

_____

when his brother asked him to pass the dishtowel, their
90 communal napkin. His sister said, "It's your turn to do dishes," and he said, "Nothing's wrong. I can see." His dog, Queenie, begged him for more than water and a dog biscuit. He touched his dog's own hairy beard and said, "Nothing's wrong. I can see."

One warm spring night, Robert lay on his back in the backyard, counting shooting stars. He was up to three when David, a friend who was really his brother's friend, hopped the fence and asked, "What's the matter with you?" ◄

"Nothing's wrong. I can see," Robert answered. He sat up,
100 feeling good because the line came naturally, without much thought. He leaned back on his elbow and asked David what he wanted to be when he grew up.

"I don't know yet," David said, plucking at the grass. "Maybe a fighter pilot. What do you want to be?"

"I want to guard the president. I could wrestle the assassins and be on television. But I'd pin those dudes, and people would say, 'That's him, our hero.'" David plucked at a stalk of grass and thought deeply.

Robert thought of telling David that he really wanted to
110 be someone with a supergreat memory, who could recall facts that most people thought were unimportant. He didn't know if there was such a job, but he thought it would be great to sit at home by the telephone waiting for scientists to call him and ask hard questions. ◄

The three weeks passed quickly. The day before the play, Robert felt happy as he walked home from school with no homework. As he turned onto his street, he found a dollar floating over the currents of wind.

"A buck," he screamed to himself. He snapped it up and
120 looked for others. But he didn't find any more. It was his lucky day, though. At recess he had hit a home run on a

fluke bunt—a fluke because the catcher had kicked the ball, another player had thrown it into center field, and the pitcher wasn't looking when Robert slowed down at third, then burst home with dust flying behind him.

That night, it was his sister's turn to do the dishes. They had eaten enchiladas with the works, so she slaved with suds up to her elbows. Robert bathed in bubble bath, the suds peaked high like the Donner Pass. He thought about how 130 full he was and how those poor people had had nothing to eat but snow. I can live on nothing, he thought and whistled like wind through a mountain pass, raking flat the suds with his palm.

The next day, after lunch, he was ready for the play, red beard in hand and his one line trembling on his lips. Classes herded into the auditorium. As the actors dressed and argued about stepping on each other's feet, Robert stood near a cardboard barrel full of toys, whispering over and over to himself, "Nothing's wrong. I can see." He was hot, itchy, 140 and confused when he tied on the beard. He sneezed when a strand of the beard entered his nostril. He said louder, "Nothing's wrong. I can see," but the words seemed to get caught in the beard. "Nothing, no, no. I can see great," he said louder, then under his breath because the words seemed wrong. "Nothing's wrong, can't you see? Nothing's wrong. I can see you." Worried, he approached Belinda and asked if she remembered his line. Balling her hand into a fist, Belinda warned, "Sucka, I'm gonna bury your ugly face in the ground if you mess up." ▶

150 "I won't," Robert said as he walked away. He bit a nail and looked into the barrel of toys. A clown's mask stared back at him. He prayed that his line would come back to him. He would hate to disappoint his teacher and didn't like the thought of his face being rubbed into spiky grass. ▶

The curtain parted slightly, and the principal came out smiling onto the stage. She said some words about pioneer history and then, stern faced, warned the audience not to

💡 TestSmart

The events in the boxed text are part of the story's

(A) rising action

(B) resolution

(C) falling action

(D) exposition

TIP If a test question asks you how story events relate to **stages of the plot**, you'll need to **classify events** based on what you know about plot. In the boxed passage, Robert's **conflict** gets more difficult. In what stage of a plot does this occur?

ANALYZE

Underline three details in lines 134–154 that **foreshadow** what will happen when Robert is onstage.

scrape the chairs on the just-waxed floor. The principal then introduced Mrs. Bunnin, who told the audience about how they had rehearsed for weeks.

Meanwhile, the class stood quietly in place with lunchtime spaghetti on their breath. They were ready. Belinda had swallowed her gum because she knew this was for real. The snowflakes clumped together and began howling.

Robert retied his beard. Belinda, smoothing her skirt, looked at him and said, "If you know what's good for you, you'd better do it right." Robert grew nervous when the curtain parted and his classmates who were assigned to do snow, wind, and hail broke into song. ◀

Alfonso stepped forward with his **narrative** about a blot on American history that would live with us forever. He looked at the audience, lost for a minute. He continued by saying that if the Donner party could come back, hungry from not eating for over a hundred years, they would be sorry for what they had done.

The play began with some boys in snowshoes shuffling around the stage, muttering that the blizzard would cut them off from civilization. They looked up, held out their hands, and said in unison, "Snow." One stepped center stage and said, "I wish I had never left the prairie." Another one said, "California is just over there." He pointed, and some of the first graders looked in the direction of the piano. ◀

"What are we going to do?" one kid asked, brushing pretend snow off his vest.

"I'm getting pretty hungry," another said, rubbing her stomach.

The audience seemed to be following the play. A ribbon of sweat ran down Robert's face. When his scene came up, he staggered to center stage and dropped to the floor, just as Mrs. Bunnin had said, just as he had seen Robert De Niro do in that movie about a boxer. Belinda, bending over with an "Oh, my," yanked him up so hard that something clicked in his elbow. She boomed, "Is there anything wrong with your eyes?"

CLASSIFY

Circle details in lines 161–169 that help build **suspense**.

narrative (năr′ə-tĭv) *n.* a story

🔆 **TestSmart**

VOCABULARY
To speak in *unison* means to speak

Ⓐ in turn
Ⓑ as one
Ⓒ in anger
Ⓓ for others

TIP When a test question asks about a word you don't know, **think about similar words** you do know. Words that look alike are often related in meaning. The word *unison* in line 179 is related to the words *unit*, *unicycle*, and *unicorn*. Write the word part they have in common on the line below.

_____

The Latin root *uni* means "one." Look for the answer choice that means "one."

Robert rubbed his elbow, then his eyes, and said, "I can see nothing wrong. Wrong is nothing, I can see."

"How are we going to get through?" she boomed, wringing her hands together at the audience, some of whom had their mouths taped shut because they were known talkers. "My husband needs a doctor." The drama advanced through snow, 200 wind, and hail that sounded like chattering teeth.

Belinda turned to Robert and muttered, "You mess-up. You're gonna hate life."

But Robert thought he'd done okay. At least, he reasoned to himself, I got the words right. Just not in the right order.

With his part of the play done, he joined the snowflakes and trees, chattering his teeth the loudest. He howled wind like a baying hound and snapped his fingers furiously in a snow flurry. He trembled from the cold. ▶

The play ended with Alfonso saying that if they came back to 210 life, the Donner party would be sorry for eating each other. "It's just not right," he argued. "You gotta suck it up in bad times."

Robert figured that Alfonso was right. He remembered how one day his sister had locked him in the closet and he didn't eat or drink for five hours. When he got out, he hit his sister, but not so hard as to leave a bruise. He then ate three sandwiches and felt a whole lot better.

The cast then paraded up the aisle into the audience. Belinda pinched Robert hard, but only once because she was thinking that it could have been worse. As he passed a smiling 220 and relieved Mrs. Bunnin, she patted Robert's shoulder and said, "Almost perfect."

Robert was happy. He'd made it through without passing out from fear. Now the first and second graders were looking at him and clapping. He was sure everyone wondered who the actor was behind that smooth voice and red, red beard. ▶

Reading Comprehension

DIRECTIONS *Answer these questions about "The School Play" by filling in the correct ovals.*

1. Belinda's threats are important to the story's plot because they
   - (A) add to the conflict
   - (B) lead to the resolution
   - (C) hint about the ending
   - (D) reveal the setting

2. Which event is the story's climax?
   - (A) Robert falls down on stage.
   - (B) Belinda pulls Robert to his feet.
   - (C) Robert says his line.
   - (D) Belinda threatens Robert.

3. Which event is part of the story's resolution?
   - (A) Robert prays that his line will come back to him.
   - (B) Belinda pinches Robert hard, but only once.
   - (C) Belinda threatens to bury Robert's face in the ground.
   - (D) Robert's beard itches, and he starts to sweat.

4. Reread lines 222–225. Which word *best* describes Robert's emotions after the play is over?
   - (A) confused
   - (B) relieved
   - (C) gloomy
   - (D) proud

5. Which event helps increase suspense in the story?
   - (A) The snowflakes clump together and howl.
   - (B) Robert staggers onstage and drops to the floor.
   - (C) Robert asks Belinda if she remembers his line.
   - (D) The actors argue backstage while getting dressed.

6. What does foreshadowing do in a story?
   - (A) It reveals the conflict.
   - (B) It tells how a story ends.
   - (C) It hints at an upcoming event.
   - (D) It explains what happened earlier.

7. What does the word *chops* mean in line 9?
   - (A) meat slices
   - (B) quick cuts
   - (C) hand movements
   - (D) lower jaws

8. Using related words, such as *community*, you can guess that a *communal* napkin (line 90) is one that
   - (A) is used by everyone
   - (B) has an exact double
   - (C) is easily packable
   - (D) has lost its usefulness

For help, use the *Test-Taker's Toolkit* below.

Responding in Writing

9. Short Response Write a paragraph that summarizes "The School Play."

_____

_____

_____

_____

_____

_____

_____

Test-Taker's Toolkit

ACADEMIC VOCABULARY When you're asked to **summarize** a story, you need to identify its setting and characters. You also need to briefly explain the conflict, main events, and resolution in your own words.

GRAPHIC ORGANIZER Use the story map below to plan your response. Look back at the story to help you remember the details.

TITLE:	AUTHOR:
SETTING:	
CHARACTERS:	
CONFLICT:	

MAIN PLOT EVENTS:

RESOLUTION:

- **Through Children's Eyes**
  MAGAZINE ARTICLE
- **Trail Basics**
  ONLINE ARTICLE

Use with "The School Play," p. 2

What's the Connection?

In "The School Play," Robert's class performs a play about the terrible struggles a group of pioneers faced on the way to California. The *Cobblestone Magazine* article "Through Children's Eyes" describes what the trip west was like for children. The online article "Trail Basics" reveals details about the everyday life of people heading for California.

WEB IT With a small group, discuss what you know or imagine about what life was like for pioneers. Add words and phrases to the web to record your thoughts.

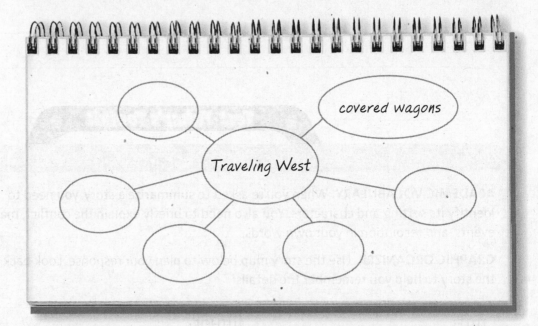

LEARN THE SKILL: USE TEXT FEATURES

Nonfiction writing often includes design elements called **text features.** Text features help organize ideas and emphasize key information. Here are some different kinds of text features:

- A **title** suggests the topic of an article.
- **Subheadings** show where different sections begin and what topics they cover.
- **Bulleted lists** (like this one) display details of equal importance.
- **Graphic aids,** such as diagrams, illustrations, and schedules, present details in a visual way.
- **Pullout quotes** in large type emphasize important ideas in the text.
- **Sidebars** give further details on the main topic. They can be read at any time.

For more on text features, see *Nonfiction Handbook* page R22.

Through Children's Eyes

BY SANDRA WEBER

YOUNG PIONEERS ON THE CALIFORNIA TRAIL FACED
DANGERS AND HARDSHIPS, BUT THEY HAD FUN, TOO.
"TO ME THE JOURNEY WAS A 'PLEASURE-TRIP,'—SO
MANY BEAUTIFUL WILD FLOWERS, SUCH WILD SCENERY,
MOUNTAINS, ROCKS, AND STREAMS—SOMETHING NEW
AT EVERY TURN," RECALLED SARAH IDE, WHO MADE
THE TRIP WEST IN 1845.

New Experiences ▶

Along the trail, children enjoyed the first time they set eyes on
10   prairie dogs, buffalo, Chimney Rock, and cactus, among other
encounters. Sarah also had the thrill of riding her own pony and
herding cattle.

While on the trail, small children rode inside the wagons.
Some were stowed in saddlebags. The first child to cross the
Sierra Nevada Mountains into California was carried in her

SET A PURPOSE
My purpose for reading is

_____

_____

_____

TEXT FEATURES

Preview each article by reading
the titles and scanning the
**subheadings, illustrations,
sidebars,** and **diagrams.**
Based on your preview, decide
which article would cover
the following topics:

- details about covered
  wagons
- the route pioneers took west
- how children amused
  themselves

List each topic under the
correct title.

"Through Children's Eyes"

_____

_____

"Trail Basics"

_____

_____

mother's arms: Ann Kelsey, of the Bidwell-Bartleson party, was only six months old.

Thirteen-year-old Mary Murphy tried to walk across the snowy mountains, but "the snow was soft and we would almost sink to our neck." Seven-year-old Benjamin Bonney walked barefoot on the plains. Later he recalled "how we limped across the desert, for we cut the soles of our feet on the prickly pears." ◀

Keeping Busy

Even on the trail, children did chores. They milked cows and tended livestock. In the evening, the children gathered sagebrush and buffalo chips to fuel the cooking fires. Younger members of the Stephens party shot wild ducks, geese, sage hens, antelope, and deer.

After the work was done, "we waded the creek, made mud pies, and gathered posies," wrote Eliza Donner. Sometimes the older girls would invite little children to sit behind them on their horses, "and away we would canter with the breeze playing through our hair."

Some children sent letters to relatives. Virginia Reed, age twelve, wrote her cousin Mary from Independence Rock: "paw treated the company and we all had some leminade. maw and pau is well and sends there best love to you all."

Dangerous Journey

Not everything was always "well," however. Benjamin Bonney said that there was a good deal of sickness at Fort Sutter and "a large number of the natives died as well as some of the emigrants, mainly children." Another danger was the possibility of falling off a wagon and getting run over by its wheels. One of the Donner wagons tipped over while going down a hill. It landed on Eliza and Georgia, but luckily, they were not hurt.

One day, thirteen-year-old Edward Breen was galloping along on his saddle pony when it stepped into a prairie dog burrow. Edward tumbled to the ground and broke his left leg. . . . The leg healed in a few weeks. ◀

CONNECT

How are the experiences described in lines 18–22 different from the lives of children today?

💡 **TestSmart**

VOCABULARY

Which word below is related to the Latin word *migrare*, meaning "to change location"?

Ⓐ adults
Ⓑ canters
Ⓒ natives
Ⓓ emigrants

TIP Tests often include questions about a Latin word and a vocabulary word. Remember that words that are related in spelling and structure are often **related in meaning.** In this case, look for the answer choice that has a **base word** similar to *migrare*. Check your answer by using a dictionary.

50   As traveling parties moved farther west, food supplies dwindled. Parents did whatever they could to feed their children. Two men stole food from the Fort Hall trading post. Some families ate animal hides that were boiled to soften them until they jelled into a "pot of glue." . . .

Holding onto Hope

Despite some horrible situations, the children found moments of delight. Little girls "used to fill the pretty porcelain tea-cups with freshly fallen snow, daintily dip it out with teaspoons and eat it, playing it was custard." Patty Reed held onto a wooden doll and a
60 lock of her grandmother's hair to remind her of happier times.

    When they finally reached California, emigrants found good weather and food. "The ground was covered with fine green grass and there was a very fat beef hanging from the branch of an oak tree," wrote John Breen, age fifteen. "The birds were singing . . . and the journey was over."

Terms to Know:

Saddlebags are a pair of pouches hung across a saddle.

Prickly pears are a kind of cactus with sharp needles.

A **canter** is the gait of a horse that is slower than a gallop but faster than a trot.

A **burrow** is a hole dug in the ground by a small animal and used as its home. ▶

TEXT FEATURES

Circle each term from the sidebar where it appears in the article.

Would it have been easier to find the words if they had been listed in alphabetical order? Why or why not?

TestSmart

In which year did the greatest number of people travel west?

(A) 1841

(B) 1843

(C) 1848

(D) 1850

TIP When a test question asks you about the dates that events occurred, **skim the text to locate the dates** listed in the question. Replace phrases like "two years later" or "the following year" with a numeric date. To answer this question, find and circle each date reference in the text. Replace time phrases with dates. Then underline the number of travelers given for each year. Use this information to choose the correct answer.

SPECIALIZED Vocabulary

If the word artisans in line 20 is new to you, try to figure out its meaning by analyzing its root. *Artisans* comes from the Latin word *artitus*, which means "skilled in the arts." Circle this word root in the word *artisans*.

Based on this root, what kind of work do artisans do? Use a dictionary to check your answer. *WORD ANALYSIS*

HOME HISTORICAL TRAILS EXPERIENCE THE TRAIL THE TRAIL CENTER LINKS

http://www.oregontrailcenter.org/HistoricalTrails/

1 | 2 | 3 | 4 ▶

Trail Basics

The Trek West

During the nineteenth century, over 200,000 men, women, and children traveled the Oregon and California trails in search of new homes in the West. The trek was a difficult journey, and it took five months to travel the 2,000 miles by ox-drawn wagon. Today, you could make the same trip by car in four days or by jet in four hours.

At first the emigrant flood was a trickle. It began in 1841 as a small, lonely caravan of only 58 people—the Bidwell/Bartleson company—followed the trail. Near Soda Springs, half of the party continued to 10 Fort Hall and across southern Idaho to Oregon, while the other half followed the Bear River, crossed the Great Salt Lake Desert and over the Sierra Nevada Mountains to become the first emigrants to follow a land route to California. This first group established what would become the Oregon and the California trails.

This was the beginning of the Great Migration. Two years later, 875 farmers went to Oregon, while 38 split at Soda Springs and followed the new California Trail to California. After the Mexican War was over in 1847, another 4,000 ventured west on the trail. ◀

Who were the people who dared to leave home and hearth and venture 20 into the wilderness? Most were farmers; a few were artisans. After selling their farms, machinery, draft animals, and household goods, most had a sizeable amount of cash to invest in their trip and to settle on new land. . . . The discovery of gold in California in 1848 dramatically changed the character and experience of traveling the trail. ◀

Men dropped everything in a rush to get to California. By the end of 1849, over 25,000 more people traveled the trail. The Gold Rush didn't end in 1849. The following year another 55,000 migrated to California and 50,000 more came in 1852. By the 1860s, when interest waned due to Native American raids, over 300,000 had moved west.

30 The Starting Point

The country that lay ahead of the pioneers contained no towns or settlements. For weeks emigrants crossed vast grassland, which was hot by day and cold at night. Often violent thunderstorms swept down on the hapless travelers. Eventually, they crossed the snow-capped Rocky Mountains. Beyond the mountains lay a vast wilderness of scrubby desert sagebrush, canyons, and forests.

The trail began at the old Independence Landing north of Independence, Missouri. Here emigrants left steamboats after a five- or six-day journey from St. Louis. The center of activity in the
40 small town of Independence was the bustling square. Most of the new pioneers camped a mile or two from the square and were busily purchasing supplies needed for their four- to five-month trek. . . . ▶

The Wagon

Nothing contributed more to the success or failure of a Western wagon trek than the wagons that carried the pioneers across 2,000 miles of jolting wilderness. Pioneers needed wagons strong enough to haul people and supplies for five months or more. To outlast the rugged trail and months of wear, the wagon needed to be constructed of seasoned hardwood. Most pioneers used the typical farm wagon
50 with a canvas cover stretched over hooped frames. A family of four could manage with a single wagon. It would be very tight on space since supplies would take up almost the entire space within the wagon. If they could afford it, many families took more than one wagon. Although most emigrants on the trail went west in their farm wagons, modified to take the punishment, others bought rigs specifically built for the one-way journey.

A wagon had to be light enough to not overtax the mules or oxen that pulled it and strong enough not to break down under loads of as much as 2,500 pounds. For these reasons wagons were constructed
60 of such hardwoods as maple, hickory, and oak. Iron was used only to reinforce parts that took the greatest beating, such as tires, axles,

TEXT FEATURES

Underline the sentence that reveals the starting point mentioned in the **subheading.**

http://www.oregontrailcenter.org/HistoricalTrails/

and hounds. An emigrant wagon was not comfortable to ride in, since wagons lacked springs and there was little room to sit because most space was taken up with cargo.

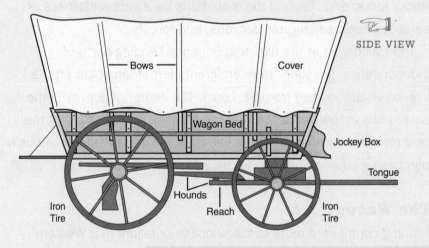

Parts of a Prairie Schooner

SIDE VIEW

Bows　　　Cover

Wagon Bed

Jockey Box

Tongue

Iron
Tire

Hounds

Reach

Iron
Tire

Find and circle each term on the **diagram** in which it appears.

- jockey box
- axle assembly
- bows

In which of the three main parts of a wagon is each of the above elements located? Use the **bulleted list** to complete the lines below.

The bed includes the

_____

The undercarriage includes the

_____

The cover includes the

_____

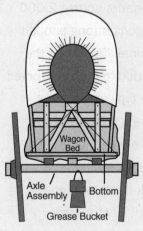

Wagon
Bed

Axle
Assembly　　Bottom

Grease Bucket

BACK VIEW

The three main parts of a prairie wagon were the bed, the undercarriage, and the cover.

- BED—a rectangular wooden box, usually 4 feet wide by 10 feet long. At its front end was a jockey box to hold tools.

- UNDERCARRIAGE—composed of the wheels, axle assemblies, the reach (which connected the two axle assemblies), the hounds (which fastened the rear axle to the reach and the front axle to the wagon tongue), and the bolsters (which supported the wagon bed). Dangling from the rear axle was a bucket containing a mixture of tar and tallow to lubricate the wheels.

- COVER—made of canvas or cotton and was supported by a frame of hickory bows and tied to the sides of the bed. It was closed by a drawstring. The cover served the purpose of shielding the wagon from rain and dust, but when the summer heat became stifling, the cover could be rolled back and bunched to let in more fresh air. ◄

A Day on the Trail

Eighteen to twenty miles a day over prairie was considered a good day's travel. After several days on the trail, certain routines were followed:

4:00 A.M.	A bugler blows a trumpet, or a rifle is fired by the night guards to wake up the camp.
5:00 A.M.	Cattle are rounded up after being allowed to graze during the night.
5:30 A.M.	Women and children are up and fixing breakfast of bacon, corn porridge, or "Johnny Cakes," made of flour and water.
6:30 A.M.	Women rinse plates and mugs and stow bedding, while the men haul down tents and load them in the wagons.
7:00 A.M.	After every family has gathered their teams and hitched them to wagons, a trumpeter signals a "Wagons Ho" to start the wagons down the trail. Average distance covered in a day was usually fifteen miles.
7:30 A.M.	Men ride ahead on horses with shovels to clear out a path, if needed.
"Nooning Time"	Animals and people stop to eat, drink, and rest.
1:00 P.M.	Get back on the trail.
5:00 P.M.	When a good campsite with ample water and grass is found, pioneers stop to set up camp for the evening. Wagons are formed into a corral.
6:00 P.M.	Families unpack and make supper.
7:00 P.M.	Mothers do chores, men talk to each other, and young people dance.
8:00 P.M.	Camp settles down for the night, and guards go out on duty.
Midnight	Night guards are changed. ▶

CLASSIFY

Put a W next to the times of day that were mostly focused on working. Put a P next to the times that were mostly focused on resting or playing.

MAKE GENERALIZATIONS

Based on your responses to the above activity, what general statements can you make about life on the trail?

_____

_____

_____

_____

_____

Reading Comprehension

DIRECTIONS *Answer these questions about the three selections in this lesson by filling in the correct ovals.*

1. Under which subheading of "Through Children's Eyes" would you find details about chores?

   (A) New Experiences

   (B) Keeping Busy

   (C) Dangerous Journey

   (D) Holding onto Hope

2. Which text feature *best* indicates the main topic of "Through Children's Eyes"?

   (A) subheading

   (B) illustration

   (C) sidebar

   (D) title

3. According to "Trail Basics," what was most important to the success of the journey west?

   (A) adequate food and supplies

   (B) the strength of the wagon

   (C) the mules and oxen

   (D) strict daily routines

4. According to the diagram in "Trail Basics," a prairie schooner's *bow* is part of the

   (A) cover

   (B) bed

   (C) undercarriage

   (D) jockey box

5. Based on information in both articles, which of the following statements is true?

   (A) Children had no time to play.

   (B) Children always rode in the wagons.

   (C) Children helped push the wagons.

   (D) Children helped with daily chores.

6. Which idea is supported by all three selections?

   (A) The trip west was filled with hardships and dangers.

   (B) Children on the trail had plenty of time to play.

   (C) Many pioneers shared the fate of the Donner party.

   (D) Prairie schooners were a remarkable innovation.

7. What is the meaning of the word *canter* in line 32 of "Through Children's Eyes"?

   (A) to pick flowers

   (B) to swim upstream

   (C) to change location

   (D) to jog on horseback

8. Which word has a similar base word as *migration* in line 15 of "Trail Basics"?

   (A) relatives

   (B) militant

   (C) emigrate

   (D) vacation

Timed Writing Practice

PROMPT

How often do you set aside your fears and just take a chance? Write a ⟨personal narrative⟩ about a time when you did something you didn't think you could do. End your narrative by telling what you learned about yourself along the way.

BUDGET YOUR TIME

You have 30 minutes to complete this assignment. Decide how much time to spend on each step.

Analyze _____

Plan _____

Write _____

Review _____

Test-Taker's Toolkit

1. ANALYZE THE PROMPT

A. **Circle the words** that tell you what you are being asked to write.

B. **Underline the words** that tell you what topic to write about, and how your narrative should end.

C. **Restate the prompt** in your own words to make sure you understand it.

2. PLAN YOUR RESPONSE

A. **Make notes** Now it's time to get more specific. Use a chart like this one to take notes.

B. **Organize your information** Your narrative should begin by telling readers what you will be writing about. Then retell what you did and explain what you learned. Include vivid details to help readers understand the challenge you faced and how you felt about your experience.

What I Did

What I Learned

Details

3. WRITE AND REVIEW

A. **Write a catchy opening** that will grab your reader's interest. You can try one of the sentence starters here.

- *Have you ever surprised yourself? When I tried to* _____ ,

  I surprised myself by _____

- *If someone had described me as* _____ ,

  I would have said _____ . *That is, until I managed to*

  _____

B. **Write your complete narrative** Leave enough time to read through it. Make sure you did all the things you were asked to do in the prompt.

Ghost of the Lagoon
BY ARMSTRONG SPERRY

RELATED NONFICTION
Great White Shark Attacks: Defanging the Myths

Corals

What makes a
HERO?

When we think of heroes, we often think of extraordinary people with unusual skills and talents. However, ordinary people who bravely face great challenges can also be considered heroes. In "Ghost of the Lagoon," you'll meet a boy who faces a difficult situation with heroic skill and courage.

CHART IT Think of three people whom you consider to be heroes. Write their names in a chart like the one at the right. Then identify the actions and personal qualities that make them heroes to you.

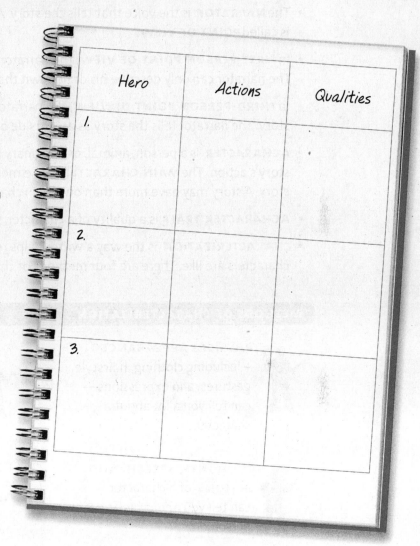

Hero	Actions	Qualities
1.		
2.		
3.		

ASSESSMENT GOALS

By the end of this lesson, you will be able to . . .

• analyze character and point of view in a work of fiction

• apply critical thinking skills to analyze text

• determine the author's purpose in nonfiction texts

• analyze a writing prompt and plan a descriptive essay

Character and Point of View

Like real people, the characters in literature have different personalities. As you read "Ghost of the Lagoon," use the following terms to help uncover the details that reveal the character's behavior, actions, and feelings:

- The **NARRATOR** is the voice that tells the story. A writer's choice of narrator is called **POINT OF VIEW**.

- In **FIRST-PERSON POINT OF VIEW**, the narrator is a character in the story. The narrator can only describe his or her own thoughts and feelings.

- In **THIRD-PERSON POINT OF VIEW**, the narrator is not a character in the story. The narrator tells the story as an outside observer would.

- A **CHARACTER** is a person, animal, or imaginary being who takes part in the story's action. The **MAIN CHARACTER** is the most important character in a story. A story may have more than one main character.

- A **CHARACTER TRAIT** is a quality of a character, such as honesty or bravery.

- **CHARACTERIZATION** is the way a writer helps readers understand what characters are like. There are four methods of characterization.

METHODS OF CHARACTERIZATION

 PHYSICAL APPEARANCE—including clothing, hairstyle, gestures, and expressions—can tell you a lot about a character.

 OTHER CHARACTERS can give clues to what a character is like through their reactions.

 THOUGHTS, SPEECH, AND ACTIONS of a character can tell you about his or her personality.

 NARRATOR'S COMMENTS sometimes tell you directly what a character is like.

ADDITIONAL TERMS FOR CRITICAL ANALYSIS

- **MINOR CHARACTERS** are not the focus of the story, but they help keep the plot moving.

- The word *omniscient* means "all knowing." In a story told from the **THIRD-PERSON OMNISCIENT POINT OF VIEW**, the narrator knows what each character thinks and feels. In a story told from the **THIRD-PERSON LIMITED POINT OF VIEW**, the narrator reveals the thoughts and feelings of only one character.

GHOST
of the
LAGOON

Armstrong Sperry

BACKGROUND This story takes place on Bora Bora. The island is almost completely surrounded by coral reefs and is known for the crystal clear waters of its lagoon.

The island of Bora Bora, where Mako lived, is far away in the South Pacific. It is not a large island—you can paddle around it in a single day—but the main body of it rises straight out of the sea, very high into the air, like a castle. Waterfalls trail down the faces of the cliffs. As you look upward, you see wild goats leaping from crag to crag.

Mako had been born on the very edge of the sea, and most of his waking hours were spent in the waters of the **lagoon**, which was nearly enclosed by the two outstretched arms of the island. He was very clever with his hands; he had made a harpoon that was as straight as an arrow and tipped with five pointed iron spears. He had made a canoe, hollowing it out of a tree. It wasn't a very big canoe—only a little longer than his own height. It had an outrigger, a sort of balancing pole, fastened to one side to keep the boat from tipping over. The canoe was just large enough to hold Mako and his little dog, Afa. They were great companions, these two. ▶

10

lagoon (lə-gōon′) *n.* a shallow body of water separated from a larger body of water by sandbars or other barriers

ANALYZE

Knowing what happens later in the story, which details in the boxed description seem especially important? Put a star next to these details. ✐

One evening Mako lay stretched at full length on the pandanus mats,[1] listening to Grandfather's voice. Overhead,
20 stars shone in the dark sky. From far off came the thunder of the surf on the **reef**.

The old man was speaking of Tupa, the ghost of the lagoon. Ever since the boy could remember, he had heard tales of this terrible monster. Frightened fishermen, returning from the reef at midnight, spoke of the ghost. Over the evening fires, old men told endless tales about the monster. ◄

Tupa seemed to think the lagoon of Bora Bora belonged to him. The natives left presents of food for him out on the reef: a dead goat, a chicken, or a pig. The presents always
30 disappeared mysteriously, but everyone felt sure that it was Tupa who carried them away. Still, in spite of all this food, the nets of the fishermen were torn during the night, the fish stolen. What an appetite Tupa seemed to have!

Not many people had ever seen the ghost of the lagoon. Grandfather was one of the few who had.

"What does he really look like, Grandfather?" the boy asked, for the hundredth time.

The old man shook his head solemnly. The light from the cook fire glistened on his white hair. "Tupa lives in the great
40 caves of the reef. He is longer than this house. There is a sail on his back, not large but terrible to see, for it burns with a white fire. Once, when I was fishing beyond the reef at night, I saw him come up right under another canoe—"

"What happened then?" Mako asked. He half rose on one elbow. This was a story he had not heard before.

The old man's voice dropped to a whisper. "Tupa dragged the canoe right under the water—and the water boiled with white flame. The three fishermen in it were never seen again. Fine swimmers they were, too." ◄
50 Grandfather shook his head. "It is bad fortune even to speak of Tupa. There is evil in his very name."

---

1. **pandanus** (păn-dā′nəs) **mats:** mats made from the fiber of leaves from a palmlike tree.

"But King Opu Nui has offered a reward for his capture," the boy pointed out.

"Thirty acres of fine coconut land, and a sailing canoe as well," said the old man. "But who ever heard of laying hands on a ghost?"

Mako's eyes glistened. "Thirty acres of land and a sailing canoe. How I should love to win that reward!" ▶

Grandfather nodded, but Mako's mother scolded her son for such foolish talk. "Be quiet now, son, and go to sleep. Grandfather has told you that it is bad fortune to speak of Tupa. Alas, how well we have learned that lesson! Your father—" She stopped herself.

"What of my father?" the boy asked quickly. And now he sat up straight on the mats.

"Tell him, Grandfather," his mother whispered.

The old man cleared his throat and poked at the fire. A little shower of sparks whirled up into the darkness.

"Your father," he explained gently, "was one of the three fishermen in the canoe that Tupa destroyed." His words fell upon the air like stones dropped into a deep well.

Mako shivered. He brushed back the hair from his damp forehead. Then he squared his shoulders and cried fiercely, "I shall slay Tupa and win the king's reward!" He rose to his knees, his slim body <u>tense</u>, his eyes flashing in the firelight.

"Hush!" his mother said. "Go to sleep now. Enough of such foolish talk. Would you bring trouble upon us all?"

Mako lay down again upon the mats. He rolled over on his side and closed his eyes, but sleep was long in coming.

The palm trees whispered above the dark lagoon, and far out on the reef the sea thundered.

The boy was slow to wake up the next morning. The ghost of Tupa had played through his dreams, making him <u>restless</u>. And so it was almost noon before Mako sat up on the mats

MAKE JUDGMENTS

Remember what happens later in the story. Was the reward the most important reason why Mako decided to fight Tupa?

☐ yes   ☐ no

Explain your answer.

_____

_____

_____

_____

tense (tĕns) *adj.* nervous; feeling strain

restless (rĕst'lĭs) *adj.* unable to sleep or rest

TestSmart

What details are used to characterize Mako in lines 82–86?

(A) the way Mako looks

(B) Mako's thoughts and actions

(C) the narrator's comments about Mako

(D) other characters' reactions to Mako

TIP A test question may ask you to identify which method of **characterization** the author uses in a specific part of a story. To answer this kind of question, **reread** the passage to see what kinds of details are included. In this case, the narrator doesn't discuss the way Mako looks, so you know that answer is not correct. Choose the answer that *best* describes the details you find in the passage.

ANALYZE

In the boxed text, notice that the **narrator** shows you the lagoon as Mako sees it. The narrator also reveals Mako's thoughts. Circle words and phrases in these lines that remind you that you are seeing what Mako sees.

and stretched himself. He called Afa, and the boy and his dog ran down to the lagoon for their morning swim. ◄

When they returned to the house, wide-awake and hungry, Mako's mother had food ready and waiting.

"These are the last of our bananas," she told him. "I wish you would paddle out to the reef this afternoon and bring back a new bunch."

The boy agreed eagerly. Nothing pleased him more than such an errand, which would take him to a little island on the outer reef, half a mile from shore. It was one of Mako's favorite playgrounds, and there bananas and oranges grew in great plenty.

"Come, Afa," he called, gulping the last mouthful. "We're going on an expedition." He picked up his long-bladed knife and seized his spear. A minute later, he dashed across the white sand, where his canoe was drawn up beyond the water's reach.

Afa barked at his heels. He was all white except for a black spot over each eye. Wherever Mako went, there went Afa also. Now the little dog leaped into the bow of the canoe, his tail wagging with delight. The boy shoved the canoe into the water and climbed aboard. Then, picking up his paddle, he thrust it into the water. The canoe shot ahead. Its sharp bow cut through the green water of the lagoon like a knife through cheese. And so clear was the water that Mako could see the coral gardens, forty feet below him, growing in the sand. The shadow of the canoe moved over them.

A school of fish swept by like silver arrows. He saw scarlet rock cod with ruby eyes and the head of a conger eel[2] peering out from a cavern in the coral. The boy thought suddenly of Tupa, ghost of the lagoon. On such a bright day it was hard to believe in ghosts of any sort. The fierce sunlight drove away all thought of them. Perhaps ghosts were only old men's stories, anyway! ◄

---

2. **rock cod . . . conger eel:** Rock cod is a type of saltwater fish, and a conger eel is a large eel.

Mako's eyes came to rest upon his spear—the spear that he had made with his own hands—the spear that was as straight and true as an arrow. He remembered his vow of the night before. Could a ghost be killed with a spear? Some night, when all the village was sleeping, Mako swore to himself that he would find out! He would paddle out to the reef and challenge Tupa! Perhaps tonight. Why not? He caught his breath at the thought. A shiver ran down his back. His hands were tense on the paddle. ▶

As the canoe drew away from shore, the boy saw the coral reef that, above all others, had always interested him. It was of white coral—a long slim shape that rose slightly above the surface of the water. It looked very much like a shark. There was a ridge on the back that the boy could pretend was a dorsal fin, while up near one end were two dark holes that looked like eyes!

Times without number the boy had practiced spearing this make-believe shark, aiming always for the eyes, the most **vulnerable** spot. So true and straight had his aim become that the spear would pass right into the eyeholes without even touching the sides of the coral. Mako had named the coral reef Tupa.

This morning, as he paddled past it, he shook his fist and called, "Ho, Mister Tupa! Just wait till I get my bananas. When I come back, I'll make short work of you!" ▶

Afa followed his master's words with a sharp bark. He knew Mako was excited about something.

The bow of the canoe touched the sand of the little island where the bananas grew. Afa leaped ashore and ran barking into the jungle, now on this trail, now on that. Clouds of sea birds whirled from their nests into the air with angry cries.

Mako climbed into the shallow water, waded ashore, and pulled his canoe up on the beach. Then, picking up his banana knife, he followed Afa. In the jungle the light was so dense and green that the boy felt as if he were moving underwater. Ferns grew higher than his head. The branches of

CLASSIFY

Think about the narrator's voice throughout the story. Which sentence best describes the story's **point of view?** Check one.

☐ The narrator reveals the thoughts of all the characters.

☐ The narrator reveals the thoughts of only one character.

This type of point of view is called

_____

_____

vulnerable (vŭl′nər-ə-bəl) adj. open to attack or damage

ANALYZE

Underline details in the boxed text that foreshadow, or hint at, the story's ending. ◖

the trees formed a green roof over him. A flock of parakeets fled on swift wings. Somewhere a wild pig crashed through the undergrowth while Afa dashed away in **pursuit**. Mako paused anxiously. Armed only with his banana knife, he had no desire to meet the wild pig. The pig, it seemed, had no 160 desire to meet him, either.

Then, ahead of him, the boy saw the broad green blades of a banana tree. A bunch of bananas, golden ripe, was growing out of the top.

At the foot of the tree he made a nest of soft leaves for the bunch to fall upon. In this way the fruit wouldn't be crushed. Then with a swift slash of his blade he cut the stem. The bananas fell to the earth with a dull thud. He found two more bunches.

Then he thought, "I might as well get some oranges while 170 I'm here. Those little rusty ones are sweeter than any that grow on Bora Bora." ◄

So he set about making a net out of palm leaves to carry the oranges. As he worked, his swift fingers moving in and out among the strong green leaves, he could hear Afa's excited barks off in the jungle. That was just like Afa, always barking at something: a bird, a fish, a wild pig. He never caught anything, either. Still, no boy ever had a finer companion.

The palm net took longer to make than Mako had realized. By the time it was finished and filled with oranges, the jungle 180 was dark and gloomy. Night comes quickly and without warning in the islands of the tropics.

Mako carried the fruit down to the shore and loaded it into the canoe. Then he whistled to Afa. The dog came bounding out of the bush, wagging his tail.

"Hurry!" Mako scolded. "We won't be home before the dark comes."

The little dog leaped into the bow of the canoe, and Mako came aboard. Night seemed to rise up from the surface of the

water and swallow them. On the distant shore of Bora Bora,
190 cook fires were being lighted. The first star twinkled just over
the dark mountains. Mako dug his paddle into the water, and
the canoe leaped ahead.

The dark water was alive with phosphorus.[3] The bow of the
canoe seemed to cut through a pale liquid fire. Each dip of
the paddle trailed streamers of light. As the canoe approached
the coral reef, the boy called, "Ho, Tupa! It's too late tonight
to teach you your lesson. But I'll come back tomorrow." The
coral shark glistened in the darkness.

And then, suddenly, Mako's breath caught in his throat.
200 His hands felt weak. Just beyond the fin of the coral Tupa,
there was another fin—a huge one. It had never been there
before. And—could he believe his eyes? It was moving.

The boy stopped paddling. He dashed his hand across his
eyes. Afa began to bark furiously. The great white fin, shaped
like a small sail, glowed with phosphorescent light. Then
Mako knew. Here was Tupa—the real Tupa—ghost of the
lagoon!

His knees felt weak. He tried to cry out, but his voice died
in his throat. The great shark was circling slowly around the
210 canoe. With each circle, it moved closer and closer. Now the
boy could see the phosphorescent glow of the great shark's
sides. As it moved in closer, he saw the yellow eyes, the gill
slits in its throat. ▶

Afa leaped from one side of the canoe to the other. In
sudden anger Mako leaned forward to grab the dog and shake
him soundly. Afa wriggled out of his grasp as Mako tried to
catch him, and the shift in weight tipped the canoe on one
side. The outrigger rose from the water. In another second
they would be overboard. The boy threw his weight over
220 quickly to balance the canoe, but with a loud splash Afa fell
over into the dark water. ▶

---

3. **phosphorus** (fŏs′fər-əs): a substance that glows with a yellowish or white light.

ANALYZE

How would this paragraph be different if it were written in **first-person point of view?** Change words and phrases by marking corrections in the text.

ANALYZE

Think about what happens next in the story. How do Afa's actions help move the plot toward its climax? Explain your answer.

Mako stared after him in dismay. The little dog, instead of swimming back to the canoe, had headed for the distant shore. And there was the great white shark—very near.

"Afa! Afa! Come back! Come quickly!" Mako shouted.

The little dog turned back toward the canoe. He was swimming with all his strength. Mako leaned forward. Could Afa make it? Swiftly the boy seized his spear. Bracing himself, he stood upright. There was no weakness in him now. His dog, his companion, was in danger of instant death.

Afa was swimming desperately to reach the canoe. The white shark had paused in his circling to gather speed for the attack. Mako raised his arm, took aim. In that instant the shark charged. Mako's arm flashed forward. All his strength was behind that thrust. The spear drove straight and true, right into the great shark's eye. Mad with pain and rage, Tupa whipped about, lashing the water in fury. The canoe rocked back and forth. Mako struggled to keep his balance as he drew back the spear by the cord fastened to his wrist.

He bent over to seize Afa and drag him aboard. Then he stood up, not a moment too soon. Once again the shark charged. Once again Mako threw his spear, this time at the other eye. The spear found its mark. Blinded and weak from loss of blood, Tupa rolled to the surface, turned slightly on his side. Was he dead?

Mako knew how clever sharks could be, and he was taking no chances. Scarcely daring to breathe, he paddled toward the still body. He saw the faintest motion of the great tail. The shark was still alive. The boy knew that one flip of that tail could overturn the canoe and send him and Afa into the water, where Tupa could destroy them.

Swiftly, yet calmly, Mako stood upright and braced himself firmly. Then, murmuring a silent prayer to the shark god, he threw his spear for the last time. Downward, swift as sound, the spear plunged into a white shoulder. ◄

Peering over the side of the canoe, Mako could see the great fish turn over far below the surface. Then slowly, slowly,

230

240

250

ANALYZE

Think about how Tupa is **characterized** in lines 231–255. Match each **character trait** with the method of characterization used to reveal it. Write the letter of the method next to each trait.

Methods used to reveal traits

A. Tupa's actions

B. Mako's responses

C. the narrator's comments

Tupa's traits

1. clever _____

2. fast _____

3. frightening _____

the great shark rose to the surface of the lagoon. There he floated, half on one side.

260   Tupa was dead. ▶

Mako flung back his head and shouted for joy. Hitching a strong line about the shark's tail, the boy began to paddle toward the shore of Bora Bora. The dorsal fin, burning with the white fire of phosphorus, trailed after the canoe.

Men were running down the beaches of Bora Bora, shouting as they leaped into their canoes and put out across the lagoon. Their cries reached the boy's ears across the water.

"It is Tupa—ghost of the lagoon," he heard them shout. "Mako has killed him!" ▶

270   That night, as the tired boy lay on the pandanus mats listening to the distant thunder of the sea, he heard Grandfather singing a new song. It was the song which would be sung the next day at the feast which King Opu Nui would give in Mako's honor. The boy saw his mother bending over the cook fire. The stars leaned close, winking like friendly eyes. Grandfather's voice reached him now from a great distance, "Thirty acres of land and a sailing canoe . . ."

MAKE JUDGMENTS

In your opinion, is Tupa a **main character** or a **minor character**? Explain your answer.

_____

_____

_____

MAKE JUDGMENTS

Notice that the **third-person limited point of view** only provides the actions of the islanders in lines 265–269. What can you guess about their feelings as they see Mako paddling toward the shore?

I think the islanders feel

_____

because_____

_____

_____

_____

Big Question

Was Mako's fight with Tupa heroic? Or was Mako simply trying to win a generous reward? Use specific examples to support your answer.
MAKE JUDGMENTS

_____

_____

_____

_____

Reading Comprehension

DIRECTIONS *Answer these questions about "Ghost of the Lagoon" by filling in the correct ovals.*

1. Which method does the author use to characterize Mako in lines 52–58?

   (A) Mako's words

   (B) Mako's actions

   (C) other characters' reactions to Mako

   (D) the narrator's comments about Mako

2. A minor character is

   (A) an animal companion

   (B) usually the narrator

   (C) important to the plot

   (D) the focus of the plot

3. Which statement is *not* always true of a story in first-person point of view?

   (A) The narrator can only reveal his or her thoughts.

   (B) The narrator uses the pronouns *I* and *me*.

   (C) The narrator is a character in the story.

   (D) The narrator is the hero of the story.

4. You know this story is told from the third-person point of view because

   (A) the story has a narrator

   (B) Mako is the main character

   (C) the narrator speaks as an outside observer

   (D) the narrator is part of the action

5. Which character trait does *not* describe Mako?

   (A) forgiving

   (B) adventurous

   (C) strong

   (D) good with his hands

6. Which statement *best* explains third-person limited point of view?

   (A) The narrator describes one character's thoughts.

   (B) The narrator describes all characters' thoughts.

   (C) The narrator is a minor character in the story.

   (D) The narrator is the main character.

7. In line 108, what is the meaning of the word *bow*?

   (A) the front of a boat

   (B) a ribbon tied on a gift

   (C) to bend from the waist

   (D) what a violin is played with

8. What is the meaning of the word *true* in line 137?

   (A) honest

   (B) accurate

   (C) straight

   (D) believable

Responding in Writing

9. Short Response Write a character sketch of Mako.

_____

_____

_____

_____

_____

_____

Test-Taker's Toolkit

ACADEMIC VOCABULARY When you're asked to write a **character sketch,** you need to write a short description of the character. Include details that show what the character is like. Include details about the character's actions, personal history, and **character traits.**

GRAPHIC ORGANIZER Use the graphic organizer below to help you gather details for your character sketch.

How others react to him

What he does

MAKO

Who he is

What his personality is like

- **Great White Shark Attacks: Defanging the Myths**
  MAGAZINE ARTICLE
- **Corals**
  ONLINE ARTICLE

Use with "Ghost of the Lagoon," p. 24

What's the Connection?

"Ghost of the Lagoon" is about a shark that attacks an island community for many years. The *National Geographic* article "Great White Shark Attacks: Defanging the Myths" provides a very different view of sharks. The online article "Corals" describes how coral reefs like the one around Bora Bora form.

TAKE A QUIZ How much do you know about great white sharks? Decide whether each statement is true or false and check the correct box below. Then use the information in "Great White Shark Attacks" to check your answers.

SHARKS: FACT OR FICTION?	TRUE	FALSE
Most people do not survive shark attacks.	☐	☐
Sharks become crazed when blood is in the water.	☐	☐
Great white sharks can weigh 5,000 pounds.	☐	☐
Sharks bite things because they are curious.	☐	☐

LEARN THE SKILL: IDENTIFY AUTHOR'S PURPOSE

Every author has a **purpose,** or reason, for writing a text. An author may write for any of the following reasons:

- to inform readers about a topic or to explain something
- to persuade readers to act or think in a certain way
- to express thoughts and feelings
- to entertain readers

An author may also have more than one purpose for writing. For example, an author may seek to inform readers while also entertaining them. In this case, you must decide which purpose is the author's main reason for writing the text. This is called the **primary purpose.** The purpose that is less important is called the **secondary purpose.**

For more on author's purpose, see *Nonfiction Handbook* page R5.

Great White Shark Attacks:
Defanging the Myths ▶

by Jennifer Hile
from *National Geographic*

SET A PURPOSE
My purpose for reading is

_____

_____

_____

AUTHOR'S PURPOSE

Sometimes the title of a selection contains a clue to the author's purpose for writing it. What does the phrase "defanging the myths" tell you about the purpose of the article?

_____

_____

_____

_____

There is good and bad news for surfers regarding the great white shark (*Carcharodon carcharias*). The bad news, according to shark scientists, is that great whites are sharp-sighted, curious animals. They are prone to taking "taste tests" of unfamiliar objects that catch their eye. The good news is they generally don't like to eat people.

"In the 20th century, there were 108 authenticated, unprovoked shark attacks along the Pacific Coast of the United States," said Ralph Collier, president of the Shark Research
10 Committee in Canoga Park, California.

Of those, eight attacks were fatal. "When you consider the number of people in the water during that hundred-year period, you realize deadly strikes are very rare," said Collier.

Films like *Jaws* promote the image of great whites as mindless hunters prowling dark, coastal waters for unfortunate swimmers—an animal whipped to frenzy by the scent of human blood. Yet not only do most people survive their encounters, many suffer only moderate injuries. Swimmers dragged underwater by great whites are sometimes left with
20 puncture marks, but the animals often don't inflict more severe wounds. ▶

A great white shark can reach 20 feet in length and weigh up to 5,000 pounds. Survivors' explanations of their escapes increase misconceptions about the nature of this beast.

CLASSIFY

In lines 14–21, find one myth that the author exposes and draw a line through it. Find one fact and draw a box around it.

SPECIALIZED Vocabulary

Specialized words in science articles are usually explained somewhere in the text. Underline the words that explain what pinnipeds are.

WORD ANALYSIS

Mistaken Identity

The most common myth is that great whites, with their poor vision, attack divers and surfers in wet suits, mistaking them for <u>pinnipeds</u> (seals and sea lions), their main prey. In this scenario, once the animal realizes its mistake, it releases the victim and
30 swims away. ◀

"Completely false," said R. Aidan Martin, director of ReefQuest Centre for Shark Research in Vancouver, Canada. A shark's behavior while hunting a pinniped differs markedly from how it approaches people. This suggests that the animal does not confuse surfers for seals.

"I spent five years in South Africa and observed over 1,000 predatory attacks on sea lions by great whites," said Martin. "The sharks would rocket to the surface and pulverize their prey with incredible force."
40 By comparison, sharks usually approach people with what he calls "leisurely or undramatic behavior."

Curious Animals

On August 15, 1987, Craig Rogers, a landscape contractor then living in Santa Cruz, California, paddled out to go surfing at a nearby break. It was 7:30 A.M., Rogers was sitting up on his board, legs dangling over each side, searching the horizon for the next set of waves. Abruptly, he noticed his board stopped bobbing in the water.

Comparing Sizes

17 feet

6.75 feet

"I looked down and my eyes filled with a sight of
50 instantaneous horror," said Rogers. A great white shark was
biting his board just in front of his left hand. The head was
almost three feet across. "I could have touched its eye with
my elbow."

The shark had surfaced so quietly, Rogers hadn't heard a
thing. He flung up his hands, accidentally grazing two of his
fingers along the shark's teeth. "I yelled in terror and slid off
the board to the opposite side," Rogers explained in a written
report made just after the attack.

He was bleeding when he entered the water. Submerging
60 to his shoulder, he watched the shark gently release his board
and sink like a submarine, disappearing beneath him. Later
analyses of the puncture marks on his board suggest the
shark was 17 feet in length.

"It is typical for a great white to swim up to someone at a
relaxed pace, take a bite, then swim off," said Collier. . . . ▶

Teeth Like Hands

"Great whites are curious and investigative animals," said
Martin. "That's what most people don't realize. When great
whites bite something unfamiliar to them, whether a person
70 or a crab pot, they're looking for tactile evidence about what
it is."

What is the author's primary purpose for writing this selection?

(A) to explain the truth about sharks

(B) to express admiration for sharks

(C) to entertain readers with stories of shark attacks

(D) to persuade readers that sharks are dangerous

TIP When a question asks you to state an author's primary purpose, **recall the details that the author includes** in the text. Ask yourself what purpose most of the details support. In this case, you should scan the text to recall the facts, anecdotes, and quotations the author includes. What message do most of these details communicate?

A great white uses its teeth the way humans use their hands. In a living shark, every tooth has ten to fifteen degrees of flex. When the animal opens its mouth, the tooth bed is pulled back, "causing their teeth to splay out like a cat's whiskers," said Martin.

"Combine that with the flexibility of each tooth, and you realize a great white can use its jaws like a pair of forceps. They're very adept at grabbing things that snag their curiosity."

80 Great whites are also sharp-sighted, further evidence that they do not mistake humans for other prey. Scientists believe that sharks see as well below the surface as humans do above it. And they see in color. . . .

"What we need to remember is that if great whites really liked to eat people, there would be a lot more fatalities," said Collier. "And I wouldn't interview so many survivors." ◀

How to Reduce the Risk of Shark Attack

1. Swim, surf, or dive with other people.
2. Stay out of the water at dawn, dusk, and night, when some species of sharks may move inshore to feed.
3. Do not enter the water if you have open wounds or are bleeding.
4. Avoid murky waters, harbor entrances, and areas near stream mouths (especially after heavy rains), channels, or steep dropoffs. These are frequented by sharks.
5. Do not wear high-contrast clothing or shiny jewelry. Sharks see contrast very well.
6. Refrain from excessive splashing; keep pets, which swim erratically, out of the water. Sharks are known to be attracted to such activity.
7. Do not enter the water if sharks are known to be present, and leave the water quickly and calmly if one is sighted. Do not provoke or harass a shark, even a small one.
8. If fish or turtles start to behave erratically, leave the water. Be alert to the presence of dolphins, as they are prey for some large sharks.
9. Do not swim near people fishing or spearfishing.
10. Swim or surf at beaches patrolled by lifeguards. ◀

HOME | CORAL REEFS | OCEANS | COASTS | TIDES

1 | 2 | 3 ▶

Corals

WHAT ARE CORALS? ▶

When corals are mentioned, most people immediately think about clear, warm tropical seas and fish-filled reefs. In fact, the stony, shallow-water corals—the kind that build reefs—are only one type of coral. There are also soft corals and deep water corals that live in dark, cold waters.

10   Almost all corals are colonial organisms. This means that they are composed of hundreds to hundreds of thousands of individual animals, called polyps. Each polyp has a stomach that opens at only one end. This opening, called the mouth, is surrounded by a circle of tentacles. The polyp uses these tentacles for defense, to capture small animals for food, and to clear away debris. Food enters the stomach through the mouth. After the food is consumed, waste products are expelled through the same opening.

    Most corals feed at night. To capture their food, corals use
20 stinging cells called nematocysts. These cells are located in the coral polyp's tentacles and outer tissues. If you've ever been "stung" by a jellyfish, you've encountered nematocysts.

    Nematocysts are capable of delivering powerful, often lethal toxins, and are essential in capturing prey. A coral's prey ranges in size from nearly microscopic animals called zooplankton to small fish, depending on the size of the coral polyps. In addition to capturing zooplankton and larger animals with their tentacles, many corals also collect fine organic particles in mucous film and strands, which they then draw into their mouths.

AUTHOR'S PURPOSE

Preview this online article by reading the title and subheadings. Use what you learn from previewing to complete each sentence.

1. The author wants to inform readers about

_____

_____

2. The author wants to persuade readers that

_____

_____

30 HOW DO CORAL REEFS FORM?

Coral reefs begin to form when free-swimming coral larvae attach to submerged rocks or other hard surfaces along the edges of islands or continents. As the corals grow and expand, reefs take on one of three major characteristic structures— fringing, barrier, or atoll.

40 Fringing reefs, which are the most common, project seaward directly from the shore, forming borders along the shoreline and surrounding islands. Barrier reefs also border shorelines, but at a greater distance. They are separated from their neighboring land mass by a lagoon of open, often deep water. If a fringing 50 reef forms around a volcanic island that sinks completely below sea

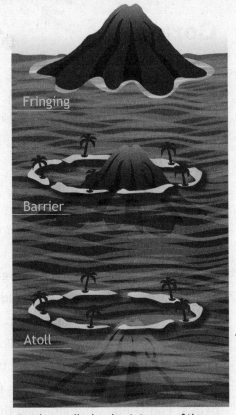

Corals usually develop into one of three forms.

level while the coral continues to grow upward, an atoll forms. Atolls are usually circular or oval, with a central lagoon. Parts of the reef platform may emerge as one or more islands, and gaps in the reef provide access to the central lagoon. ◀

In addition to being some of the most beautiful and biologically diverse habitats in the ocean, barrier reefs and atolls also are some of the oldest. With growth rates of 0.3 to 2 centimeters per year for massive corals, and up to 10 centimeters per year for branching corals, 60 it can take up to 10,000 years for a coral reef to form from a group of larvae. Depending on their size, barrier reefs and atolls can take from 100,000 to 30,000,000 years to fully form.

DRAW CONCLUSIONS

Draw a box around the name of each type of coral reef. Underline details that help you remember each type.

Based on this information, which type of reef surrounds Mako's island in "Ghost of the Lagoon"?

IMPORTANCE OF CORAL REEFS

Coral reefs are some of the most diverse and valuable ecosystems on Earth. Coral reefs support more species per unit area than any other marine environment, including about 4,000 species of fish, 800 species of hard corals, and hundreds of other species. Scientists estimate that there may be another 1 to 8 million undiscovered species of organisms living in and around reefs. This biodiversity is
70 considered key to finding new medicines for the 21st century. Many drugs are now being developed from coral reef animals and plants as possible cures for cancer, arthritis, human bacterial infections, viruses, and other diseases.

Reefs are storehouses of immense biological wealth. They also provide economic and environmental services to millions of people. Coral reefs may provide goods and services worth $375 billion each year. This is an amazing figure for an environment that covers less than 1 percent of Earth's surface. ▶

Healthy reefs contribute to local economies through tourism. Diving
80 tours, fishing trips, hotels, restaurants, and other businesses based near reef systems provide millions of jobs and contribute billions of dollars all over the world. Recent studies show that millions of people visit coral reefs in the Florida Keys every year. These reefs alone are estimated to have a value of $7.6 billion.

The commercial value of U.S. fisheries from coral reefs is over $100 million. In addition, the annual value of recreational fisheries that depend on reefs probably exceeds $100 million per year. In developing countries, coral reefs contribute about one-quarter of the total fish catch, providing critical food resources for tens of millions of
90 people.

Coral reefs buffer adjacent shorelines from wave action and prevent erosion, property damage, and loss of life. Reefs also protect the highly productive wetlands along the coast, as well as ports and harbors and the economies they support. Globally, half a billion people are estimated to live within 100 kilometers of a coral reef and benefit from its production and protection. ▶

💡 **TestSmart**

VOCABULARY
What is the meaning of the word *biological* in line 74?

Ⓐ closely guarded

Ⓑ located underwater

Ⓒ based on scientific data

Ⓓ affecting life and living things

TIP A test question may ask you to define a **scientific term.** Knowing a few common **prefixes** can help you figure out the meaning of many science words. The word *biological* includes the prefix *bio-*, which means "life." Use this information to choose the best answer.

AUTHOR'S PURPOSE

Think about the details the author includes in this section. Which statement best describes the purpose of this section?

☐ to persuade readers that coral reefs are valuable

☐ to inform readers about the uses of coral reefs

Reading Comprehension

DIRECTIONS *Answer these questions about the three selections in this lesson by filling in the correct ovals.*

1. If the primary purpose of "Great White Shark Attacks" were to entertain, what details would it most likely include?

   Ⓐ statistics about shark attacks

   Ⓑ quotations from survivors of shark attacks

   Ⓒ interesting stories about sharks

   Ⓓ scientific explanations of shark behavior

2. According to "Great White Shark Attacks," why do sharks attack people?

   Ⓐ They see people as threats.

   Ⓑ They mistake swimmers for seals.

   Ⓒ They are cold-blooded killers.

   Ⓓ They are curious about an unfamiliar creature.

3. What is the primary purpose of "Corals"?

   Ⓐ to persuade readers to visit a coral reef

   Ⓑ to explain that there are many kinds of coral

   Ⓒ to provide general information about corals

   Ⓓ to persuade readers that corals are important

4. What is one difference between a fringing reef and a barrier reef?

   Ⓐ Barrier reefs protect shorelines from waves and erosion.

   Ⓑ Barrier reefs are separated from land by a lagoon.

   Ⓒ Fringing reefs provide homes for millions of fish.

   Ⓓ Fringing reefs border the shoreline.

5. Which statement is supported by details in both "Ghost of the Lagoon" and "Great White Shark Attacks"?

   Ⓐ Sharks use their teeth to explore.

   Ⓑ Sharks are the enemies of humans.

   Ⓒ Sharks are fast and powerful.

   Ⓓ Sharks can hunt the same waters for years.

6. What does "Coral" help you understand about "Ghost of the Lagoon"?

   Ⓐ why reefs are popular with tourists

   Ⓑ how a reef formed around the island

   Ⓒ why Tupa hunted in the coral reef for so long

   Ⓓ what makes the reef appear to have Tupa's shape

7. Which words in the text explain what *nematocysts* are in line 20 of "Corals"?

   Ⓐ tentacles   Ⓒ polyps

   Ⓑ outer tissues   Ⓓ stinging cells

8. Based on the meaning of the prefix *bio-*, what does *biodiversity* mean in line 69?

   Ⓐ medical research

   Ⓑ undiscovered species

   Ⓒ deep sea environment

   Ⓓ variety of plant and animal life

Timed Writing Practice

PROMPT

What does it mean to be a hero? Write an essay that describes (two different heroes.) Include one example from the selections you just read and another example from your own experience.

BUDGET YOUR TIME

You have **30 minutes** to respond. Decide how much time to spend on each step.

Analyze _____

Plan _____

Write _____

Review _____

Test-Taker's Toolkit

1. ANALYZE THE PROMPT

A. **Read the prompt** slowly so you know what you must do.

B. **Circle key words** that tell you what your writing must include. One phrase has been circled for you.

C. **Make a list** of what's important so you don't forget anything. Write out a list like the one started here.

I must write an essay about _____

that includes _____

_____

_____

2. PLAN YOUR RESPONSE

A. **Make notes** Choose examples that meet the requirements of the prompt.

B. **Organize your information** Use your notes to help plan your essay. You might try organizing it in four paragraphs, as shown here.

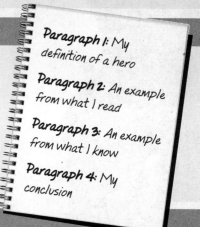

Paragraph 1: My definition of a hero

Paragraph 2: An example from what I read

Paragraph 3: An example from what I know

Paragraph 4: My conclusion

3. WRITE AND REVIEW

A. **Finish your essay** with a strong conclusion that restates the main point of your essay. Try something like this:

These examples taught me that a hero _____

There are different kinds of heroes, but all heroes _____

B. **Write your full response** on a separate piece of paper. Be sure to leave time to check your spelling and grammar.

Nadia the Willful
BY SUE ALEXANDER

RELATED NONFICTION

Sahara

Bedouins: The Desert's Nomadic Hosts

Can MEMORIES
keep the past alive?

Memories are how we hold on to people we have known, places we have been, and things we have done. As time goes by, those memories can fade unless we find ways to keep them fresh. In "Nadia the Willful," a character takes action to protect precious memories.

SKETCH IT Think about a happy or important event you want to remember. It might be a birthday, a holiday, or a day spent with friends. In the notebook shown, plan a scrapbook entry for your memory. Be sure to label the items you plan to include, such as photos, postcards, or other souvenirs.

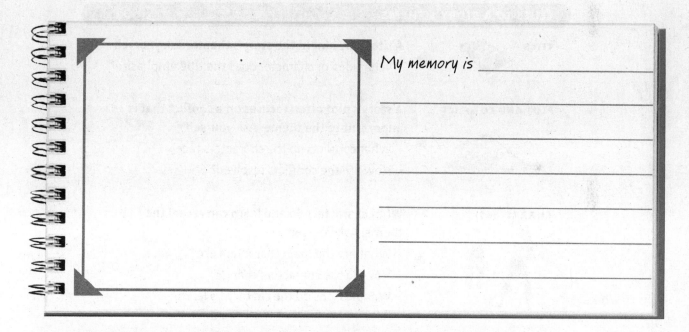

My memory is _____

_____

_____

_____

_____

_____

_____

ASSESSMENT GOALS

By the end of this lesson, you will be able to . . .

- analyze theme in a work of fiction
- apply critical thinking skills to analyze text
- identify main ideas and details in nonfiction texts
- analyze a writing prompt and plan a description

Theme

"Nadia the Willful" is a story about how one family faces a terrible loss. Like many stories, it has a THEME—a message about life or human nature that a writer wants you to understand. Use these tips to identify a story's theme:

- A story's theme can usually be expressed in a sentence, such as "Winning isn't everything" or "Be true to yourself."

- Sometimes the theme of a story is directly stated by the writer. However, most of the time, it is simply implied. You will have to discover the theme on your own.

- A story may have more than one theme.

As you read, you may find clues to the theme in the story's title, plot, characters, and setting. Use the chart below to help recognize these clues.

CLUES TO A STORY'S THEME

TITLE
> A title may hint at the story's theme. Ask yourself
> - What idea or character does the title emphasize?

PLOT AND CONFLICT
> A story's plot often focuses on a conflict that is important to the theme. Ask yourself
> - What conflicts do the characters face?
> - How are the conflicts resolved?

CHARACTERS
> What characters do and learn can reveal the theme. Ask yourself
> - What are the main characters like?
> - How do the characters change?
> - What lessons do the characters learn?

SETTING
> A setting can suggest a theme because of the conflicts it creates. Ask yourself
> - What conflicts does the setting create?
> - How does the setting affect the characters?

ADDITIONAL TERM FOR CRITICAL ANALYSIS

Here's a term that will help you interpret the deeper meaning of Sue Alexander's story.

- A SYMBOL is a person, a place, an object, or an activity that stands for something beyond itself. For example, a white dove is a symbol of peace.

NADIA ✦THE✦ WILLFUL

SUE ALEXANDER

BACKGROUND This story is about a Bedouin girl named Nadia. The Bedouin live in the deserts of North Africa and the Middle East. They are nomads, or wanderers, who move from place to place to find food for the animals they raise. In Bedouin culture, people try not to show strong emotions.

In the land of the drifting sands where the Bedouin move their tents to follow the fertile grasses, there lived a girl whose stubbornness and flashing temper caused her to be known throughout the desert as Nadia the Willful.

Nadia's father, the sheik[1] Tarik, whose kindness and **graciousness** caused his name to be praised in every tent, did not know what to do with his willful daughter.

Only Hamed, the eldest of Nadia's six brothers and Tarik's favorite son, could calm Nadia's temper when it flashed. "Oh, angry one," he would say, "shall we see how long you can stay that way?" And he would laugh and tease and pull at her dark hair until she laughed back. Then she would follow Hamed wherever he led. ▶

One day before dawn, Hamed mounted his father's great white stallion and rode to the west to seek new grazing

10

---

1. **sheik** (shēk): a leader of an Arab family or village.

graciousness (grā′shəs-nəs) *n.* the condition of being pleasant, courteous, and generous

MARK & ANALYZE

Read this selection once on your own, marking the text in any way that is helpful to you.

Then read the story a second time, using the questions in the margins to help you analyze the literature. When you see this pencil, you'll be asked to mark up the text.

ANALYZE

Underline details in the boxed text that help you understand why Tarik and Nadia were so deeply affected by Hamed's death.

console (kən-sōl′) *v.* to ease someone's sorrow; to comfort

clan (klăn) *n.* a family group; a group united by common interests or qualities

ground for the sheep. Nadia stood with her father at the edge of the oasis[2] and watched him go.

Hamed did not return.

20   Nadia rode behind her father as he traveled across the desert from oasis to oasis, seeking Hamed.

Shepherds told them of seeing a great white stallion fleeing before the pillars of wind that stirred the sand. And they said that the horse carried no rider.

Passing merchants, their camels laden with spices and sweets for the bazaar, told of the emptiness of the desert they had crossed. ◀

Tribesmen, strangers, everyone whom Tarik asked, sighed and gazed into the desert, saying, "Such is the will of Allah."[3]

At last Tarik knew in his heart that his favorite son,

30   Hamed, had been claimed, as other Bedouin before him, by the drifting sands. And he told Nadia what he knew—that Hamed was dead.

Nadia screamed and wept and stamped the sand, crying, "Not even Allah will take Hamed from me!" until her father could bear no more and sternly bade her to silence.

Nadia's grief knew no bounds. She walked blindly through the oasis neither seeing nor hearing those who would **console** her. And Tarik was silent. For days he sat inside his tent, speaking not at all and barely tasting the meals set before him.

40   Then, on the seventh day, Tarik came out of his tent. He called all his people to him, and when they were assembled, he spoke. "From this day forward," he said, "let no one utter Hamed's name. Punishment shall be swift for those who would remind me of what I have lost."

Hamed's mother wept at the decree. The people of the **clan** looked at one another uneasily. All could see the hardness that

---

2. **oasis:** a fertile or green spot in a desert or wasteland, made so by the presence of water.

3. **Allah** (äl′ə): the name for God in the Islamic religion.

had settled on the sheik's face and the coldness in his eyes, and so they said nothing. But they obeyed. ▶

Nadia, too, did as her father decreed, though each day 50 held something to remind her of Hamed. As she passed her brothers at play, she remembered games Hamed had taught her. As she walked by the women weaving patches for the tents and heard them talking and laughing, she remembered tales Hamed had told her and how they had made her laugh. And as she watched the shepherds with their flock, she remembered the little black lamb Hamed had loved.

Each memory brought Hamed's name to Nadia's lips, but she stilled the sound. And each time that she did so, her unhappiness grew until, finally, she could no longer 60 contain it. She wept and raged at anyone and anything that crossed her path. Soon everyone at the oasis fled at her approach. And she was more lonely than she had ever been before.

One day, as Nadia passed the place where her brothers were playing, she stopped to watch them. They were playing one of the games that Hamed had taught her. But they were playing it wrong.

Without thinking, Nadia called out to them. "That is not the way! Hamed said that first you jump this way and then 70 you jump back!"

Her brothers stopped their game and looked around in fear. Had Tarik heard Nadia say Hamed's name? But the sheik was nowhere to be seen.

"Teach us, Nadia, as our brother taught you," said her smallest brother.

And so she did. Then she told them of other games and how Hamed had taught her to play them. And as she spoke of Hamed, she felt an easing of the hurt within her.

So she went on speaking of him. ▶

COMPARE

Compare the characters' actions in lines 45–48 with their actions later in the story. Describe the patterns of behavior that you begin to see here.

Hamed's mother

_____

_____

Tarik

_____

_____

people of the clan

_____

_____

INTERPRET

How do the events in lines 71–79 reflect the story's **theme?**

_____

_____

_____

_____

She went to where the women sat at their loom[4] and spoke of Hamed. She told them tales that Hamed had told her. And she told how he had made her laugh as he was telling them.

At first the women were afraid to listen to the willful girl and covered their ears, but after a time, they listened and laughed with her. ◀

"Remember your father's promise of punishment!" Nadia's mother warned when she heard Nadia speaking of Hamed. "Cease, I implore you!"

90 Nadia knew that her mother had reason to be afraid, for Tarik, in his grief and bitterness, had grown quick-tempered and sharp of tongue. But she did not know how to tell her mother that speaking of Hamed eased the pain she felt, and so she said only, "I will speak of my brother! I will!" And she ran away from the sound of her mother's voice.

She went to where the shepherds tended the flock and spoke of Hamed. The shepherds ran from her in fear and hid behind the sheep. But Nadia went on speaking. She told of Hamed's love for the little black lamb and how he had taught it to leap at his whistle. Soon the shepherds left off their 100 hiding and came to listen. Then they told their own stories of Hamed and the little black lamb. ◀

The more Nadia spoke of Hamed, the clearer his face became in her mind. She could see his smile and the light in his eyes. She could hear his voice. And the clearer Hamed's voice and face became, the less Nadia hurt inside and the less her temper flashed. At last, she was filled with peace.

But her mother was still afraid for her willful daughter. Again and again she sought to quiet Nadia so that Tarik's bitterness would not be turned against her. And again and 110 again Nadia tossed her head and went on speaking of Hamed.

Soon, all who listened could see Hamed's face clearly before them.

---

4. **loom:** a tool used for making thread or yarn into cloth by weaving strands together at right angles.

CLASSIFY

Think about the way different characters act throughout the story. Who are the leaders and who are the followers? On the lines below, label each character L for leader or F for follower.

_____ Nadia

_____ Nadia's mother

_____ Tarik

_____ people of the clan

MAKE INFERENCES

Reread the boxed text. What might the little black lamb be a **symbol** of? Give details to support your answer.

It's a symbol of _____

_____

Why I think so:

_____

_____

_____

_____

One day, the youngest shepherd came to Nadia's tent, calling, "Come, Nadia! See Hamed's black lamb, it has grown so big and strong!" ▶

But it was not Nadia who came out of the tent.

It was Tarik.

On the sheik's face was a look more fierce than that of a desert hawk, and when he spoke, his words were as sharp as a
120 scimitar.

"I have forbidden my son's name to be said. And I promised punishment to whoever disobeyed my command. So shall it be. Before the sun sets and the moon casts its first shadow on the sand, you will be gone from this oasis—never to return."

"No!" cried Nadia, hearing her father's words.

"I have spoken!" roared the sheik. "It shall be done!"

Trembling, the shepherd went to gather his possessions.

And the rest of the clan looked at one another uneasily and muttered among themselves.
130 In the hours that followed, fear of being **banished** to the desert made everyone turn away from Nadia as she tried to tell them of Hamed and the things he had done and said.

And the less she was listened to, the less she was able to recall Hamed's face and voice. And the less she recalled, the more her temper raged within her, destroying the peace she had found.

By evening, she could stand it no longer. She went to where her father sat, staring into the desert, and stood before him.

"You will not rob me of my brother Hamed!" she cried,
140 stamping her foot. "I will not let you!"

Tarik looked at her, his eyes colder than the desert night.

But before he could utter a word, Nadia spoke again. "Can you recall Hamed's face? Can you still hear his voice?"

Tarik started in surprise, and his answer seemed to come unbidden to his lips. "No, I cannot! Day after day I have sat in this spot where I last saw Hamed, trying to remember the look, the sound, the happiness that was my beloved son—but I cannot."

TestSmart

Which sentence *best* states the theme of this story?

Ⓐ A sheik's eldest son has died.

Ⓑ Life in the desert can be harsh.

Ⓒ Memories can keep the past alive.

Ⓓ Silence is the best way to deal with loss.

TIP A test question may ask you about a story's **theme**. Remember that a story's theme is often **revealed by what a character learns**. To answer this question, think about what Nadia and Tarik have learned as they try to cope with their loss.

INTERPRET

Remember that a story can have more than one **theme**. What message can you find in Nadia's personality and behavior?

_____

_____

_____

Put stars by details in the story that support your interpretation. ✏

Big Question

According to the story, what is one way to keep memories alive? *CLARIFY*

_____

_____

And he wept.

150 Nadia's tone became gentle. "There is a way, honored father," she said. "Listen."

And she began to speak of Hamed. She told of walks she and Hamed had taken, and of talks they had had. She told how he had taught her games, told her tales, and calmed her when she was angry. She told many things that she remembered, some happy and some sad.

And when she was done with the telling, she said gently, "Can you not recall him now, Father? Can you not see his face? Can you not hear his voice?"

160 Tarik nodded through his tears, and for the first time since Hamed had been gone, he smiled.

"Now you see," Nadia said, her tone more gentle than the softest of the desert breezes, "there is a way that Hamed can be with us still." ◀

The sheik pondered what Nadia had said. After a long time, he spoke, and the sharpness was gone from his voice.

"Tell my people to come before me, Nadia," he said. "I have something to say to them."

When all were assembled, Tarik said, "From this day 170 forward, let my daughter Nadia be known not as Willful, but as Wise. And let her name be praised in every tent, for she has given me back my beloved son." ◀

And so it was. The shepherd returned to his flock, kindness and graciousness returned to the oasis, and Nadia's name was praised in every tent. And Hamed lived again—in the hearts of all who remembered him.

Reading Comprehension

DIRECTIONS *Answer these questions about "Nadia the Willful" by filling in the correct ovals.*

1. Based on the title, what is one possible theme of the story?

    Ⓐ It is reckless to disobey laws.

    Ⓑ Being willful can lead to conflict.

    Ⓒ It is important to think for yourself.

    Ⓓ Those who are truly wise are obedient.

2. Which of the following is *not* an effect of Tarik's decree?

    Ⓐ It causes conflict in the family.

    Ⓑ It makes Nadia lonely and angry.

    Ⓒ It makes members of the clan afraid.

    Ⓓ It brings peace to the clan.

3. In this story, all of the following give you clues to the theme *except*

    Ⓐ Nadia's response to Hamed's death

    Ⓑ Tarik's response to Hamed's death

    Ⓒ the main character's appearance

    Ⓓ the conflicts caused by the decree

4. Why does Tarik change Nadia's name?

    Ⓐ because she outsmarted everyone

    Ⓑ because she taught him an important lesson

    Ⓒ because she is now the leader of the clan

    Ⓓ because she has changed her behavior

5. The black lamb is most likely a symbol of

    Ⓐ Hamed's death

    Ⓑ Bedouin culture

    Ⓒ Hamed's memory

    Ⓓ Nadia's willfulness

6. Why does Nadia stand up to her father?

    Ⓐ She wants to protect the traditions of her people.

    Ⓑ She decides that Tarik should take back his order.

    Ⓒ She refuses to let him take Hamed's memory away from her.

    Ⓓ She is upset because the shepherd has been banished.

7. Based on context clues, what is the meaning of the word *scimitar* in line 120?

    Ⓐ a desert hawk

    Ⓑ a sword

    Ⓒ a sharp word

    Ⓓ a harsh decree

8. Based on context clues, what is the meaning of the word *pondered* in line 165?

    Ⓐ looked for

    Ⓑ thought about

    Ⓒ disagreed with

    Ⓓ turned away from

For help, use
the **Test-Taker's
Toolkit** below.

Responding in Writing

9. Short Response By the end of the story, Nadia's way of dealing with her sadness
has changed. What important lesson has she learned? Write a paragraph describing
Nadia's experiences and what she learned from them.

_____

_____

_____

_____

_____

_____

Test-Taker's Toolkit

GRAPHIC ORGANIZER Use the graphic organizer below to plan your response. As you
fill in the chart, look back at the story to find details that support your explanations.

RESPONSE EARLY IN THE STORY	RESPONSE LATER IN THE STORY	LESSON LEARNED

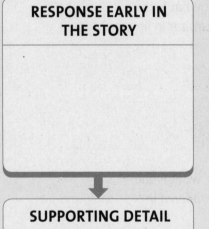  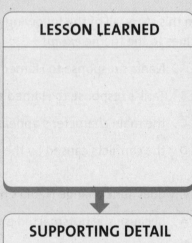

SUPPORTING DETAIL	SUPPORTING DETAIL	SUPPORTING DETAIL

What's the Connection?

Nadia and her family are Bedouins who live in the deserts of North Africa and the Middle East. The brochure "Sahara" describes the mix of traditional and modern ways of life in the desert. The magazine article "Bedouins: The Desert's Nomadic Hosts" describes Bedouin customs.

TEST YOURSELF If you visited the Sahara today, what do you think you would see? With a group, discuss each cultural detail listed below. Decide whether it is part of the past, the present, or both. Record your responses in the first column of the chart. After reading the selections, review your responses and note any changes in the last column.

- *Sahara*
  BROCHURE
- *Bedouins: The Desert's Nomadic Hosts*
  MAGAZINE ARTICLE

Use with "Nadia the Willful," p. 48

LIFE IN THE SAHARA: THEN AND NOW		
Response Before Reading	**Cultural Detail**	**Response After Reading**
	camel caravans	
	salt traders	
	huge cities	
	goat herds	
	living in tents	
	long, flowing robes	

LEARN THE SKILL: IDENTIFY MAIN IDEAS AND DETAILS

The **main ideas** in a nonfiction text are the most important points the writer makes about a topic. **Supporting details,** such as facts or examples, give more information about a main idea. Recognizing the main ideas and understanding supporting details can help you remember the key points of any text you read.

You can use these text features to help identify main ideas:

- The **title** gives or suggests the topic of a nonfiction text.
- **Subheadings** tell the main idea in each section of the text. Often a sentence near the beginning of a section states its main idea.

As you read each section, look for supporting details that tell more about the main idea.

For more on main ideas and supporting details, see *Nonfiction Handbook* page R14.

Sahara

SPECIALIZED
Vocabulary

When you read about different cultures, you should expect to come across unfamiliar words. One example is the word caravans in line 10. Circle context clues in the text that can help you figure out the meaning of this word. One has been done for you.

The Sahara has amazed outsiders for centuries. It is the world's largest desert, and its size is difficult to imagine: 3.3 million square miles, or around 25 percent of Africa. Not surprisingly, the Sahara's name in Arabic means simply "desert."

10   Camel **caravans** looking for gold, ivory, grain, salt, and slaves made the Sahara the world's first gateway to Africa. These endless trains, run by Tuaregs, Arabs, and others, gave rise to the legendary era of trans-Saharan trade— a phenomenon that still defines the Sahara to many outsiders.

20   Today, the Sahara still serves as a border between the continent's black African south and Arab-influenced north. Its scorching heat and size still influence the cycle of drought and rainfall in sub-Saharan Africa. With one

of the planet's lowest population densities, its people—Tuareg, Arab, Tubu, Moor—can seem afloat in vast seas of sand. Blue-robed Tuaregs still run salt caravans and herd goat, sheep, and camels. Moors farm date palms.

But much has changed. The Arabs have retreated to Saharan cities like Cairo; at roughly 10 million people, Africa's largest. Trucks are replacing camels in the salt trade. Tuaregs are acting as guides to Western adventure tourists, and oil and gas operations promise far greater riches than gold and ivory ever could. Political unrest has gripped the region. In the late 1990s, armed Tuareg rebel groups blazed across the desert. Nor has the Sahara escaped the Internet revolution. Rissani, Morocco, a tiny desert oasis, offers several Internet cafés, primarily for tourists about to begin their own exploration of the most famous of deserts. ▶

Bedouins:
THE DESERT'S NOMADIC HOSTS

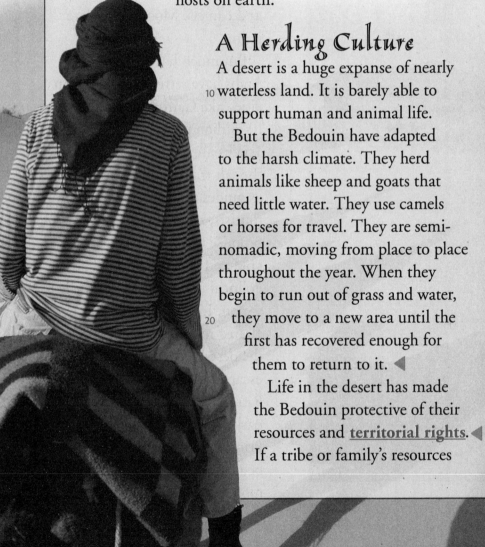

Lost and thirsty in the desert sands, a traveler in North Africa or the Middle East would be wise to seek shelter in a Bedouin tent. These desert people live in areas that cover the Sahara, Sinai, Negev, and Arabian deserts. Their tribes are used to finding resources in a challenging land. Because of this, they are some of the most famous hosts on earth.

A Herding Culture

A desert is a huge expanse of nearly
10 waterless land. It is barely able to support human and animal life.

But the Bedouin have adapted to the harsh climate. They herd animals like sheep and goats that need little water. They use camels or horses for travel. They are semi-nomadic, moving from place to place throughout the year. When they begin to run out of grass and water,
20 they move to a new area until the first has recovered enough for them to return to it.

Life in the desert has made the Bedouin protective of their resources and **territorial rights**. If a tribe or family's resources

MAIN IDEAS AND DETAILS

Underline the main idea in lines 12–22. Circle the supporting details.

SPECIALIZED
Vocabulary

Social studies articles will often use legal or political terms, such as territorial rights in line 25. This term is related to the word *territory*, which means "land." On the lines below, use this information to guess the meaning of *territorial rights*.
WORD ANALYSIS

are used outside of those rights, tribal law has been broken. Those breaks are remembered and corrected.

Hospitality

30 The Bedouin may protect their own rights, but they also protect the rights of strangers. The desert can be dangerous for travelers. The Bedouin make sure to provide food and shelter to anyone who needs them.

Arrive at a Bedouin tent and you'll be given a cup of sweet hot tea made from tea 40 leaves and the desert herbs *habuck* and *marmaraya* to indicate that you are welcome. The Bedouin will take care of you for up to three days, according to their custom. That should give you enough time to recover before you head back out into the vast and solitary desert. ▶

Shelter, Food, and Clothing

50 The tent where you'd stay for those days would be made with materials that came from the Bedouins' herd animals. Tents are traditionally woven from goat or camel hair. A woven curtain divides them into two separate areas. One is a men's section, or *mag'ad*, and the other is a women's area called the *maharama*.

Bedouins raise or grow most of their own food. They cook their bread on an open fire. Meat, especially lamb, is cooked in an underground oven called a *zaarp*.
60 They also eat rice and vegetables. They drink goat and camel milk, and coffee spiced with cardamom.

Their traditional dress is similar to clothing worn by people throughout Egypt. They wear a long, hooded robe called a *jalabiyya*. The extra fabric shelters them from the relentless desert
70 sun and keeps them warm when the temperature drops at night.

Changes to the Bedouin Way of Life

As the world around them changes, some aspects of Bedouin life are changing too. In the last 100 years, many of the Bedouin have given up their solitude and moved into homes in cities and towns. Some have left the desert because of droughts or government programs.

80 But the lives of traditional Bedouins can serve as an example in our time of scarce resources and global climate change. The Bedouin use what they make. They consume little water. They care for their land and conserve resources so they can be used by future generations. ◄

MAIN IDEAS AND DETAILS

Identify the main idea and supporting details in lines 80–85.

The Blue People of the Desert

BY LESLEY REED

The Tuareg people have been called warriors, pirates of the Sahara, and the "blue people" of the desert. Sounds scary, but the day I met them, they were so happy to see us. The women clapped and sang, while the men danced in their dark-blue veils that cover everything but their eyes.

I had come, bumping and shaking over roadless sand dunes, in a jeep full of aid workers, food, and blankets. We were in

10 the African country of Niger during a terrible drought (a long period without rain). There were no green pastures for the Tuareg's herds of camels, goats, and cattle. The animals and the people were going

20 hungry. Some were even dying. Life was so hard that these Tuareg were doing the unthinkable—they were settling into camps near almost dry ponds to learn how to farm. ▶

We ate and slept in a low leather tent, and in the morning, I woke to a surprise. Outside, a crowd of Tuareg men waited with a camel. I had mentioned at dinner that I had always wanted to ride a camel, and they brought me my wish. The camel shook me back and forth as it stood up, front legs then back, but then it settled into an easy walk. It was like riding a rocking horse high above the desert. It was

30 wonderful.

The Tuareg have continued to lose their nomadic ways due to droughts and the growing desert. Now, only a few travel with their herds. The way of the caravan is disappearing, but I will always remember the kindness of the blue people of the desert and the beauty of their ways. ▶

MAIN IDEAS AND DETAILS

Find three details in lines 1–22 of this sidebar that support the idea that life is hard for the Tuareg. Draw a box around each detail. Then number them.

USE PRIOR KNOWLEDGE

Recall the meaning of the word *caravan*. Use your knowledge of this word and how it is used in line 33 to figure out the meaning of *nomadic* in line 31.

I know that <u>caravan</u> means

_____

_____

The idea that these words have in common is

_____

_____

<u>Nomadic</u> probably means

_____

_____

Reading Comprehension

DIRECTIONS *Answer these questions about the three selections in this lesson by filling in the correct ovals.*

1. Which sentence *best* states the main idea of lines 20–35 in "Sahara"?

   (A) The Sahara is the border between northern and southern Africa.

   (B) The Sahara affects the climate of sub-Saharan Africa.

   (C) Population is very spread out in the Sahara.

   (D) Many parts of life in the Sahara have changed little over time.

2. In the brochure, which details are used as examples of recent changes in the Sahara?

   (A) camel caravans

   (B) tourism and political unrest

   (C) trade in ivory, gold, and salt

   (D) the heat and size of the desert

3. What generalization can you make about the Bedouin people, based on details in "Bedouins"?

   (A) They have separate areas for men and women.

   (B) They do not welcome strangers.

   (C) They do not enjoy life in the desert.

   (D) They are no longer nomads.

4. According to the sidebar on page 65, what made some nomadic groups change their lifestyle?

   (A) a terrible drought

   (B) a population increase

   (C) fighting in the region

   (D) economic changes

5. Which detail from "Nadia the Willful" is *not* supported by facts in "Bedouins"?

   (A) Bedouins move from place to place.

   (B) Bedouins live in tents.

   (C) Bedouins often banish people.

   (D) Bedouins keep herds of sheep.

6. According to the articles, all of the following are threats to the nomadic lifestyle *except*

   (A) severe droughts

   (B) modern transportation

   (C) date farming

   (D) the growth of nearby cities

7. Using your knowledge of the Latin root *sol*, you can guess that *solitude* in line 76 of "Bedouins" means

   (A) a card game

   (B) being alone

   (C) a large group

   (D) the height of a place

8. Based on context clues, what is the most likely meaning of the word *indicate* in line 42 of "Bedouins"?

   (A) show

   (B) maintain

   (C) increase

   (D) insure

Timed Writing Practice

PROMPT

If you took a trip to the Sahara, what would you see? Write a description of this region. Include (physical details) about what it looks and feels like. Also include cultural details about how people live in the region. Make sure to choose details from all three selections.

BUDGET YOUR TIME

You have 30 minutes to complete this assignment. Decide how much time to spend on each step.

Analyze _____

Plan _____

Write _____

Review _____

30

Test-Taker's Toolkit

1. ANALYZE THE PROMPT

A. **Read the prompt twice** to make sure you understand it.

B. **Circle key words** in each sentence. One phrase has been circled for you. These words tell you what you must include to get a good score.

C. **Write down a list** of the key elements you need to include.

2. PLAN YOUR RESPONSE

A. **Make notes** Use your list to create a chart that gives a detail or example for each main idea. Review your list to make sure you've included details from each selection.

B. **Organize your information** Use your notes to help organize your description. For this prompt you could begin by giving general facts about the Sahara's geography and climate. Then you could continue by showing how people have adapted to these conditions.

Geography & Climate
-
-
-

How People Live
-
-
-

3. WRITE AND REVIEW

A. A good description uses carefully chosen details that create vivid images in the reader's mind. Instead of saying "huge area," try saying "25 percent of Africa."

B. Be sure to leave time to read through your description to check your spelling and grammar.

The All-American Slurp
BY LENSEY NAMIOKA

RELATED NONFICTION
Potstickers

Jiaoze Dumplings or Potstickers

Are people more ALIKE *or different?*

Have you ever been somewhere and found that the language, food, or customs were different from what you were used to? You may have felt out of place. Or perhaps you discovered that you actually had a lot in common with the people you met. In "The All-American Slurp," a Chinese-American girl learns that people can share similarities even when they appear very different at first.

SURVEY Complete the survey below by marking your favorite in each category. Then survey three to five people you don't know well. Share the results of your surveys to see how much you do (or don't) have in common.

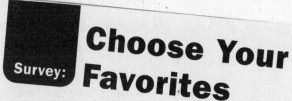

Survey: **Choose Your Favorites**

Choose your favorite from each grouping. Then find out how your classmates answered.

Holidays
- Thanksgiving
- Halloween
- Valentine's Day
- Fourth of July

Seasons
- Winter
- Spring
- Summer
- Fall

Food
- Desserts
- Spicy Foods
- Salty Snacks

Movies
- Dramas
- Comedies
- Musicals
- Sci-Fi
- Action

Music
- Rock 'n' Roll
- Country
- Hip Hop

ASSESSMENT GOALS

By the end of this lesson, you will be able to...

- analyze mood, tone, and style in a work of fiction
- apply critical thinking skills to analyze text
- use text features and signal words to trace steps in a process
- analyze a writing prompt and plan a fiction story

Mood, Tone, and Style

Every story has its own "personality"—characteristics that make it unique. Like an individual's personality, a story's personality can affect how you respond to it. Knowing the following terms can help you figure out the personality of "The All-American Slurp."

- **MOOD** is the feeling that a writer creates for readers. For example, a mood can be tense, relaxed, spooky, or joyful.

- **TONE** is a writer's attitude toward his or her subject. For example, a writer's tone can be affectionate, disgusted, sarcastic, or sincere.

- **STYLE** is a writer's unique way of communicating ideas. Such things as word choice, sentence structure, imagery, and point of view are all part of a writer's style.

MOOD, TONE, AND STYLE	
MOOD (the feeling a writer creates)	**TONE** (a writer's attitude toward the subject)
WORDS TO DESCRIBE MOOD: peaceful, scary, exciting	**WORDS TO DESCRIBE TONE:** humorous, serious, sentimental

STYLE
(not *what* is said, but *how* it is said)

HOW A WRITER REVEALS STYLE:

- **WORD CHOICE** types of nouns and verbs the writer chooses to use (For example: casual and informal, or precise and descriptive)

- **SENTENCE STRUCTURE** sentence length and type (For example: short and simple, or long and complex)

- **IMAGERY** language that appeals to the five senses (vivid descriptions)

ADDITIONAL TERM FOR CRITICAL ANALYSIS

Knowing this additional term will help you discuss Lensey Namioka's story more precisely.

ONOMATOPOEIA is the use of words that sound like their meanings, such as *buzz*, *whisper*, and *gurgle*.

The All-American Slurp

Lensey Namioka

BACKGROUND This story deals with a Chinese family's unfamiliarity with American etiquette. *Etiquette* is a system of rules and traditions that guide behavior in social situations. Different cultures often have different rules. In China, suffering public humiliation—"losing face"—is considered one of the worst things that can happen to a person. Public displays of emotion are frowned upon. It is also considered impolite to brag about one's accomplishments.

MARK & ANALYZE

Read this selection once on your own, marking the text in any way that is helpful to you.

Then read the story a second time, using the questions in the margins to help you. When you see this pencil (✎), you'll be asked to mark up the text.

The first time our family was invited out to dinner in America, we disgraced ourselves while eating celery. We had emigrated to this country from China, and <u>during our early days here we had a hard time with American table manners.</u> ▶

In China we never ate celery raw, or any other kind of vegetable raw. We always had to disinfect the vegetables in boiling water first. When we were presented with our first relish tray, the raw celery caught us unprepared.

We had been invited to dinner by our neighbors, the

10 Gleasons. After arriving at the house, we shook hands with our hosts and packed ourselves into a sofa. As our family of four sat stiffly in a row, my younger brother and I stole glances at our parents for a clue as to what to do next.

Mrs. Gleason offered the relish tray to Mother. The tray looked pretty, with its tiny red radishes, curly sticks of carrots, and long, slender stalks of pale green celery. "Do try some of

COMPARE

Reread the underlined statement. What other embarrassing events in the story support this claim by the narrator?

_____

_____

_____

_____

_____

slurp! z-z-zip! crunch! shloop!

the celery, Mrs. Lin," she said. "It's from a local farmer, and it's sweet."

Mother picked up one of the green stalks, and Father 20 followed suit. Then I picked up a stalk, and my brother did too. So there we sat, each with a stalk of celery in our right hand.

Mrs. Gleason kept smiling. "Would you like to try some of the dip, Mrs. Lin? It's my own recipe: sour cream and onion flakes, with a dash of Tabasco sauce."

Most Chinese don't care for dairy products, and in those days I wasn't even ready to drink fresh milk. Sour cream sounded perfectly **revolting**. Our family shook our heads in unison. ◄

Mrs. Gleason went off with the relish tray to the other 30 guests, and we carefully watched to see what they did. Everyone seemed to eat the raw vegetables quite happily.

Mother took a bite of her celery. *Crunch.* "It's not bad!" she whispered.

Father took a bite of his celery. *Crunch.* "Yes, it *is* good," he said, looking surprised. ◄

I took a bite, and then my brother. *Crunch, crunch.* It was more than good; it was delicious. Raw celery has a slight sparkle, a zingy taste that you don't get in cooked celery. When Mrs. Gleason came around with the relish tray, we each took 40 another stalk of celery, except my brother. He took two.

There was only one problem: long strings ran through the length of the stalk, and they got caught in my teeth. When I help my mother in the kitchen, I always pull the strings out before slicing celery.

I pulled the strings out of my stalk. *Z-z-zip, z-z-zip.* My brother followed suit. *Z-z-zip, z-z-zip, z-z-zip.* To my left, my parents were taking care of their own stalks. *Z-z-zip, z-z-zip, z-z-zip.* ◄

Suddenly I realized that there was dead silence except for 50 our zipping. Looking up, I saw that the eyes of everyone in the room were on our family. Mr. and Mrs. Gleason, their daughter Meg, who was my friend, and their neighbors the

revolting (rĭ-vōl′tĭng) *adj.* causing disgust **revolt** *v.*

MAKE JUDGMENTS

According to American etiquette, what would have been a more polite way for the Lins to turn down the offer of the sour cream dip?

_____

_____

_____

EVALUATE

Which word in lines 32–35 is an example of **onomatopoeia**? Circle it.

CLASSIFY

Reread the boxed text and notice how the author uses **imagery** to help you visualize the scene. Write an *S* next to details about sounds. Write a *T* next to images that relate to taste.

Badels—they were all staring at us as we busily pulled the strings of our celery. ▶

That wasn't the end of it. Mrs. Gleason announced that dinner was served and invited us to the dining table. It was <u>lavishly</u> covered with platters of food, but we couldn't see any chairs around the table. So we helpfully carried over some dining chairs and sat down. All the other guests just

60 stood there.

Mrs. Gleason bent down and whispered to us, "This is a buffet dinner. You help yourselves to some food and eat it in the living room."

Our family beat a retreat back to the sofa as if chased by enemy soldiers. For the rest of the evening, too <u>mortified</u> to go back to the dining table, I nursed a bit of potato salad on my plate. ▶

Next day Meg and I got on the school bus together. I wasn't sure how she would feel about me after the spectacle[1]

70 our family made at the party. But she was just the same as usual, and the only reference she made to the party was, "Hope you and your folks got enough to eat last night. You certainly didn't take very much. Mom never tries to figure out how much food to prepare. She just puts everything on the table and hopes for the best."

I began to relax. The Gleasons' dinner party wasn't so different from a Chinese meal after all. My mother also puts everything on the table and hopes for the best.

80 Meg was the first friend I had made after we came to America. I eventually got acquainted with a few other kids in school, but Meg was still the only real friend I had.

My brother didn't have any problems making friends. He spent all his time with some boys who were teaching him

MAKE INFERENCES

How would you describe the story's **mood** as the Lin family sits in the Gleason's living room?

_____

Predict whether the family's experience is about to get better or worse.

☐ better
☐ worse

lavishly (lăv′ĭsh-lē) *adv.* in a rich or plentiful way; abundantly

mortified (môr′tə-fīd′) *adj.* ashamed, humiliated
mortify *v.*

ANALYZE

Later in the story, a scene that is similar to the Gleasons' dinner party occurs—but the characters switch roles. What is that scene? How are the roles switched?

_____

_____

_____

_____

---

1. **spectacle:** public display of bad behavior.

baseball, and in no time he could speak English much faster than I could—not better, but faster.

I worried more about making mistakes, and I spoke carefully, making sure I could say everything right before opening my mouth. At least I had a better accent than my parents, who never really got rid of their Chinese accent, even years later. My parents had both studied English in school before coming to America, but what they had studied was mostly written English, not spoken.

Father's approach to English was a scientific one. Since Chinese verbs have no tense, he was fascinated by the way English verbs changed form according to whether they were in the present, past imperfect, perfect, pluperfect, future, or future perfect tense. He was always making diagrams of verbs and their inflections,[2] and he looked for opportunities to show off his mastery of the pluperfect and future perfect tenses, his two favorites. "I shall have finished my project by Monday," he would say smugly.[3] ◄

Mother's approach was to memorize lists of polite phrases that would cover all possible social situations. She was constantly muttering things like "I'm fine, thank you. And you?" Once she accidentally stepped on someone's foot, and hurriedly blurted, "Oh, that's quite all right!" Embarrassed by her slip, she resolved to do better next time. So when someone stepped on *her* foot, she cried, "You're welcome!" ◄

In our own different ways, we made progress in learning English. But I had another worry, and that was my appearance. My brother didn't have to worry, since Mother bought him blue jeans for school, and he dressed like all the other boys. But she insisted that girls had to wear skirts. By the time she saw that Meg and the other girls were wearing jeans, it was too late. My school clothes were bought already, and we didn't have money left to buy new outfits for me. We had too many other things to buy first, like furniture, pots, and pans.

---

2. **inflections** (ĭn-flĕk'shənz): different tenses.
3. **smugly:** with self-satisfaction; self-righteously.

SYNTHESIZE

What other details in the story support the narrator's statement that her father has a scientific approach to things?

_____

_____

_____

INTERPRET

Underline the "polite phrases" Mrs. Lin uses.

What effect do these details have on the story's **mood**?

_____

_____

_____

The first time I visited Meg's house, she took me upstairs to her room, and I wound up trying on her clothes. We were pretty much the same size, since Meg was shorter and thinner than average. Maybe that's how we became friends in the first place. Wearing Meg's jeans and T-shirt, I looked at myself in the mirror. I could almost pass for an American—from the back, anyway. At least the kids in school wouldn't stop and stare at me in the hallways, which was what they did when they saw me in my white blouse and navy blue skirt that went a couple of inches below the knees. ▶

When Meg came to my house, I invited her to try on my Chinese dresses, the ones with a high collar and slits up the sides. Meg's eyes were bright as she looked at herself in the mirror. She struck several sultry poses, and we nearly fell over laughing.

The dinner party at the Gleasons' didn't stop my growing friendship with Meg. Things were getting better for me in other ways too. Mother finally bought me some jeans at the end of the month, when Father got his paycheck. She wasn't in any hurry about buying them at first, until I worked on her. This is what I did. Since we didn't have a car in those days, I often ran down to the neighborhood store to pick up things for her. The groceries cost less at a big supermarket, but the closest one was many blocks away. One day, when she ran out of flour, I offered to borrow a bike from our neighbor's son and buy a ten-pound bag of flour at the big supermarket. I mounted the boy's bike and waved to Mother. "I'll be back in five minutes!"

Before I started pedaling, I heard her voice behind me. "You can't go out in public like that! People can see all the way up to your thighs!"

"I'm sorry," I said innocently. "I thought you were in a hurry to get the flour." For dinner we were going to have pot-stickers (fried Chinese dumplings), and we needed a lot of flour. ▶

TestSmart

Which word best describes the author's tone in lines 125–128 when the narrator describes the possibility of wearing blue jeans to school?

- (A) sarcastic
- (B) sympathetic
- (C) surprised
- (D) scornful

TIP When line numbers appear in a test question, always **reread those lines.** If the answer is not directly stated, you have to **infer** the answer by combining clues from the text with what you already know to make an educated guess. The narrator says that the kids at school wouldn't stare at her if she wore jeans. How would most people feel if they stood out in a crowd? Try to infer the author's **tone,** or attitude about this situation.

USE PRIOR KNOWLEDGE

Reread the boxed text. In what ways does the narrator show that she is just like many other kids?

_____

_____

_____

_____

"Couldn't you borrow a girl's bicycle?" complained Mother. "That way your skirt won't be pushed up."

"There aren't too many of those around," I said. "Almost all the girls wear jeans while riding a bike, so they don't see any point buying a girl's bike."

We didn't eat pot-stickers that evening, and Mother was thoughtful. Next day we took the bus downtown and she bought me a pair of jeans. In the same week, my brother made the baseball team of his junior high school, Father started taking driving lessons, and Mother discovered rummage sales. We soon got all the furniture we needed, plus a dart board and a 1,000-piece jigsaw puzzle (fourteen hours later, we discovered that it was a 999-piece jigsaw puzzle). There was hope that the Lins might become a normal American family after all. ◄

Then came our dinner at the Lakeview Restaurant. ◄

The Lakeview was an expensive restaurant, one of those places where a headwaiter dressed in tails conducted you to your seat, and the only light came from candles and flaming desserts. In one corner of the room a lady harpist played tinkling melodies.

Father wanted to celebrate, because he had just been promoted. He worked for an electronics company, and after his English started improving, his superiors decided to appoint him to a position more suited to his training. The promotion not only brought a higher salary but was also a tremendous boost to his pride.

Up to then we had eaten only in Chinese restaurants. Although my brother and I were becoming fond of hamburgers, my parents didn't care much for Western food, other than chow mein.[4]

---

4. **chow·mein** (chou' mān'): Chinese-American dish of vegetables and meat served over fried noodles.

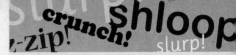

But this was a special occasion, and Father asked his coworkers to recommend a really elegant restaurant. So there we were at the Lakeview, stumbling after the headwaiter in the murky dining room.

At our table we were handed our menus, and they were so big that to read mine I almost had to stand up again. But why 190 bother? It was mostly in French, anyway. ▶

Father, being an engineer, was always systematic. He took out a pocket French dictionary. "They told me that most of the items would be in French, so I came prepared." He even had a pocket flashlight, the size of a marking pen. While Mother held the flashlight over the menu, he looked up the items that were in French.

"Pâté en croûte," he muttered. "Let's see . . . *pâté* is paste . . . *croûte* is crust . . . hmm . . . a paste in crust."

The waiter stood looking patient. I squirmed and died at 200 least fifty times.

At long last Father gave up. "Why don't we just order four complete dinners at random?" he suggested.

"Isn't that risky?" asked Mother. "The French eat some rather peculiar things, I've heard." ▶

"A Chinese can eat anything a Frenchman can eat," Father declared.

The soup arrived in a plate. How do you get soup up from a plate? I glanced at the other diners, but the ones at the nearby tables were not on their soup course, while the more 210 distant ones were invisible in the darkness.

Fortunately my parents had studied books on Western **etiquette** before they came to America. "Tilt your plate," whispered my mother. "It's easier to spoon the soup up that way."

She was right. Tilting the plate did the trick. But the etiquette book didn't say anything about what you did after the soup reached your lips. As any respectable Chinese knows, the correct way to eat your soup is to slurp. This helps to cool the liquid and prevent you from burning your lips. It also shows your appreciation. ▶

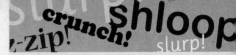

VISUALIZE

Underline the details in lines 169–190 that help you picture the Lakeview Restaurant.

Based on these details, do you think the narrator feels comfortable there?

☐ yes   ☐ no

MAKE GENERALIZATIONS

Circle the judgment the narrator's mother makes about French people.

What general truth about people does this statement reveal?

_____

_____

_____

etiquette (ĕt'ĭ-kĕt') *n*. the practice of social manners

EVALUATE

Reread the boxed text. Why is slurping important in this story? Consider the story's ending as you respond.

_____

_____

_____

_____

consumption (kən-sŭmp′shən) *n.* the act of taking in, eating, or drinking **consume** *v.*

220 We showed our appreciation. *Shloop,* went my father. *Shloop,* went my mother. *Shloop, shloop,* went my brother, who was the hungriest.

The lady harpist stopped playing to take a rest. And in the silence, our family's <u>consumption</u> of soup suddenly seemed unnaturally loud. You know how it sounds on a rocky beach when the tide goes out and the water drains from all those little pools? They go *shloop, shloop, shloop.* That was the Lin family, eating soup.

At the next table a waiter was pouring wine. When a
230 large *shloop* reached him, he froze. The bottle continued to pour, and red wine flooded the tabletop and into the lap of a customer. Even the customer didn't notice anything at first, being also hypnotized by the *shloop, shloop, shloop.*

It was too much. "I need to go to the toilet," I mumbled, jumping to my feet. A waiter, sensing my urgency, quickly directed me to the ladies' room.

I splashed cold water on my burning face, and as I dried myself with a paper towel, I stared into the mirror. In this perfumed ladies' room, with its pink-and-silver wallpaper and
240 marbled sinks, I looked completely out of place. What was I doing here? What was our family doing in the Lakeview Restaurant? In America? ◄

The door to the ladies' room opened. A woman came in and glanced curiously at me. I retreated into one of the toilet cubicles and latched the door.

Time passed—maybe half an hour, maybe an hour. Then I heard the door open again, and my mother's voice. "Are you in there? You're not sick, are you?"

There was real concern in her voice. A girl can't leave her
250 family just because they slurp their soup. Besides, the toilet cubicle had a few drawbacks as a permanent residence. "I'm all right," I said, undoing the latch.

Mother didn't tell me how the rest of the dinner went, and I didn't want to know. In the weeks following, I managed to push the whole thing into the back of my mind, where it

TestSmart

The use of repeated questions in lines 240–242 helps to reveal the narrator's

- (A) curiosity about America
- (B) confusion over the menu
- (C) humiliation about being different
- (D) anger at the waiter

TIP A test question may ask you about an author's choice of **sentence structure.** To answer a **style** question like this, reread the passage you are being asked about. **Pay attention to the author's use of sentence structure, while keeping the plot events in mind.** A series of questions can reveal many different states of mind, but the plot events in this story support only one of the answer choices.

jumped out at me only a few times a day. Even now, I turn hot all over when I think of the Lakeview Restaurant.

But by the time we had been in this country for three months, our family was definitely making progress toward becoming Americanized. I remember my parents' first PTA[5] meeting. Father wore a neat suit and tie, and Mother put on her first pair of high heels. She stumbled only once. They met my homeroom teacher and beamed as she told them that I would make honor roll soon at the rate I was going. Of course Chinese etiquette forced Father to say that I was a very stupid girl and Mother to protest that the teacher was showing favoritism toward me. But I could tell they were both very proud. ▶

INTERPRET

During the PTA meeting, Mr. and Mrs. Lin show that they are now a part of two cultures—Chinese and American. Circle the Chinese behavior and underline the American behavior.

The day came when my parents announced that they wanted to give a dinner party. We had invited Chinese friends to eat with us before, but this dinner was going to be different. In addition to a Chinese-American family, we were going to invite the Gleasons.

"Gee, I can hardly wait to have dinner at your house," Meg said to me. "I just *love* Chinese food."

That was a relief. Mother was a good cook, but I wasn't sure if people who ate sour cream would also eat chicken gizzards[6] stewed in soy sauce.

Mother decided not to take a chance with chicken gizzards. Since we had Western guests, she set the table with large dinner plates, which we never used in Chinese meals. In fact we didn't use individual plates at all, but picked up food from the platters in the middle of the table and brought it directly to our rice bowls. Following the practice of Chinese-American restaurants, Mother also placed large serving spoons on the platters.

---

5. **PTA:** Parent Teacher Association.
6. **gizzards:** A gizzard is the muscular pouch behind a bird's stomach that helps with its digestion.

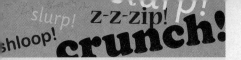

TestSmart

What does the author's use of imagery in lines 296–306 help readers do?

- Ⓐ picture the messy piles of foods
- Ⓑ picture a beautifully arranged meal
- Ⓒ smell the delicious mix of scents
- Ⓓ hear the noisy sounds of dinner

TIP A test question may ask you about an author's use of **imagery**. To answer a **style** question like this, **reread the lines, looking for colorful phrases or unusual comparisons that create a vivid picture.** The author compares Mrs. Gleason's treatment of the food to mixing up a batch of cement. What does this comparison help you do?

ANALYZE

Reread the boxed text. Is it the Gleasons' actions, the narrator's responses, or both that add to the humorous **mood** of the story? Explain.

_____

_____

_____

_____

cope (kōp) v. to struggle to overcome difficulties

The dinner started well. Mrs. Gleason exclaimed at the beautifully arranged dishes of food: the colorful candied fruit in the sweet-and-sour pork dish, the noodle-thin shreds of
290 chicken meat stir-fried with tiny peas, and the glistening pink prawns[7] in a ginger sauce.

At first I was too busy enjoying my food to notice how the guests were doing. But soon I remembered my duties. Sometimes guests were too polite to help themselves and you had to serve them with more food.

I glanced at Meg, to see if she needed more food, and my eyes nearly popped out at the sight of her plate. It was piled with food: the sweet-and-sour meat pushed right against the chicken shreds, and the chicken sauce ran into the prawns.
300 She had been taking food from a second dish before she finished eating her helping from the first!

Horrified, I turned to look at Mrs. Gleason. She was dumping rice out of her bowl and putting it on her dinner plate. Then she ladled prawns and gravy on top of the rice and mixed everything together, the way you mix sand, gravel, and cement to make concrete. ◄

I couldn't bear to look any longer, and I turned to Mr. Gleason. He was chasing a pea around his plate. Several times he got it to the edge, but when he tried to pick it up with his
310 chopsticks, it rolled back toward the center of the plate again. Finally he put down his chopsticks and picked up the pea with his fingers. He really did! A grown man! ◄

All of us, our family and the Chinese guests, stopped eating to watch the activities of the Gleasons. I wanted to giggle. Then I caught my mother's eyes on me. She frowned and shook her head slightly, and I understood the message: the Gleasons were not used to Chinese ways, and they were just **coping** the best they could. For some reason I thought of celery strings.

---

7. **prawns** (prônz): large seafood, similar to shrimp.

320 When the main courses were finished, Mother brought out a platter of fruit. "I hope you weren't expecting a sweet dessert," she said. "Since the Chinese don't eat dessert, I didn't think to prepare any." ▶

"Oh, I couldn't possibly eat dessert!" cried Mrs. Gleason. "I'm simply stuffed!"

Meg had different ideas. When the table was cleared, she announced that she and I were going for a walk. "I don't know about you, but I feel like dessert," she told me, when we were outside. "Come on, there's a Dairy Queen down the
330 street. I could use a big chocolate milkshake!"

Although I didn't really want anything more to eat, I insisted on paying for the milkshakes. After all, I was still hostess.

Meg got her large chocolate milkshake and I had a small one. Even so, she was finishing hers while I was only half done. Toward the end she pulled hard on her straws and went *shloop, shloop.*

"Do you always slurp when you eat a milkshake?" I asked, before I could stop myself.

Meg grinned. "Sure. All Americans slurp." ▶

TestSmart

VOCABULARY
What does the word *courses* mean in line 320?

(A) available options
(B) the classes at a college
(C) the routes of a race
(D) the parts of a meal

TIP A test question may ask you to identify the meaning of a word that has more than one possible meaning. To answer a question about a **multiple-meaning word,** reread the sentence in which the word appears. **Use context clues** to figure out how the word is being used. Then look for the answer choice that matches this meaning.

Big Question

What is this story's answer to the question of whether people are more alike or different? Explain.

_____

_____

_____

_____

Reading Comprehension

DIRECTIONS *Answer these questions about "The All-American Slurp" by filling in the correct ovals.*

1. What mood does the author create in lines 158–167?

   (A) serious and somber

   (B) moody and depressed

   (C) embarrassing and funny

   (D) cheerful and lively

2. Which words best sum up the author's tone in lines 296–312?

   (A) shocked and disgusted

   (B) impressed and proud

   (C) angry and resentful

   (D) curious and enthusiastic

3. Which words best describe the author's style in "The All-American Slurp"?

   (A) formal and stern

   (B) bland and unemotional

   (C) casual and conversational

   (D) scientific and analytical

4. What does the end of the story show about the rules of etiquette?

   (A) The rules never change.

   (B) The rules change, based on the situation.

   (C) Everyone has the same rules after all.

   (D) The rules don't matter during dessert.

5. Which word below sounds like the action it describes?

   (A) table

   (B) spectacle

   (C) accent

   (D) slurp

6. Which word in lines 49–54 is an example of onomatopoeia?

   (A) silence

   (B) zipping

   (C) daughter

   (D) neighbors

7. Based on context clues, what does the word *nursed* mean in line 66?

   (A) ate very slowly

   (B) took care of

   (C) drank milk from a mother

   (D) brought back to good health

8. What does *conducted* mean in the context of line 170?

   (A) carried electricity

   (B) directed musicians

   (C) behaved badly

   (D) solemnly guided

Responding in Writing

9. Short Response Choose one memorable scene from "The All-American Slurp." Write a paragraph that describes the mood of the scene.

_____

_____

_____

_____

_____

_____

Test-Taker's Toolkit

ACADEMIC VOCABULARY When you're asked to write a **descriptive essay** about a story scene, you need to begin by writing a main idea sentence that tells which scene you are going to discuss. Then write a sentence that identifies the mood in that scene. Follow with several sentences that give supporting details—in this case, include examples of words and phrases from the story that help to create the mood.

GRAPHIC ORGANIZER Use the graphic organizer below to help you plan your response. Look back at the story to gather the examples you need.

> **Scene:**
>
> **Mood:**

Example:	**Example:**	**Example:**	**Example:**

Use with "The All-American Slurp," p. 68

What's the Connection?

"The All-American Slurp" tells how a family of Chinese immigrants adjusts to American culture. The newspaper article "Potstickers" shows how one traditional Chinese treat represents elements of Chinese culture. The recipe "Jiaoze Dumplings or Potstickers" explains how to make this common but delicious dish.

DISH IT UP Think of a food that is important in your family or culture. It could be a food that is prepared for special occasions, or a food that is a regular part of your meals. In the center of the web below, draw a picture of that food (or write its name). In the surrounding spaces, write the different ways in which this dish is important to your family or culture. Then form a group and compare your responses.

LEARN THE SKILL: TRACE STEPS IN A PROCESS

Informational text often presents steps for how to do or make something. The following tips can help you follow the **steps in a process.**

- **Text features** such as headings and lists can help you identify key information. They can tell you which part of a recipe gives the ingredients and which part lists the instructions.

- **Signal words** such as *first, before,* and *when* can help you understand the sequence, or order in which the steps should be followed.

- **Visual aids** such as photographs and diagrams can show the steps in a process so they are easier to visualize.

For more on tracing steps in a process, see *Nonfiction Handbook* page R22.

SECTION C · **LIFE** · NOVEMBER 5

Potstickers

by Bill Daley
from *The San Francisco Chronicle*

*In one small package, these dumplings link past
to present, rich to poor, mother to daughter.*

Amy Tan and her siblings will gather Nov. 22 to mark the anniversary of their mother's death. They will do so by making potstickers.

These humble pork dumplings, pan-fried until the bottoms of their pleated wrappers are golden and crisp, 10 are a way to remember their mother, a woman known for her potstickers.

"We try to make the potstickers and then we criticize the potstickers and say how bad they are," says Tan, a San Francisco resident who grew up in the Bay Area and is the best-selling author 20 of *The Joy Luck Club* and *The Bonesetter's Daughter,* among other books.

With potstickers, both the filling and the wrapper are crucial. "It's very easy to fail on both levels. My mother was a real big critic." ▶

Potstickers, Tan says, are "the original ravioli, the original 30 taco." And, just like those foods, the potsticker provides much more than nourishment. It can soothe the soul, spur memory, and spark many a passionate debate on how it should be made. Not bad for something that costs about $5 for a half-dozen in local restaurants.

40 When Rhoda Yee was a little girl in China, her grandmother would tell her a story about how potstickers came to be. It's a legend Yee, a chef-instructor at the California Culinary Academy in San Francisco, tells her students today.

INTERPRET

Underline the sentences in lines 1–27 that give examples of how potstickers "link . . . mother to daughter."

According to Amy Tan, in what ways is making potstickers a meaningful way of remembering her mother?

SET A PURPOSE
My purpose for reading is

According to the tale, recounted in Yee's cookbook, *Dim Sum,* the aged chef to the royal household left a pot of dumplings on the stove too long and discovered the bottoms had burned. The horrified chef thought he would be killed for this, but his smart son decided to present the dumplings to the emperor himself. When the emperor asked why the dumplings were burned, the son quickly explained it was a new recipe for something called potstickers. The emperor liked the crunchiness of the browned bottoms and a new dish was born.

Around for centuries—the crescent form is said to have been popularized 1,500 years ago—potstickers have become deeply ingrained in Chinese culture. The similarity in form between these *guotie* and the gold and silver ingots[1] of ancient China has turned these treats into edible metaphors for wealth and prosperity. It is traditional to eat potstickers during the symbol-laden feasts of Chinese New Year, but people also eat them year-round. . . .

Tan says potstickers are so appealing because they are so accessible to so many.

"You can have the most glorious potstickers and be poor. They transcend class and money," she explains. "Anyone can enjoy them and everyone throughout China makes them. You can go to the most humble dwellings with outdoor kitchens and the wok resting on a pile of rocks and they make them." ◀

Tan's mother, for example, would make potstickers every few weeks and for birthdays.

DRAW CONCLUSIONS

Underline the way in which potstickers "link present to past" and the way in which they "link . . . rich to poor."

Why do you think potstickers "transcend class and money"?

---

1. **ingot:** metal that is molded into a bar or other shape and used as a form of currency.

100 "She would count on us eating 25 of them and she would make hundreds of these things. They were always our favorite meal," the author recalls . . . .

Making potstickers takes skill, practice, and patience. Often dozens, if not hundreds, have to be made. It frequently is a family project—another 110 element that lends to the continuing appeal of potstickers in family-centered China. ▶

Throwing a potsticker party is great for entertaining because you need provide little else, chef Martin Yan says. The dumpling is a one-meal dish with meat, vegetable, and starch combined. . . .

120 Yan looks for a plump potsticker—plumpness means a lot of filling. "When I bite into it, it should be very juicy," he says. "There should be a very good percentage of vegetable and meat. I want to make sure (the filling) is marinated properly. It should be nice and savory and not bland." . . .

130 While Yan says many restaurant chefs can do a very good job with dumplings, Tan insists no one can make a potsticker like her mother.

They were evenly gold on the bottom, never black or charred. The filling had the right meat-to-vegetable ratio, so the potsticker didn't get 140 soggy and it emerged cooked through but "not a little hard meatball." The shape was so consistent that if she made 100 dumplings they all looked identical. ▶

So critical was her mother of potstickers that Tan never tried to make them while growing up, contenting herself with 150 trying to roll out the dough as consistently as possible. Now, though the family tries, the potstickers still don't compare. "I have to say no one makes them quite like my mother," Tan says, even though she and her siblings continue to make potstickers in her mother's memory. "They (her mother's 160 dumplings) are lost to the world."

MAKE INFERENCES

Reread the boxed text. According to this passage, what other elements of life are linked through potstickers?

_____

_____

TRACE STEPS IN A PROCESS

Reread lines 120–145. What are the basic steps required for making potstickers?

_____

_____

_____

_____

_____

Jiaoze Dumplings or Potstickers *(Guotie)*

by Olivia Wu

You may freeze the just-wrapped dumplings: Place them on a baking sheet and put in the freezer. When frozen solid, transfer to plastic freezer bags. To cook: Boil or steam an extra minute or two to make sure they're cooked through.

INGREDIENTS:

The Dough

1½ pounds (6 cups) all-purpose flour

about 1½ cups water

The Filling

10   ¾ pound (about ½ large head) napa cabbage, finely minced

¾ cup garlic chives, cut into ⅛-inch segments (optional)

1 pound ground pork (preferably not too lean)

1 garlic clove, minced

½ teaspoon minced fresh ginger

4 teaspoons light soy sauce

2 teaspoons rice wine

1 teaspoon sesame oil

½ to ¾ teaspoon kosher salt

The Dipping Sauce

20   2 tablespoons vinegar (preferably black vinegar)

1 tablespoon light soy sauce

1 tablespoon sesame oil

about 1 tablespoon hot bean paste (optional) ◀

TRACE STEPS IN A PROCESS

Why are the ingredients for potstickers divided into three categories?

_____

_____

_____

Circle the **text features** that help you understand why the ingredients are organized this way.

INSTRUCTIONS:

The dough: Put flour in a bowl; make a well in the center. Gradually pour in the water, stirring with a wooden spoon. When dough forms in small pieces, knead it together with one hand, adding more water to make a soft, sticky dough. Knead on a flat surface for about 5 minutes. Return to bowl, cover with a towel and set aside for at

30 least 30 minutes. ▶

The filling: You may cut cabbage into 1-inch segments and pulse in a processor. You may do the same with garlic chives. But it's better to cut both by hand. Take cabbage by the handful; gently squeeze out some of the moisture. Stir both vegetables into pork. Add garlic, ginger, soy sauce, rice wine, sesame oil and salt. Stir until you have a light mixture.

The dumplings: Separate dough into 3 or 4 equal pieces. Roll each into a log, ½ to ¾ inch in diameter. Cut each log into ½ to ¾ inch segments, about ⅓-ounce each. Roll each segment into a ball, then

40 gently flatten it into a disk. Using a 1-inch diameter rolling pin, roll

TRACE STEPS IN A PROCESS

Underline the phrase that explains how you can tell the dough is ready to be kneaded.

What **signal word** begins this phrase?

each disk into a 2½-inch-diameter circle. Work with 1 dough circle at a time, keeping the rest covered with plastic wrap so they don't dry out. Hold a pastry circle in the curve of your fingers; place a rounded teaspoon of filling in the center. Form dumplings.

To boil jiaoze: Bring 1½ to 2 quarts water to a rolling boil in a wok. Place 1 cup of cold tap water on the side. Drop about 25 dumplings into the water—don't crowd them. Bring to a boil and add ½ cup cold water to cool the boiling water. Bring to a boil, cool again with remaining cold water, then scoop out dumplings and serve.

50 **To make potstickers:** This is what you do with leftover, boiled jiaoze—fry them. However, if you want to fry uncooked dumplings (fresh or frozen), here's how: Heat a 10-inch nonstick skillet; add 2 to 4 tablespoons oil and heat until almost smoking. Place dumplings in pan in a circle with a few in the center. Fry until bottoms brown. Shake pan often so dumplings don't stick. Add enough water to come up ¼-inch on the dumplings, then cover pan immediately. ◀ Cook over high heat for 5 to 8 minutes. Uncover and if wrappers look <u>translucent</u>, keep cooking until all water has evaporated and only oil remains. Shake pan often. Invert pan on a plate to keep circular form

60 of dumplings and to present browned bottom sides up. ◀

The sauce: Stir together all ingredients. Or, more authentically, place separate ingredients out for diners to make their own concoction. Vinegar and sesame oil are the critical components.

Yields about 60 dumplings.

PER DUMPLING (dipping sauce not included): 45 calories, 2 g protein, 5 g carbohydrate, 2 g fat (1 g saturated), 5 mg cholesterol, 43 mg sodium, 0 fiber.

TRACE STEPS IN A PROCESS

When can you make potstickers out of *jiaoze* dumplings? Circle one answer.

before or after the jiaoze *have been boiled*

only after the jiaoze *have been boiled*

Underline the part of the recipe that tells you this.

SPECIALIZED Vocabulary

If you are unfamiliar with the word <u>translucent</u> in line 58, try breaking the word into parts. The prefix *trans-* means "through." The word part *lucent* comes from the Latin word *lucere*, meaning "to shine." Based on this information, what is the most likely meaning of *translucent*? *WORD ANALYSIS*

_____

_____

_____

Dumpling How-To

Here's one way to shape dumplings:

Shaping the disks	Roll dough into the size of a large cherry. On a lightly floured surface, flatten the dough into a disk. Roll the disk with a rolling pin, at the same time turning the disk with your other hand to create a 2½-inch circle. This technique yields a thinner edge and slightly thicker center.	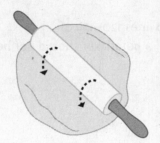
Adding the filling	Cup the disk in the palm of your hand with your fingers slightly curved. Place a rounded teaspoon of filling in the center of the dough. Tugging the dough slightly, bring it together to create a taco-like shape and pinch at the top midpoint to seal.	
Sealing the ends	Close off the ends by pulling each corner down, pushing up into the filling from the rear and pinching closed.	
Creating the shape	Grab the dough halfway between the corners and the top midpoint, pulling it from the rear to meet the front. Pinch it closed. You will have created two gaps on each side of the top.	
Pleating the potsticker	Pinch each gap closed, forming pleats, and making sure the filling is contained.	
The finished dumpling	The dumpling should be completely sealed, with the flatter side in front, and be able to stand in a crescent. Don't be frustrated if your first one isn't perfect; it gets easier with practice. ▶	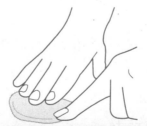

Reading Comprehension

DIRECTIONS *Answer these questions about the three selections in this lesson by filling in the correct ovals.*

1. According to lines 120–129 of "Potstickers," a potsticker should *not* be

   (A) plump

   (B) juicy

   (C) savory

   (D) bland

2. According to "Potstickers," dumplings with identical shapes are

   (A) boring, because they are all the same

   (B) ideal, because they reflect skill

   (C) unappealing, because they are bland

   (D) rare, because they are a specialty

3. In the introduction to the recipe, what signal words tell you when you may transfer potstickers to a freezer bag?

   (A) just-wrapped

   (B) When frozen solid

   (C) an extra minute

   (D) cooked through

4. When making dipping sauce for potstickers, which ingredient can you leave out?

   (A) vinegar

   (B) soy sauce

   (C) sesame oil

   (D) hot bean paste

5. "The All-American Slurp" and "Potstickers" both reflect the Chinese value of

   (A) beautifully crafted food

   (B) perfectly shaped dumplings

   (C) symbol-laden feasts

   (D) popular crescent shapes

6. The article "Potstickers" and the recipe for making them both emphasize the importance of

   (A) woks

   (B) legends

   (C) practice

   (D) family

7. Using word parts, you can determine that the word *authentically* in line 61 of *"Jiaoze* Dumplings or Potstickers" means

   (A) proven to be right

   (B) true to traditional ways

   (C) invented later

   (D) automatically

8. In line 62 of "Jiaoze Dumplings or Potstickers," a *concoction* is

   (A) an invented mix

   (B) an authentic mix

   (C) an exact ratio

   (D) a cooking disaster

BUDGET YOUR TIME

You have **30 minutes** to respond. Decide how much time to spend on each step.

Analyze _____

Plan _____

Write _____

Review _____

30

Timed Writing Practice

PROMPT

Write a (fiction story) about two friends from different backgrounds who find out that they are more alike than different. Draw upon examples of differences and similarities from your own life, as well as from two of the selections you have read.

Test-Taker's Toolkit

1. ANALYZE THE PROMPT

A. **Read the prompt** carefully.

B. **Circle key words** in each sentence. One has been done for you. These words tell you what you must include to get a good score.

C. **Restate the prompt** in your own words to make sure you understand it. You may use the lines on the right.

2. PLAN YOUR RESPONSE

A. **Make a story map** A **story map** shows the elements that most stories include. Before beginning to write, fill in the story map with the names of the characters, the setting, the differences between characters (this can be the story's conflict), and the similarities they discover (the resolution).

B. **Organize your information** Use your story map to structure your story.

STORY MAP

CHARACTERS: _____
SETTING: _____
PLOT:
conflict _____
_____
_____
resolution _____

3. WRITE AND REVIEW

A. **Let your voice come through** You can give your story a humorous, thoughtful, or critical tone, based on how you feel about the characters at different points in the story. Practice rewriting the sentence below in a different tone.

I saw the chopsticks by my bowl and wondered if I was expected to eat my rice with them.

_____

_____

_____

B. **Write out your full response** Leave enough time to read through it and make sure you have met all the requirements of the prompt.

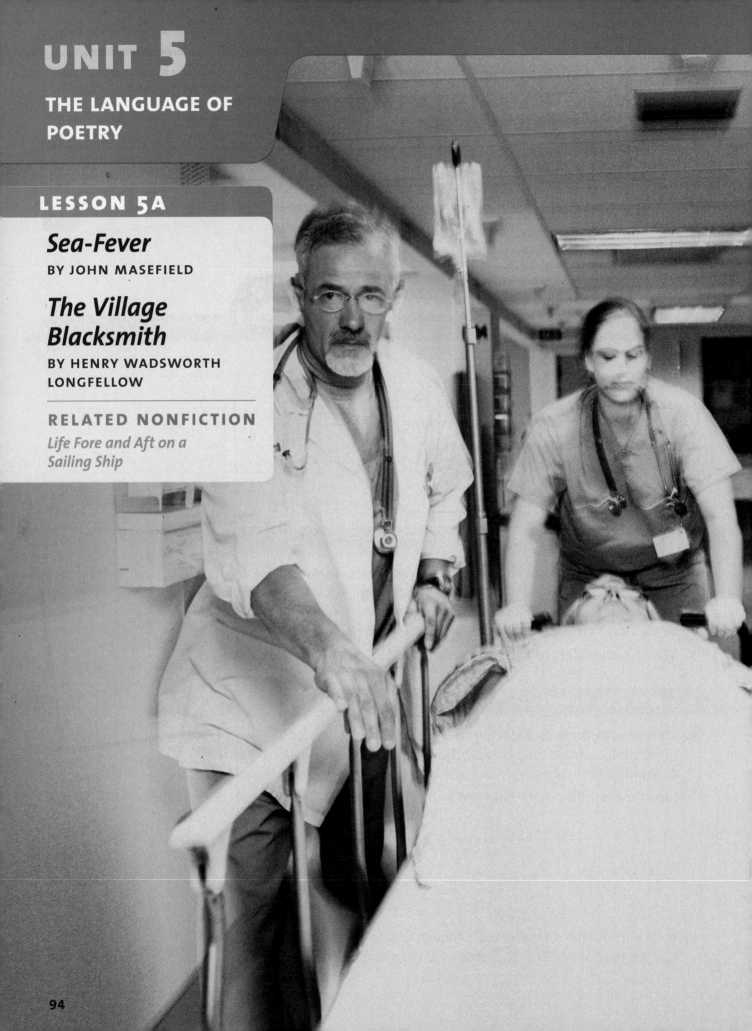

LESSON 5A

Sea-Fever
BY JOHN MASEFIELD

The Village Blacksmith
BY HENRY WADSWORTH LONGFELLOW

RELATED NONFICTION
Life Fore and Aft on a Sailing Ship

When is your WORK your life?

What do you think of when you hear the word *work*? If your experience with projects or chores hasn't been pleasant, then words like *boring* and *dull* might come to mind. When you love what you do, however, work is more than just a job. It is an exciting and challenging way to spend your time. The two poems you will read explore different ways in which work adds meaning to life.

DISCUSS What jobs might be interesting enough to build your life around? With a group, brainstorm a list of jobs that seem rewarding, fascinating, or fun. Write each one in the first column of the chart shown. In the second column, briefly describe the reasons why each job might be fulfilling.

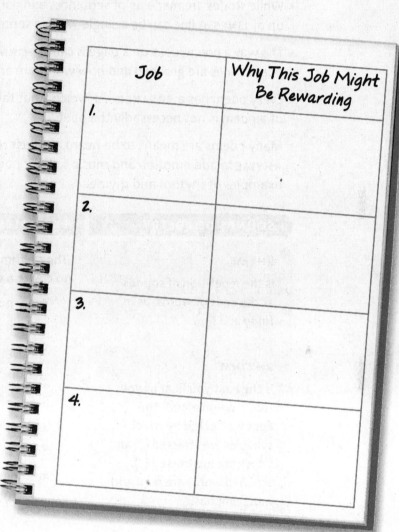

Job	Why This Job Might Be Rewarding
1.	
2.	
3.	
4.	

ASSESSMENT GOALS

By the end of this lesson, you will be able to...

- analyze form, rhythm, and rhyme in a poem
- apply critical thinking skills to analyze text
- analyze the organization of information in a nonfiction article
- analyze a writing prompt and plan an opinion essay

Analyzing Poetry: Form, Rhythm, and Rhyme

Have you ever heard a song that you couldn't get out of your head? Like songs, poems and stories have the power to get inside your heart and mind. However, poems are different from stories in some important ways.

- While stories are made up of sentences and paragraphs, poems are made up of LINES. A line can be a single word, a sentence, or part of a sentence.

- The way a poem looks on a page is called FORM. Form includes how the poem's lines are grouped and how words are arranged on the page.

- Every poem has a SPEAKER—a "voice" that talks to readers. The speaker of a poem is not necessarily the poet.

- Many poems are meant to be heard, not just read. Poets use RHYTHM and RHYME to add emotion and music to their poems. The chart below gives examples of rhythm and rhyme.

SOUNDS OF POETRY	EXAMPLES
RHYME is the repetition of sounds at the ends of words, as in *thing* and *sing*. **RHYTHM** is the beat you hear as you read a poem aloud. The beat is affected by which syllables are stressed (´) and which are unstressed (˘). Stressed words are read with more emphasis.	The rhythm and rhyme in this poem help to create a singsong sound. Some people talk and talk and never say a thing Some people look at you and birds begin to sing. Some people laugh and laugh and yet you want to cry. Some people touch your hand and music fills the sky. —"People" by Charlotte Zolotow

ADDITIONAL TERMS FOR CRITICAL ANALYSIS

Knowing these additional terms will help you discuss poetry more precisely.

- The place where a line ends is called a LINE BREAK. The poet carefully chooses the breaks to enhance rhythm, rhyme, and meaning.

- In many poems, lines are arranged into groups called STANZAS. The stanzas within a poem can have the same or different forms. Each stanza will reveal more about the speaker or about the topic of the poem.

Sea-Fever

John Masefield

I must go down to the seas again, to the lonely sea and
  the sky,
And all I ask is a tall ship and a star to steer her by,
And the wheel's kick and the wind's song and the white
  sail's shaking,
And a grey mist on the sea's face and a grey dawn breaking. ▶

5 I must go down to the seas again, for the call of the
  running tide
Is a wild call and a clear call that may not be denied;
And all I ask is a windy day with the white clouds flying,
And the flung spray and the blown spume,[1] and the
  sea-gulls crying.

I must go down to the seas again to the <u>vagrant</u> gypsy life,
10 To the gull's way and the whale's way where the wind's like
  a whetted[2] knife;
And all I ask is a merry yarn[3] from a laughing fellow-rover,
And a quiet sleep and a sweet dream when the long
  trick's[4] over. ▶

---

1. **spume** (spyo͞om): foam or froth on a liquid.
2. **whetted** (hwĕt′ĭd): sharpened.
3. **yarn:** long, entertaining tale.
4. **trick:** term of work or duty.

ANALYZE

Reread lines 1–4. Underline the
words that **rhyme.**

What pattern do you notice?

_____

_____

_____

vagrant (vā′grənt) *adj.*
wandering from place to
place; unrestrained

INTERPRET

Does the **speaker** of the
poem describe a sailor's life
in a positive or negative way?
Explain why you think so.

_____

_____

_____

_____

ANALYZE

Draw a box around the poem's first two **stanzas.**

What does the blacksmith look like? Quote from the poem to support your answer.

_____

_____

_____

_____

TestSmart

Which example correctly shows the rhythm of this line?

Ⓐ Week in, week out, from morn till night

Ⓑ Week in, week out, from morn till night

Ⓒ Week in, week out, from morn till night

Ⓓ Week in, week out, from morn till night

TIP When a test question includes **academic vocabulary,** review the meaning of any terms you are unsure of. In this case, reread the definitions of **rhythm** and **line** on page 96 and review the example. Then read line 13 of the poem aloud and mark its stressed and unstressed syllables in your book.

Then review each answer choice and choose the correct one.

THE VILLAGE BLACKSMITH

HENRY WADSWORTH LONGFELLOW

Under a spreading chestnut-tree
    The village smithy stands;
The smith, a mighty man is he,
    With large and <u>sinewy</u> hands;
5 And the muscles of his <u>brawny</u> arms
    Are strong as iron bands.

His hair is crisp, and black, and long,
    His face is like the tan;
His brow is wet with honest sweat,
10   He earns whate'er he can,
And looks the whole world in the face,
    For he owes not any man. ◄

Week in, week out, from morn till night,
    You can hear his bellows[1] blow;
15 You can hear him swing his heavy sledge,
    With measured beat and slow,
Like a sexton[2] ringing the village bell,
    When the evening sun is low. ◄

And children coming home from school
20   Look in at the open door;
They love to see the flaming forge,
    And hear the bellows roar,

---

1. **bellows:** a device for providing air to feed a fire.
2. **sexton:** an employee of a church, responsible for maintaining the building and ringing the church bells.

And catch the burning sparks that fly
    Like chaff from a threshing-floor.[3]

25 He goes on Sunday to the church,
    And sits among his boys;
He hears the parson pray and preach,
    He hears his daughter's voice,
Singing in the village choir,
30   And it makes his heart rejoice.

It sounds to him like her mother's voice,
    Singing in Paradise!
He needs must think of her once more,
    How in the grave she lies;
35 And with his hard, rough hand he wipes
    A tear out of his eyes. ▶

Toiling, —rejoicing, —sorrowing,
    Onward through life he goes;
Each morning sees some task begin,
40   Each evening sees it close;
Something attempted, something done,
    Has earned a night's <u>repose</u>. ▶

Thanks, thanks to thee, my worthy friend,
    For the lesson thou hast taught!
45 Thus at the flaming forge of life
    Our fortunes must be wrought;
Thus on its sounding anvil[4] shaped
    Each burning deed and thought.

---

3. **chaff from a threshing-floor:** Chaff is the dry coating on grains of wheat. It is discarded during threshing, when the wheat and straw are separated.

4. **sounding anvil:** An anvil is a heavy block of iron on which metals are hammered into shape. *Sounding* refers to the ringing noise the hammering makes.

ANALYZE

Reread lines 31–36 and mark each **line break** with a slash.

What is the effect of the breaks?

_____

_____

INTERPRET

Which parts of the blacksmith's life reflect each of the following words from line 37?

toiling: _____

_____

rejoicing: _____

_____

sorrowing: _____

_____

repose (rĭ-pōz') *n.* freedom from work or worry; rest

Big Question ?

Look back at the Big Question on page 95. What do you think the **speaker** in each poem would say about his work? *DRAW CONCLUSIONS*

"Sea-Fever"

_____

_____

"The Village Blacksmith"

_____

_____

Reading Comprehension

DIRECTIONS *Answer these questions about "Sea-Fever" and "The Village Blacksmith" by filling in the correct ovals.*

1. Who is the speaker in "Sea-Fever"?

   Ⓐ the poet John Masefield

   Ⓑ a vagrant gypsy

   Ⓒ a sailor who misses the sea

   Ⓓ a sailor who is at sea

2. How many stanzas does "Sea-Fever" have?

   Ⓐ 1

   Ⓑ 3

   Ⓒ 12

   Ⓓ none

3. Which lines from "Sea-Fever" rhyme?

   Ⓐ lines 6 and 7

   Ⓑ lines 7 and 8

   Ⓒ lines 8 and 9

   Ⓓ lines 9 and 11

4. Which example correctly shows the rhythm of this line?

   Ⓐ His hair is crisp, and black, and long

   Ⓑ His hair is crisp, and black, and long

   Ⓒ His hair is crisp, and black, and long

   Ⓓ His hair is crisp, and black, and long

5. Which description *best* characterizes the form of "The Village Blacksmith"?

   Ⓐ 8 stanzas of 6 lines each

   Ⓑ 48 lines of text

   Ⓒ 8 paragraphs of 6 lines each

   Ⓓ no regular pattern

6. What main point do you think Longfellow is making about the blacksmith?

   Ⓐ He is strong, sinewy, and brawny.

   Ⓑ He is a model for how to live.

   Ⓒ He is lucky to have children.

   Ⓓ He is an important man.

7. Which sentence *best* sums up the message of both poems?

   Ⓐ Blacksmiths and sailors teach important lessons.

   Ⓑ Blacksmiths and sailors are honest workers.

   Ⓒ Work can be rewarding.

   Ⓓ Work is better than relaxation.

8. In line 46 of "The Village Blacksmith," the word *wrought* means

   Ⓐ wreaked   Ⓒ fought

   Ⓑ formed   Ⓓ wronged

For help, use the **Test-Taker's Toolkit** below.

Responding in Writing

9. Short Response Choose which of the two poems you prefer. Write a paragraph explaining what you like about it. Include examples of lines, word choice, or rhyme that you found especially effective or interesting. Also discuss the poem's message.

____

____

____

____

____

____

Test-Taker's Toolkit

GRAPHIC ORGANIZER Use the graphic organizer below to help you plan your paragraph.

Poem title: ______________________________

Why I liked it: ______________________________

____

____

Examples of elements I especially liked:

lines: ______________________________

____

word choice: ______________________________

rhyming words: ______________________________

message: ______________________________

____

Life Fore and Aft on a Sailing Ship
MAGAZINE ARTICLE

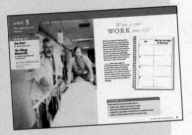

Use with "Sea-Fever" and "The Village Blacksmith," p. 94

What's the Connection?

The poem "Sea-Fever" describes one man's love of a life at sea. The *Cobblestone Magazine* article "Life Fore and Aft on a Sailing Ship" gives facts about what daily life aboard a sailing ship in the 1800s was really like.

TEST YOUR SAILING IQ Underline one or more answers to each question below. After you have read the selection, come back and circle the correct answers. How many answers did you know? What did you learn?

1. What duties would a young crew member be expected to perform?
   a. scrub decks   *b.* scrape metal   *c.* steer the ship

2. Which word or words describe a crew member's job?
   a. dull   *b.* dangerous   *c.* exciting

3. Which word names a common food for sailors in the 1800s?
   a. scuttlebutt   *b.* lobscouse   *c.* gimbals

4. The relationships between crew members and officers were often
   a. very close   *b.* disagreeable   *c.* distant

LEARN THE SKILL: ANALYZE ORGANIZATION OF INFORMATION

Writers of nonfiction usually arrange the information in ways that show how ideas are related. Often, the information is in **part-by-part order.** This means that each idea presented is related to the ideas before and after it.

- Individual parts of an article might also have a **compare-contrast organization.** This method of organization is used to compare characteristics of two subjects.

- Other parts of an article might present information about **spatial relations,** or where things are in relation to one another. This can help you visualize the information.

For more on methods of organization, see *Nonfiction Handbook* page R15.

LIFE FORE AND AFT ON A

Sailing Ship

BY LUCIE GERMER

Many nineteenth-century youths dreamed of going to sea on a whaling ship, man-of-war, or merchant vessel. They imagined a life of excitement, adventure, and escape from their dull routine. But those who became sailors were surprised at the reality.

SET A PURPOSE
My purpose for reading is
_____
_____
_____

A Ship's Crew

A boy who signed on with a ship's crew became part of a small group, one of two onboard ship. These two groups
10   lived next to and depended on each other, but they knew very little about each other and, even at the end of the voyage, rarely trusted each other. On one side were the captain and officers, on the other the crew. ▶

ANALYZE ORGANIZATION

Based on lines 8–13, what two groups will this magazine article focus on?

_____
_____

When a voyage was about to begin, the crew consisted of "green" boys, who often began to feel seasick even before the anchor was raised, older recruits from the local area, and a few sailors who actually knew what they were in for. The officers depended on these last few sailors to get the sails rigged and the anchor up. The rest would in time find their sea legs and learn the routine.

20 The captain and other officers could have a good or bad relationship with the crew. The officers had the authority to send the crew into the **rigging** during a storm, order punishments or rewards, and allow the men to sleep or force them to wake up. In general, the sailors preferred to avoid the officers, but doing so was difficult. ◀

A sailor's work was done primarily on deck or in the rigging, which needed constant adjusting to keep the ship moving properly with the wind. The crew was divided into two shifts, or watches, with four-hour duty schedules around the clock.
30 The crew also took turns standing lookout and steering the vessel. A sailor spent a lot of time scrubbing the decks and scraping metal to counteract the effects of wind, salt, and water. Everything had to be put away and fastened down after it was used, another time-consuming task. When it was not terrifying, most of a sailor's work was dull and routine—and always performed under the officers' watchful eyes. ◀

Fore: At the Front

Two places in the forward part of the ship gave the sailors a brief escape. On deck was the scuttlebutt, or water barrel. It
40 was filled each day from the precious supply stored for the voyage. The water itself was often rationed and brackish (salty or distasteful). But trips to get a drink gave the sailors a chance to relax and trade rumors, which themselves became known as scuttlebutt.

The other special place for the sailors was the forecastle, a crowded, dirty room in the bow of the ship. Here the sailors had their bunks or hammocks and gathered in their free time to rest

---

SPECIALIZED *Vocabulary*

Since this article is about sailing, it contains many terms related to that subject. For example, rigging is not defined, but line 18 provides context clues for the word. It tells us that sailors *rigged* the sails.

When you encounter specialized terms like these, look for definitions, explanations, or graphic aids that explain them. If a specialized term is not explained, **use a dictionary** to clarify its meaning. *WORD ANALYSIS*

CONTRAST

What were two important differences between the crew and the officers?

1. _____

_____

_____

2. _____

_____

_____

or mend their clothes. One sailor was usually known as the reader. He would read not only books but also letters for those who could not read. The storyteller could keep a yarn going for days, and the joker often played practical jokes. This was the sailors' space, and the captain almost never went inside. ▶

Aft: In the Back

The captain and the officers had their own territory as well, usually aft (in the after, or back, part of the ship). Besides the captain, two or three mates directed the work of the crew. The other officers onboard depended on the type of ship. A man-of-war had military officers, and a merchant ship sometimes had a super-cargo responsible for the goods carried by the ship. Ranking between the officers and crew were the cook, sail maker, carpenter, and harpooners on a whaler.

The captain's spaces were his cabin and the quarterdeck, an upper deck in the aft of the ship. His cabin was cramped but

NINETEENTH-CENTURY SAILING SHIP ▶

AFT

FORE

ANALYZE ORGANIZATION

Underline the words and phrases in lines 38–52 that help give you a sense of **spatial relations,** or where things are on the ship.

INTERPRET

Label the model of a sailing ship on this page with the following terms mentioned in the text: *rigging, bow, deck, forecastle,* and *quarterdeck.* You may want to underline each term's usage in the text first, to help you label the model correctly.

Which topic overlaps the two sections called "Fore: At the Front" and "Aft: In the Back"?

(A) where each group relaxed

(B) who the groups reported to

(C) what jobs the groups had

(D) who led the groups

TIP A test may ask you about the organization of a passage you have just read. In text organized in **part-by-part order,** each section leads into the next. Sometimes the subheadings will help you identify the connections. Other times you will find the topic identified at or near the beginning of a section. **Underline the first sentence under each subheading** listed in the question to help you identify what is being discussed.

private and had a few luxuries, such as a bed mounted on gimbals, a device that helped counteract the motion of the ship. Other officers either shared cabins or had tiny rooms of their own. ◄

Food and Living Conditions

All the officers dined together at a table. The food was
70 limited to what could be stored and prepared at sea. Fresh vegetables did not last long and there was no cow's milk. Still, the officers ate better than the crew, whose diet consisted of all the lobscouse they could eat and plum duff

This photograph from the late 1800s shows the fore of the deck of an American ship called the U.S.S. *Hartford.*

on Sundays. Lobscouse was made with salt meat, potatoes, onions, and hardtack (very hard bread). Plum duff was made of flour, water, molasses, and prunes. It probably tasted delicious after a week of lobscouse.

Most sailors died at a relatively young age, probably because of the bad food and living conditions, the constant hard work, and the danger of life at sea. Mortality tables from the 1850s show that sailors on clipper ships had the shortest life expectancy of men in any trade—twelve years from the time they signed on—and many first signed on in their teens.

The crew worked hard to always keep the ship's sails in good condition.

Although officers had slightly better living conditions and food and were subject to less physical labor and danger, they had more responsibility. They had to fulfill the contract with the owners of the ship, deliver undamaged cargo, and do so as quickly as possible. They had to keep the men alive, under control, and more or less healthy. They also were responsible for keeping the ship itself in good condition. ▶

The officers and crew knew that they needed each other to get the ship to its destination and back home again, but this knowledge led at best to toleration, not friendship or understanding. Despite the close quarters and mutual dependence, the two groups led separate and distinct lives onboard ship. ▶

COMPARE AND CONTRAST

Food and living conditions were not the same for ships' officers and crew members. List two ways in which the conditions differed and two ways in which they were alike.

Differences

1. _____

_____

2. _____

_____

Similarities

1. _____

_____

2. _____

_____

EVALUATE

This article presents some harsh details about life at sea. Why do you think the speaker in "Sea-Fever" has such a positive view of life at sea despite these realities?

_____

_____

_____

_____

_____

Reading Comprehension

DIRECTIONS *Answer these questions about "Sea-Fever" and "Life Fore and Aft on a Sailing Ship" by filling in the correct ovals.*

1. According to "Life Fore and Aft . . ." new sailors were surprised by the

   Ⓐ excitement and adventure

   Ⓑ kindness of their bosses

   Ⓒ drudgery, danger, and boredom

   Ⓓ trust between officers and crew

2. Why was it difficult for crew members to avoid the ship's officers?

   Ⓐ The officers were always watching them work.

   Ⓑ They ate, worked, and slept in the same quarters.

   Ⓒ The officers monitored the fore.

   Ⓓ The crew worked directly with them.

3. What does the last section of the magazine article compare?

   Ⓐ who made up the groups

   Ⓑ what the groups ate and how they lived

   Ⓒ where the groups slept and relaxed

   Ⓓ what the groups did for work

4. The main point made in the section called "The Ship's Crew" is that

   Ⓐ the crew included both "green" boys and sailors

   Ⓑ officers had authority over the crew

   Ⓒ sailors worked primarily on deck

   Ⓓ sailors spent a lot of time scrubbing

5. Which sentence is *not* true?

   Ⓐ "Sea-Fever" gives a romantic view of life at sea.

   Ⓑ "Life Fore and Aft on a Sailing Ship" gives a realistic view of life at sea.

   Ⓒ Both selections reflect knowledge of a sailor's life and work.

   Ⓓ Both selections emphasize the freedom and adventure that were part of a sailor's life.

6. The author uses part-by-part order to show that officers and crew

   Ⓐ had the same responsibilities

   Ⓑ had no privacy or luxuries

   Ⓒ depended on each other

   Ⓓ shared the same living conditions

7. According to lines 64–66 of "Life Fore and Aft on a Sailing Ship," gimbals are meant to

   Ⓐ steady a bed

   Ⓑ punish a crew member

   Ⓒ feed a captain

   Ⓓ clean a deck

8. According to lines 72–77 of "Life Fore and Aft on a Sailing Ship," plum duff was a

   Ⓐ spatial relation

   Ⓑ "green" sailor

   Ⓒ sweet treat

   Ⓓ hard bread

Timed Writing Practice

PROMPT

Write an opinion essay about (what is important in life.) Draw from your own experience as well as from ideas expressed in the poems "Sea-Fever" and "The Village Blacksmith."

BUDGET YOUR TIME

You have **30 minutes** to respond. Decide how much time to spend on each step.

Analyze _____

Plan _____

Write _____

Review _____

Test-Taker's Toolkit

1. ANALYZE THE PROMPT

A. Circle key words in the prompt. This has been started for you. These words tell you what to include to get a good score.

B. Write down a list of the key elements you need to include in your essay. You may use the space to the right.

_____

_____

_____

_____

2. PLAN YOUR RESPONSE

A. Gather ideas Use your list of key elements to help you gather ideas. You might begin by listing things *you* think are important in life. Then look back at the two poems for other ideas. A list like the one shown can help.

B. Organize your ideas Use your notes to help you structure your essay. For example, you might begin with a paragraph that states two things that *you* think are important in life. Then write one paragraph about something described in "Sea-Fever," such as the desire for freedom. Write a third paragraph about ideas in "The Village Blacksmith." End with a conclusion that sums up your essay.

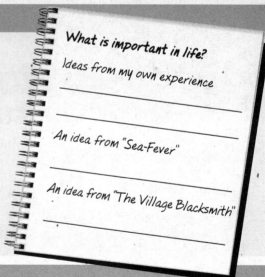

What is important in life?

Ideas from my own experience

_____

_____

An idea from "Sea-Fever"

_____

An idea from "The Village Blacksmith"

_____

3. WRITE AND REVIEW

A. Craft an ending Try to write a thoughtful conclusion that your readers will remember. Here is one idea:

Some people think that _____ is the most important thing in life, but I think that _____ and _____ are even more important. Without them, life would be _____. As __(poet's name)__ said in the poem " __(poem's title)__ ," " __(a line from the poem)__ ."

B. Write your full response Leave yourself enough time to reread your essay and correct any errors.

UNIT 5

THE LANGUAGE OF POETRY

LESSON 5B

Something Told the Wild Geese

BY RACHEL FIELD

Change

BY CHARLOTTE ZOLOTOW

RELATED NONFICTION

Canada Goose

What are
NATURE'S *mysteries?*

The natural world is full of both power and beauty. A terrifying tornado might be followed by a beautiful sunset. Many of these fascinating displays of nature are also mysterious. The poems you are about to read explore two of these mysteries—changes in the seasons and changes in ourselves.

WEB IT What natural mystery do you find amazing? Think of a remarkable animal, plant, or natural event you have seen or heard about and write it in the center of the web shown. Then fill in the rest of the web with words and phrases that describe this element of nature.

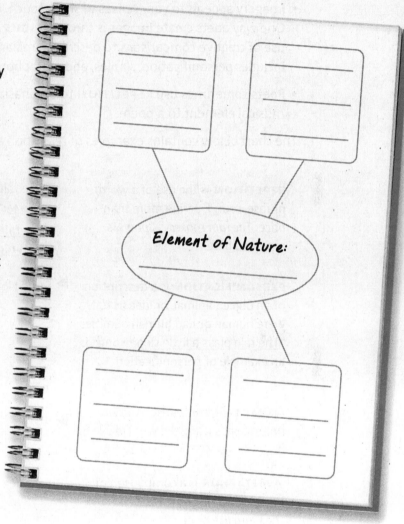

Element of Nature: _____

ASSESSMENT GOALS

By the end of this lesson, you will be able to...

- analyze figurative language and repetition in poetry
- apply critical thinking skills to analyze text
- identify the treatment of a topic in nonfiction text
- analyze a writing prompt and plan a cause-effect essay

Figurative Language and Repetition

The poems "Something Told the Wild Geese" and "Change" both present views of nature. Each poet has carefully chosen the speaker's words to help readers form vivid mental pictures of what is being described. Knowing the following terms will help you understand how poets create mental pictures for readers.

- Imagery appeals to your senses of sight, touch, hearing, smell, and taste. One way poets create images is through FIGURATIVE LANGUAGE—the use of creative comparisons to describe familiar things in new ways. This includes personification, similes, and metaphors.

- Poets sometimes use REPETITION to emphasize a word or idea or to add a musical element to a poem.

The chart below contains examples of repetition and figurative language.

REPETITION is the use of a word, phrase, sound, or line more than once. *The rain makes . . . pools* is repeated here.	The rain makes still pools on the sidewalk The rain makes running pools in the gutter The rain plays a little sleep-song on our roof at night
PERSONIFICATION is a description of an object, animal, or idea as if it were human or had human qualities. "The rain plays a little sleep-song" is an example of personification.	▶ And I love the rain. —from "April Rain Song" by Langston Hughes
A **SIMILE** is a comparison of two unlike things using the word *like* or *as*.	▶ blossoms whirl like children dancing
A **METAPHOR** is a comparison of two unlike things that does not use the word *like* or *as*.	▶ the sea was a plate of blue glass

ADDITIONAL TERMS FOR CRITICAL ANALYSIS

Knowing these additional terms will help you discuss poetry more precisely:

- Poets use rhyme, rhythm, and onomatopoeia to give their poems a musical quality. These techniques are called SOUND DEVICES.

- Another type of sound device is ALLITERATION. Alliteration is the repetition of consonant sounds at the beginning of words. One example is the *s* in *sleep-song* in the Hughes poem above. Here, the alliteration mimics the rain's soothing sound.

SOMETHING TOLD THE WILD GEESE

RACHEL FIELD

Something told the wild geese
    It was time to go.
Though the fields lay golden
    Something whispered,—"Snow."
5 Leaves were green and stirring,
    Berries, luster-glossed,[1]
But beneath warm feathers
    Something cautioned,—"Frost."
All the sagging orchards
10   Steamed with amber spice,
But each wild breast stiffened
    At remembered ice. ▶
Something told the wild geese
    It was time to fly,— ▶
15 Summer sun was on their wings,
    Winter in their cry. ▶

ANALYZE

Next to each image that appeals to the sense of sight, write an *S*; write a *T* for touch; an *M* for smell; and an *H* for hearing. Note that an image may appeal to more than one sense.

EVALUATE

Notice how many times *something* is **repeated** in this poem. How would the poem change if the speaker were to say exactly what "something" is?

_____

_____

_____

INTERPRET

What type of **figurative language** does the poet use in lines 15–16?

_____

1. **luster-glossed:** having a bright or shiny coating.

Change
Charlotte Zolotow

The summer
still hangs
heavy and sweet
with sunlight
5 as it did last year.

The autumn
still comes
showering gold and crimson
as it did last year.

10 The winter
still stings
clean and cold and white
as it did last year.

The spring
15 still comes
like a whisper in the dark night.

It is only I
who have changed. ◄

Reading Comprehension

DIRECTIONS *Answer these questions about "Something Told the Wild Geese" and "Change" by filling in the correct ovals.*

1. What kind of figurative language is used in line 4 of "Something Told the Wild Geese"?

   Ⓐ simile

   Ⓑ metaphor

   Ⓒ personification

   Ⓓ none of the above

2. The image in line 9 of "Something Told the Wild Geese" creates a picture of trees

   Ⓐ losing their leaves

   Ⓑ heavy with fruit

   Ⓒ dying slowly

   Ⓓ starting to bear fruit

3. Which line from "Something Told the Wild Geese" contains alliteration?

   Ⓐ line 5

   Ⓑ line 9

   Ⓒ line 13

   Ⓓ line 15

4. Which sound devices are used in line 16 of "Change"?

   Ⓐ onomatopoeia and rhythm

   Ⓑ rhyme and alliteration

   Ⓒ rhythm and rhyme

   Ⓓ alliteration and onomatopoeia

5. Which phrase from "Change" is repeated throughout the poem?

   Ⓐ It is only I

   Ⓑ The summer / still hangs

   Ⓒ as it did last year

   Ⓓ The spring / still comes

6. What does the speaker in "Change" mean by saying "It is only I / who have changed"?

   Ⓐ Both people and nature change all the time.

   Ⓑ Both people and nature change in predictable ways.

   Ⓒ Nature changes in more ways than people can.

   Ⓓ People change, but nature's cycles are ongoing.

GO ON ➡

For help, use the **Test-Taker's Toolkit** below.

Responding in Writing

7. Short Response Write a paragraph that compares "Change" with "Something Told the Wild Geese." Include an example from each poem that demonstrates their similarity. Also give one example of how the poems are different.

_____

_____

_____

_____

_____

_____

Test-Taker's Toolkit

GRAPHIC ORGANIZER Use the graphic organizer below to help you plan your paragraph.

Poem #1: _____

Poem #2: _____

How the poems are alike: _____

_____

    Example from poem #1: _____

_____

    Example from poem #2: _____

_____

How the poems are different: _____

_____

What's the Connection?

Rachel Field's poem "Something Told the Wild Geese" celebrates the mysterious ways in which nature signals the change of seasons. The guidebook "Canada Goose" gives information about the behavior of wild geese, including their annual migration.

DISCUSS CAUSES The Canada goose almost became extinct. But its numbers have increased significantly in recent years. With a partner, discuss the questions below. Use what you know about how human activity can affect wildlife to make thoughtful guesses about possible answers. Then record your ideas in the diagram.

1. What might have caused the Canada goose population to decline, or decrease?
2. What might have caused the goose population to recover, or increase again?

Canada Goose
GUIDEBOOK

Use with "Something Told the Wild Geese" and "Change," p. 110

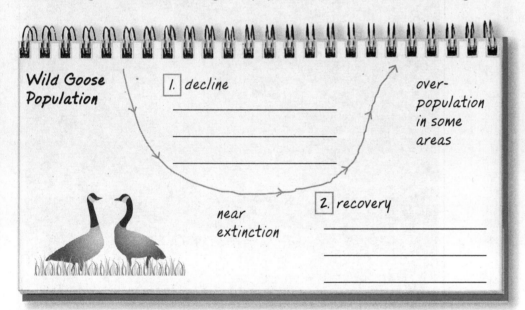

Wild Goose Population

1. decline
_____
_____
_____

over-population in some areas

near extinction

2. recovery
_____
_____
_____

LEARN THE SKILL: IDENTIFY TREATMENT

There are many different ways to write about a topic. The way a topic is handled is called **treatment.** Writers try to choose a treatment that fits their **purpose for writing.** Treatment includes the **form** the writer uses and the writer's **tone,** or attitude toward the topic. Asking these questions will help you understand a writer's treatment of a topic:

- What form does the writing take?
- What is the author's **primary purpose?** Does the author also have a **secondary purpose?**
- What is the author's tone?

For more on treatment, see *Nonfiction Handbook* page R25.

SET A PURPOSE

My purpose for reading is

_____

_____

_____

A guidebook gives detailed information about a particular topic. Underline the text feature on this page that names the topic of this guidebook. Circle the feature that gives some specific details about the topic.

Canada Goose

- **COMMON NAME:** Canada goose

- **SCIENTIFIC NAME:** *Branta canadensis*

- **FAVORITE HANGOUTS:** Golf courses and suburban lake developments ◄

You wouldn't know it to look around today, but the Canada goose was once an uncommon bird. In particular, the subspecies known as the giant Canada goose was considered extinct until a few were discovered in the early 1960s. Over-hunting and destruction of

wetlands had driven them to the brink of extinction.
10 Improved game management practices and extensive
re-introduction programs were begun. These changes
helped stabilize the subspecies and today it is doing fine.
Originally a North American bird, the Canada goose
has also been transplanted successfully to Britain and
Scandinavia. . . . ▶

Depending on whom you talk to, there are up to
eleven subspecies of Canada goose. The largest is the
giant, with a wingspan of 6 feet and weighing up to
20 pounds. Among North American waterfowl, only
20 swans are larger. The smallest version is the so-called
"cackling" goose, which weighs only 2–4 pounds. (This
is now considered a separate species.) The giant Canada
goose is native to the Great Plains. It is unique because
it is non-migratory, at least in comparison to the other
subspecies. The other subspecies nest anywhere from
southern Canada up to the high Arctic tundra. They
travel long distances in their annual migration. If the
winter is mild, the giant Canada goose may not leave its
nesting area at all.

EVALUATE

Look back at the diagram on
page 117. How does your guess
about the cause of the goose
population's decline and its
comeback compare with the
facts?

_____

_____

_____

_____

_____

What is the author's **primary purpose** for writing this guidebook?

_____

_____

How do you know?

_____

_____

_____

SPECIALIZED
Vocabulary

Reread the boxed text. Circle the words that name a male goose, a group of goose eggs, and a goose chick.

Write the words below.

male goose: _____

group of eggs: _____

goose chick: _____

Using specific terms such as these in your own writing is a good strategy for remembering them. On the lines below, write a caption for the photographs on this page. Include the terms you have learned.

_____

_____

_____

_____

30 **Family Groups**

When they do travel, Canada geese stay in family groups. The parents fly with their young. If you watch a large flock of geese come in for a landing, you can often see the different family units peel off in smaller clusters. ◀

The family bond begins at the nest. Canada geese mate for life. They begin to build their nest as early as mid-March. The nest is a large mound of vegetation such as grass and cattail stems lined with

40 down. It is usually located close to water. . . .

Four to seven eggs make up a typical clutch and incubation is done solely by the female. The male, called a gander, guards the nest and will attack any intruders. Incubation takes 25 to 30 days and the goslings are led to water within a day after hatching. ◀

After hatching, there is an amazing change in the attitude of the gander. Where he would previously chase off any other geese in the area, he now becomes much more tolerant of them. Indeed, if there are other clutches of goslings in the area, they will often be grouped together and be looked after by all the adults.

Communication ▶

Canada geese are very vocal creatures and their language is not hard to pick up if you pay close attention. Aside from vocalizations, geese have a whole vocabulary of "body language" that is also very interesting to observe. ▶

The gander has a slower, low-pitched "honk" while the goose's voice is a much quicker and higher-pitched "hink." Mated pairs will greet each other by alternating their calls so rapidly that it seems like only one is talking. A careful ear will be able to put each voice with its rightful owner, which is mighty helpful, since the male and female look alike.

The goslings have a wheezy soft call that may be either in distinct parts—"wheep-wheep-wheep"—or a drawn-out "wheee-oow." Anyone who has raised domestic geese will immediately recognize these calls. Just as with people, when the voice changes as the goose matures, it will often "crack" and sound like a cross between a honk and a wheeze. This will be noticeable when the goslings are becoming fully feathered and starting to show the distinct black and white adult coloration.

Loud, rapid calls will be made when geese are feeling threatened or excited. During land disputes or aggressive displays, some "bad grammar" will often be heard. When a flock gets ready to take off and fly away, they will usually all join in a raucous chorus. A whole flock of geese makes quite a racket! ▶

IDENTIFY TREATMENT

What do the headings on pages 120 and 121 tell you about how the author has organized the information?

_____

_____

_____

IDENTIFY TREATMENT

Underline the sentence in lines 54–58 that reveals the author's **tone,** or attitude toward the topic. 🗨

CONTRAST

How might the **form** of this selection be different if the author had written a personal narrative about an encounter with a Canada goose?

_____

_____

_____

_____

Which statement reveals the author's tone?

(A) You may have to get clear out of town to hear it, but it will be worth it.

(B) Loose dogs are about their only concern.

(C) The Canada goose has a high tolerance for people.

(D) Wichita's flock has been carefully studied.

TIP A test question may ask you about an author's **tone.** Another word for *tone* is *attitude.* A sentence that expresses tone does more than just state a fact. To identify a sentence that reveals tone, **look for a sentence that expresses an opinion, a preference, or a belief.**

EVALUATE

Underline the facts that tell how Wichita's goose population has changed.

Why do you think the author chose to include these facts?

_____

_____

_____

_____

With its interesting social behavior and high tolerance for people, the Canada goose is an appealing example of Great Plains wildlife. During spring and fall, take the time to get out and listen for the faint honking spilling down
90 from the skies from distant Vs of migrating geese. Late afternoon on a still day is a good time. It is a hallmark of the annual cycle of life on the prairie. You may have to get clear out of town to hear it, but it will be worth it. ◀

Urban Goose

In Wichita, Kansas, as well as in other cities across the lower 48 states, the phenomenon of the urban goose has become quite noticeable in the last two decades. The giant subspecies in particular has developed a great tolerance—preference even—for wintering in cities. Not only that, but some of them have taken up year-round residence in those cities!

Wichita's flock has been carefully studied. Every winter in late January a count is taken of the urban wintering geese. Between 1983 and 2007, the size of the urban wintering goose flock in Wichita grew from 1,600 to over 21,000 birds! A summer survey to track the resident population has been taken every year since 2002. There were nearly 1,700 birds in the 2006 survey. ◀

Why are cities becoming winter destinations for the Canada goose?

- More than other goose species, the Canada goose has a high tolerance for people.

- The habitat is right. Golf courses and the typical suburban housing development that includes a pond of some sort are ideal for the birds. For sleeping at night and loafing during the day, they prefer the combination of water and grassy areas with open sightlines between the two.

- In cities they are protected from predators. Loose dogs are about their only concern.

- People bring them food. Feeding the geese is an activity that many people find enjoyable. (Of course, the geese enjoy this too!) The green lawns in the areas described above are eaten by the geese also.

- The geese find other food within a short flight from town. Waste grain and new green wheat in farm fields nearby are the targets of the birds' daily foraging trips.

- And the social nature of the birds can be greatly credited for this trend. When one family of geese discovers that the city life is a good deal, they will remember and return the following year along with their youngsters and other flockmates. ▶

Canada geese in New York City

IDENTIFY TREATMENT

Something written in guidebook **form** often includes sidebars and other text features to support the main text. How does the "Urban Goose" sidebar support the main text?

_____

_____

_____

_____

Reading Comprehension

DIRECTIONS *Answer these questions about "Something Told the Wild Geese" and "Canada Goose" by filling in the correct ovals.*

1. How is the giant Canada goose different from other subspecies?

   (A) It is social.

   (B) It mates for life.

   (C) It can be non-migratory.

   (D) It is vocal.

2. According to lines 59–65 of "Canada Goose," a female makes which sound?

   (A) honk

   (B) hink

   (C) wheep-wheep-wheep

   (D) whee-ow

3. Which statement reveals the author's tone?

   (A) The Canada goose is an appealing example of Great Plains wildlife.

   (B) There were nearly 1,700 birds in the 2006 survey.

   (C) Incubation takes 25 to 30 days.

   (D) In cities they are protected from predators.

4. The last paragraph of "Canada Goose" shows that the author's *secondary* purpose is to

   (A) inform people about migration

   (B) entertain readers with a story

   (C) persuade readers to experience geese themselves

   (D) convince people to protect wild geese

5. What mystery expressed in "Something Told the Wild Geese" does "Canada Goose" help to explain?

   (A) why summer turns to fall

   (B) why some creatures remember ice

   (C) why geese like urban areas

   (D) why geese migrate in the fall

6. What idea from "Canada Goose" might surprise the author of "Something Told the Wild Geese"?

   (A) Geese fly south in the fall.

   (B) Geese get subtle clues to migrate.

   (C) Some geese do not migrate.

   (D) Some geese fly farther than others.

7. From the sentence below, you can tell that *incubation* is

   > Incubation takes 25 to 30 days and the goslings are led to water within a day after hatching.

   (A) the time between birth and death

   (B) the time it takes for an egg to hatch

   (C) the time from birth to maturity

   (D) a period of time that lasts 25 to 30 days

8. The term *phenomenon* in the third line of the sidebar probably means

   (A) an amusing spectacle

   (B) a great tragedy

   (C) a surprising incident

   (D) a serious threat

Timed Writing Practice

PROMPT

Write a cause-effect essay in which you explain why different changes occur in the natural world. Draw on ideas from your own observations, from the two poems you have read, and from the guidebook.

BUDGET YOUR TIME

You have **45 minutes** to respond. Decide how much time to spend on each step.

Analyze _____

Plan _____

Write _____

Review _____

45

Test-Taker's Toolkit

1. ANALYZE THE PROMPT

A. **Read the prompt twice** to make sure you understand it.

B. **Write down the three places** from which the prompt tells you to draw ideas.

Sources for Ideas

1. _____

2. _____

3. _____

2. PLAN YOUR RESPONSE

A. **Gather information** Begin by thinking of kinds of change that occur in nature, other than the seasons. What causes each change? Then revisit the two poems and make some notes about the changes each poem describes. What causes each change? Finally, look back at the guidebook you read and add information from that source. Record your information in a chart like the one shown.

B. **Organize your information** Think about how best to structure your essay. You could begin with a paragraph naming different kinds of change in nature and explaining what causes those changes. Then you could write a paragraph explaining what the poems say about changes and their causes. You could write a similar paragraph about the changes in the guidebook. End with a conclusion that ties everything together.

Changes in Nature		
	CAUSE	EFFECT
In nature		
In the two poems		
In the online articles		

3. WRITE AND REVIEW

A. **Create clear paragraphs** To keep your writing focused, begin or end each paragraph with a **topic sentence** that states the main idea of that paragraph. In the body of the paragraph, include supporting details such as quotations or facts from the selections.

B. **Write your response** Be sure to leave enough time to read over your response.

When is it time to
LET GO?

There are times when we have to say goodbye—to someone or something we love, or to feelings that are no longer helpful. There may also be times when we have to choose to release someone from a promise or sense of responsibility. The two folk tales in this lesson demonstrate different kinds of letting go.

DISCUSS With a group of classmates, fill out a chart with a list of stories or movies in which a character has to give up someone or something. Discuss which situation was the most difficult, and why.

Story or Movie	Character	What Character Lets Go Of
1.		
2.		
3.		
4.		

ASSESSMENT GOALS

By the end of this lesson, you will be able to...

- analyze the characteristics of myths, legends, and tales
- apply critical thinking skills to analyze text
- compare information in nonfiction text
- analyze a writing prompt and plan a compare-contrast essay

Myths, Legends, and Tales

Many stories that are still told today—such as folk tales, fairy tales, and fables—were first told hundreds, even thousands, of years ago. These TRADITIONAL STORIES are passed down from one generation to the next. They survive the test of time because they do more than entertain.

Some explain how elements in the natural world came to be. Others celebrate the deeds of legendary heroes. Many teach important lessons about how to behave in life, such as when it is time to let go. Stories from this oral tradition also provide a window into other times and cultures. The chart below describes four kinds of traditional stories. The two stories in this lesson are FOLK TALES.

TRADITIONAL STORIES

MYTH
Story that was created to explain the mysteries of the universe

- Explains how something in the natural world came to be
- Usually features gods and goddesses

LEGEND
Story that is believed to be based on real people and events

- Often tells about a hero or heroine with special powers
- Describes his or her struggle against a powerful force

TALL TALE
Humorous story about events and characters that are exaggerated

- Often features a "larger-than-life," extraordinary character
- Includes unbelievable details and events

FOLK TALE
Traditional story that may contain animal characters and supernatural events

- Characters represent human qualities, such as cleverness or greed
- Presents a lesson or message about life

ADDITIONAL TERM FOR CRITICAL ANALYSIS

Knowing this additional term will help you discuss traditional stories more precisely.

- **CULTURAL VALUES** are beliefs or traditions that are valued in a certain culture. Cultural values may differ from one group to the next. For example, some cultures value an individual's achievements while others place a higher value on what's best for the community.

THE
CRANE
MAIDEN

Retold by Rafe Martin

MARK & ANALYZE

Read this selection once on your own, marking the text in any way that is helpful to you.

Then read the story a second time, using the questions in the margins to help you. When you see this pencil 🖊, you'll be asked to mark up the text.

BACKGROUND This selection is a retelling of a Japanese folk tale about a crane. Cranes are graceful white birds with long necks. They wade in the water looking for fish, grains, and small animals on which to feed. In Japan, the crane is a symbol of long life. Because crane partners stay together for life, they are also a symbol of loyalty.

Once, long ago, an old couple lived all alone near the edges of a marsh.[1] They were hard-working but poor.

One day the man had been gathering marsh plants, cattails, and such for his wife to cook. As he walked back along the trail, he heard a sharp cry and the sounds of someone—or something—struggling. Parting the long grasses by the trail's edge, he walked carefully into the marsh. The sounds—a clacking and a flapping, whirring noise—came from up ahead. Frightened but still curious, he stepped forward and
10 looked. There on the ground before him lay a great white crane. Its leg was trapped in a **snare** and it was flapping desperately about trying to get free. Its beak was clacking open and shut. Its eye was wild with pain and fear. Its wings were muddied. Never had the man seen such desperation in

snare (snâr) *n.* a trap for catching small animals and birds

---

1. **marsh:** a wet, low-lying area, often thick with tall grasses.

COMPARE

Underline the noises the crane makes in line 8.

Where else in the **folk tale** do these same sounds appear?

_____

_____

_____

ANALYZE

Reread the boxed text. What does the crane do that a wild crane probably wouldn't do?

_____

_____

Why do you think the crane does this?

_____

_____

_____

MAKE INFERENCES

What quality or qualities do the old man and his wife demonstrate?

_____

_____

Underline details in the **folk tale** that support your answer.

a wild creature. His heart was moved. Speaking soothingly he drew closer. Somehow the crane seemed to sense his intent and grew calm. Gentle and slow were the man's movements as he approached. Then, bending down, he loosened the snare from the crane's leg and backed away. ◄

20   The crane stood up. Flexing its injured leg, it stood there gazing directly at the man. Then opening its wings, it flapped once, twice, lifted up off the muddy ground, and flew away. ◄

The man stood gazing after the great white bird as it made its way across the sky. Tears came to his eyes with the beauty of it. "I must see this clearly, and remember it, every detail," he said to himself. "How my wife will enjoy hearing of this adventure. I shall weave every detail into words for her, so she too will see."

"You are late," his wife said when her husband returned. "I
30 have been worried. Are you all right?"

"I am better than all right, dear wife. I have had an adventure. I have seen such a sight. Wait, let me remove my sandals and sit down. I shall tell you all."

Then he told her of his finding the trapped crane, of the bird's panic and pain, and of the great joy he felt as he watched the white bird fly away.

"Dear husband, I am so glad you helped that wild creature. Truly it must have been a wondrous sight to see the crane rise up from the muddied ground and soar into the heavens."
40 "It was. It was. I have told it to you as best I could. For when I saw it fly I knew it was a sight you would have loved. And I wanted to share it with you."

"Thank you, husband." Then she steamed the plants he had gathered and they ate their rice and drank their tea and, when it grew late and the moon rose up in the blackness and sailed across the night sky, they let the fire sink down and they slept. ◄

The next morning they heard a knocking at the door. The woman opened the door and there stood a young girl.

"I am lost," she said. "May I come in?"

50 "Of course. Come in, dear child," the old woman said. "Have a cup of tea. Sit down."

So the girl came in. She was alone in this world, she said, "Let me confess," she added, after drinking the tea and eating the rice the old couple gave her, "I would like to stay here with you. I am a hard worker. I no longer wish to be alone. You are kind people. Please let me stay."

The old couple had always wanted a daughter, and so it was agreed.

"Thank you," the girl said. "I do not think you will regret 60 it." She peered curiously around the house. She looked into an adjoining room. Her face lit up. "I see you have a loom.[2] May I use it from time to time?"

"Daughter," the woman said, "all that we have is yours. Of course you may use the loom."

"I am a shy weaver," the girl said. "Please, Mother, please, Father, when I am weaving do not look into the room until I am done. Will you promise me this?"

"It will be as you wish, child."

The next day their new daughter said she would go into the 70 weaving room. The door was to be shut and neither her father nor her mother were to look in until her work was completed. ▶

All day the girl sat at the loom. And all day the old couple heard the clacking and the whirring of the shuttle, the spinning of the bobbins[3] of thread.

When the sun was setting the girl emerged, pale and worn. But in her hands she held the most splendid cloth the old couple had ever seen. The pattern was perfect, the colors

ANALYZE

What clue does the author give that the girl is not who she appears to be?

---

2. **loom:** a device for making cloth by weaving strands of yarn or thread together.

3. **shuttle . . . bobbins:** A shuttle is a device used in loom weaving to carry thread back and forth between other threads held lengthwise. A bobbin is a spool that holds thread or yarn for weaving.

Why do you think the crane maiden chooses these images to spin into the cloth?

_____

_____

_____

What qualities does the girl demonstrate? Write three words that describe her character.

_____

_____

_____

glowing. Images of the marsh, the sun, the flight of cranes flowed elegantly through the finely woven material. ◄

80 "Mother, Father, please take this cloth to the market and sell it. With the money your life will become easier. I want to do this for you." ◄

The old people were astonished at their daughter's skill. The next day the man brought the cloth to the town. Immediately people began to bid for the beautiful cloth, which was sold at last for three ryo[4] of gold—an unheard of sum.

That night the old couple and their daughter, dressed in new kimonos,[5] ate a wonderful meal—all bought with a small 90 bit of the gold. For several months life was easy. But then the money was gone.

Once more the daughter entered the room, closed the door, and began to weave. *Clack clack clack, whirr whirr whirr.* Hours later she emerged, pale and worn. In her arms was a cloth that shone like silver, filled with patterns of the moon and stars, patterns of sunlight and moonlight shining on water. The old couple had never imagined a material of such stunning beauty.

But once again the girl said, "Mother, Father, do not keep 100 the cloth. I can make more. Please sell it and use the money to care for your old age."

So again the man took the cloth to town. The merchants were astonished. They bid furiously, one against the other, until the cloth had been sold for six ryo of gold.

For many months the family lived happily together. But in time, that money too was gone. The daughter went once again to the loom. But this time her mother and father were curious. Why must they not look? They couldn't bear it. They decided that they would take just a peek through a

---

4. **ryo** (ryō): a gold piece used as currency in Japan until the mid-1800s.
5. **kimonos** (kə-mō′nōz): long, wide-sleeved Japanese robes worn most often by women.

110 crack in the wall. If their daughter could not see them, they reasoned, it would not disturb her at all. ▶

Clack clack clack, whirr whirr whirr. The man and the woman walked softly along the wall, knelt down, and peered through a thin crack in the paper wall. At the loom sat a white crane pulling feathers from its own breast and wings with its long bill. It was weaving with those feathers. The crane turned toward the crack and looked with a great black <u>mournful</u> eye. The man and the woman tumbled backward. But it was too late. They had been seen. ▶

120 Later, when the door of the room opened, their daughter emerged, pale and worn. In her arms she held a most magnificent cloth. On it were images of the setting sun, the rising moon, the trees in autumn, the long migrations of the cranes. On it too were the images of a man and a woman watching a white crane fly away. ▶

"Father, Mother," she said, "I had hoped to stay with you always. But you have seen me as I truly am. I am the crane you saved, Father, from the trap. I wanted to repay you for your kindness. I shall never forget you, but now that you
130 know this truth, I cannot stay with you."

The man and the woman wept. They begged and pleaded, "We love you. Do not leave us. We do not care that you are a crane! You are our daughter. We shall tell no one."

"It is too late," whispered the girl. "The marshes call to me. The sky calls to me. The wind in the trees whispers my name. And I must follow. Perhaps all is as it should be. The debt has been repaid. I shall never forget you. Farewell."

She walked from the hut and stood out in the open air. The man and the woman watched in wonder as before their
140 eyes their beautiful pale daughter became a beautiful white crane. Flapping her wings once, twice, three times, the great crane rose slowly up off the ground and, circling the hut, flew away.

DRAW CONCLUSIONS

Reread the boxed text. Underline an example of foreshadowing—something that hints at future events.

What event is foreshadowed?

_____

mournful (môrn′fəl) *adj.* feeling or expressing sorrow or grief

CONNECT

How many times does the girl weave? _____

What other stories can you think of in which events or characters are in sets of three?

_____

_____

_____

TestSmart

The images the girl wove into the cloth in lines 120–125 reflect

- Ⓐ the beauty of the marsh
- Ⓑ the crane maiden's departure
- Ⓒ the glowing moon
- Ⓓ all of the above

TIP A test may ask you about an event in a **folk tale.** Remember that in folk tales, events are often repeated. The girl in this story spins three different cloths and creates three different images. Even if you think you know the answer, **reread the lines** referred to in the question. Which answer choice describes the *last* cloth she wove?

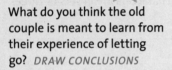

TestSmart

Which statement reveals a cultural value expressed in the story?

Ⓐ Feed migrating birds.

Ⓑ Gather plants for food.

Ⓒ Help others in need.

Ⓓ Sell fabric for gold.

TIP A **cultural value** is an idea or belief that people in a culture think is important. One of the answer choices names a cultural value.

Big Question

What do you think the old couple is meant to learn from their experience of letting go? *DRAW CONCLUSIONS*

_____

_____

_____

_____

"Farewell," said the man and the woman, watching the crane disappear over the marsh. "We shall miss you, daughter. But we are glad that you are free."

After that, every year when the cranes migrated, the old couple left a silver dish of grain out before their door. And every year a beautiful crane came to eat that grain.

150 So the story goes. ◀

AUNTY MISERY

Retold by Judith Ortiz Cofer

BACKGROUND Legends of strange happenings and supernatural forces have been part of Puerto Rican storytelling traditions for centuries. "Aunty Misery" is a retelling of a Puerto Rican folk tale about a cranky old woman who meets a sorcerer. The sorcerer's magic solves some of her problems but also creates new ones.

This is a story about an old, very old woman who lived alone in her little hut with no other company than a beautiful pear tree that grew at her door. She spent all her time taking care of her pear tree. But the neighborhood children drove the old woman crazy by stealing her fruit. They would climb her tree, shake its delicate limbs, and run away with armloads of golden pears, yelling insults at "Aunty Misery," as they called her.

One day, a pilgrim stopped at the old woman's hut and
10　asked her permission to spend the night under her roof. Aunty Misery saw that he had an honest face and bade the traveler come in. She fed him and made a bed for him in front of her hearth. In the morning while he was getting ready to leave, the stranger told her that he would show his gratitude for her <u>hospitality</u> by granting her one wish. ▶

hospitality (hŏs'pĭ-tăl'ĭ-tē) *n.* the friendly, generous treatment of guests

"There is only one thing that I desire," said Aunty Misery.

"Ask, and it shall be yours," replied the stranger, who was a sorcerer[1] in disguise.

"I wish that anyone who climbs up my pear tree should not be able to come back down until I permit it."

"Your wish is granted," said the stranger, touching the pear tree as he left Aunty Misery's house.

And so it happened that when the children came back to **taunt** the old woman and to steal her fruit, she stood at her window watching them. Several of them shimmied[2] up the trunk of the pear tree and immediately got stuck to it as if with glue. She let them cry and beg her for a long time before she gave the tree permission to let them go, on the condition that they never again steal her fruit or bother her.

Time passed and both Aunty Misery and her tree grew bent and gnarled with age. One day another traveler stopped at her door. This one looked suffocated and exhausted, so the old woman asked him what he wanted in her village. He answered her in a voice that was dry and hoarse, as if he had swallowed a desert: "I am Death, and I have come to take you with me." ◄

Thinking fast, Aunty Misery said, "All right, but before I go I would like to pluck some pears from my beloved pear tree to remember how much pleasure it brought me in this life. But, I am a very old woman and cannot climb to the tallest branches where the best fruit is; will you be so kind as to do it for me?"

With a heavy sigh like wind through a catacomb,[3] Death climbed the pear tree. Immediately he became stuck to it as if with glue. And no matter how much he cursed and threatened, Aunty Misery would not give the tree permission to release Death. ◄

---

1. **sorcerer:** a wizard or magician.
2. **shimmied:** shinnied, or scooted.
3. **catacomb** (kăt'ə-kōm'): an underground cemetery made up of tunnels full of graves.

taunt (tônt) v. to mock or insult

CLASSIFY

What characteristics of **folk tales** have been in the story so far? Name two.

1. _____

_____

2. _____

_____

EVALUATE

What doesn't Aunty Misery consider when she tricks Death? Underline upcoming story events to help you answer.

_____

_____

_____

Many years passed and there were no deaths in the world. The people who make their living from death began to protest
50 loudly. The doctors claimed no one bothered to come in for examinations or treatments anymore, because they did not fear dying; the pharmacists' business suffered too because medicines are, like magic potions, bought to prevent or postpone the **inevitable**; the priests and undertakers[4] were unhappy with the situation also, for obvious reasons. There were also many old folks tired of life who wanted to pass on to the next world to rest from the miseries of this one.

Aunty Misery realized all this, and not wishing to be unfair, she made a deal with her prisoner, Death: if he
60 promised not ever to come for her again, she would give him his freedom. He agreed. And that is why so long as the world is the world, Aunty Misery will always live. ▶

inevitable (ĭn-ĕv′ĭ-tə-bəl) *adj.* impossible to avoid or prevent

MAKE JUDGMENTS

Underline the deal Aunty Misery makes with Death.

What characteristics does Aunty Misery reveal about herself by making this deal?

_____

_____

_____

Big Question ?

Reread the Big Question on page 127. What do the main characters in each **folk tale** let go of? *CLARIFY*

"The Crane Maiden"

_____

_____

_____

"Aunty Misery"

_____

_____

_____

4. **undertakers:** funeral directors.

Reading Comprehension

DIRECTIONS *Answer these questions about "The Crane Maiden" and "Aunty Misery" by filling in the correct ovals.*

1. How are the beginning and end of "The Crane Maiden," the first folk tale, similar?

   Ⓐ The couple gains a daughter.

   Ⓑ The maiden spins a cloth.

   Ⓒ The crane is free.

   Ⓓ The old man goes to the marsh.

2. What supernatural event occurs in lines 138–143 of "The Crane Maiden"?

   Ⓐ A crane transforms itself into a girl.

   Ⓑ A girl transforms herself into a crane.

   Ⓒ A crane weaves a beautiful cloth from its feathers.

   Ⓓ An old couple adopts a strange girl.

3. Which statement does *not* reveal a cultural value expressed in "The Crane Maiden"?

   Ⓐ Appreciate good food.

   Ⓑ Value freedom.

   Ⓒ Respect nature.

   Ⓓ Love your family.

4. The last line of "Aunty Misery" reveals which Puerto Rican cultural value?

   Ⓐ acceptance of all parts of life, even misery

   Ⓑ honesty in all circumstances

   Ⓒ cleverness when solving problems

   Ⓓ acceptance of the certainty of death

5. Of the characters in both folk tales, which one demonstrates gratitude by repaying a debt?

   Ⓐ Aunty Misery

   Ⓑ the crane maiden

   Ⓒ the old man

   Ⓓ the old man's wife

6. Which of these characteristics of traditional stories appears in "The Crane Maiden" but not in "Aunty Misery"?

   Ⓐ supernatural events

   Ⓑ animal characters

   Ⓒ lesson about life

   Ⓓ focus on real people

7. What is the most likely meaning of the word *hearth* in line 13 of "Aunty Misery"?

   Ⓐ cupboard

   Ⓑ hut

   Ⓒ heart

   Ⓓ fireplace

8. What is the most likely meaning of *gnarled* in line 31 of "Aunty Misery"?

   Ⓐ cranky

   Ⓑ angry

   Ⓒ tall

   Ⓓ twisted

Responding in Writing

9. Short Response Choose one of the traditional tales you have read and write a paragraph that explains why it qualifies as a folk tale. Consider the characteristics of a folk tale and how they are demonstrated in the story you have chosen.

For help, use the **Test-Taker's Toolkit** below.

_____

_____

_____

_____

_____

_____

Test-Taker's Toolkit

ACADEMIC VOCABULARY When a prompt includes an academic term such as *characteristics*, think about the meaning of the term. **Characteristics** are features or traits that consistently appear in a type of literature. To answer this prompt, you need to review the definition of a folk tale.

GRAPHIC ORGANIZER Use the graphic organizer below to help you plan your paragraph. Write the characteristics of a folk tale in the first column. In the second column, write the ways in which the folk tale you have chosen fits each characteristic.

Characteristics of a Folk Tale	How "_____" Fits These Characteristics
1.	
2.	
3.	

- **What Is a Crane?**
  PAMPHLET
- **The Peace Crane**
  ONLINE ARTICLE

Use with "The Crane Maiden," p. 126

What's the Connection?

"The Crane Maiden" is a folk tale about a crane that becomes a human in order to repay a debt. The pamphlet "What Is a Crane?" describes the physical traits of cranes and presents some surprising facts about them. The online article "The Peace Crane" explores the roles cranes play in Japanese culture.

I KNOW / I WANT TO KNOW In the first column of the chart below, write what you know about cranes and what they symbolize. Draw your ideas from "The Crane Maiden" as well as from your own reading or viewing. In the second column, write some questions you have about these topics.

I Know . . .	I Want to Know . . .

LEARN THE SKILL: COMPARE INFORMATION

Have you ever wondered why dozens of resources are available on the same topic? Texts that cover the same topic do not necessarily present the same **information**. For example, one source may cover a large span of time and present only the most important events. Another source may focus on a shorter time span and include lots of details. How much of a topic a nonfiction selection attempts to cover is called its **scope.**

"What Is a Crane?" and "The Peace Crane" are both about the same topic—cranes. As you read these selections, compare the information they present. Think about how they differ in scope.

For more on comparing information, see *Nonfiction Handbook* page R25.

What Is a Crane?

by the International Crane Foundation

Crane Facts

- Cranes belong to a family of birds named *Gruidae*.

- Cranes are a very ancient form of bird. Scientists have discovered fossils of crane bones that are over 25 million years old!

- Cranes are found on every continent except South America and Antarctica.

- They are different from storks, egrets, and herons, even though they look similar.

10 - Cranes may choose a mate for life, and can live 20–30 years in the wild.

- Cranes are famous for their courtship dancing and loud calls.

- There are 15 different species of cranes, of which ten are now threatened by extinction.

- Two of the 15 species of cranes live in North America. Sandhill cranes are found in the Midwest, as well as many other areas
20 of North America. Whooping cranes are found in Canada and the United States.

- To many people around the world, cranes symbolize long life and happiness and have an important role in human culture.

- Most species of cranes prefer to live in wet, soggy areas called wetlands, but may also find food in grasslands or prairies. ▶

SET A PURPOSE

My purpose for reading is

_____

_____

_____

ANALYZE

Circle the sentence that has to do with **cultural values.**

What fact about cranes seems to support its role as a symbol of long life?

_____

_____

RED PATCH

Most cranes have a bright red patch on the top of their head or on their neck. They often display the red patch to another crane to warn it away from their territory.

LONG BEAKS

Cranes have long, slender beaks to probe for food in the ground. This "tool" allows cranes to find food where many other animals cannot reach. This is one adaptation that cranes have for living in wetlands. ◄

LONG TRACHEA (Wind Pipe)

Cranes are noted for their loud, bugling calls, which can be heard up to two miles away. A crane's trachea can be as long as five feet and is coiled inside the bird's breastbone to accommodate the extra length. The trachea's extra length resonates much like the tubing in a trombone and helps project the vocalization. ◄

LONG LEGS

They make it easy for cranes to walk through tall marsh grasses and wade in shallow water.

TALL

Adult sandhill cranes are about four feet tall and have a wingspan of five to eight feet. Another species, the sarus crane, is almost six feet tall and has a wingspan of nearly eight feet! The long slender neck, like a submarine periscope, allows the crane to look over tall marsh grasses to spot predators. It also allows cranes to reach into deep water to find food.

TAIL FEATHERS

Wing feathers are so long that they cover the short tail feathers when they are folded and give the appearance of a large tail. ▶

FEET

Cranes do not have webbed feet like ducks, and rarely swim. Their large feet with long, narrow toes are perfect for squishing through mud. Most cranes have a short, elevated hind toe and do not perch in trees.

INTERNATIONAL CRANE FOUNDATION

SEARCH

SYMBOLS OF PEACE | CRANE | DOVE | RAINBOW | OTHER SYMBOLS

1 | 2 ▶

The Peace Crane

by Heidi Moore

In Japan, certain birds have long been viewed as having special qualities. Stories of birds appear in ancient stories and legends. The Japanese crane, with its white feathers and the bright red spot on its head or neck, holds a lot of meaning for the Japanese people. It is known as a symbol of peace, happiness, and good fortune. ◀

For centuries, cranes have played an important role in Japanese culture. Japanese folk tales from long ago tell of cranes living for 1,000 years. That is how the crane
10 became connected with long life. It is also linked to power and leadership. The crane's loud call inspired a saying in Japan that someone who speaks forcefully has the "voice of the crane."

Because cranes partner for life, they are also linked to ideas of faithfulness and loyalty. This made them a good symbol for weddings. At traditional Japanese weddings,

COMPARE INFORMATION

How does the focus of "The Peace Crane" differ from the focus of "What Is a Crane?"

_____

_____

_____

_____

_____

the bride wore a silk robe called a *kimono*. Images of cranes were often sewn onto the bride's *kimono* with colorful silk thread.

20   Throughout Japanese history, poets, artists, and musicians have been honoring the crane. Figures of the majestic bird appear on ancient shrines and temples. Cranes are common elements in both traditional and modern Japanese paintings, as well. They often appear in a pine tree, surrounded by bamboo and plum blossoms. All three types of plant life are linked with ideas of long life, loyalty, and faithfulness, just as the crane is. There is even a series of folk songs about cranes.

    In 1952, Japan named the crane as its national bird. Today the Japanese crane is rare and threatened with extinction. However,
30 its symbol remains as popular as ever. Crane figures can be found painted on airplanes and strung from the ceiling in hotel rooms to bring good fortune to guests. In difficult times, people often fold 1,000 paper cranes as a way to bring healing and peace. ▶

TestSmart

Which phrase best describes the scope of "The Peace Crane"?

Ⓐ cranes in cultures worldwide

Ⓑ what cranes symbolize today

Ⓒ cranes in Japanese culture

Ⓓ cranes as symbols of peace

TIP A question may ask you about the **scope** of a selection. Scope refers to what aspects of a topic a selection covers. To answer a question about scope, **identify what the selection focuses on.** Then look for the answer choice that best describes that focus.

Reading Comprehension

DIRECTIONS *Answer these questions about "The Crane Maiden,"*
"What Is a Crane?" and "The Peace Crane" by filling in the correct ovals.

1. Which physical feature helps a crane find food that many other animals cannot reach?

   Ⓐ its trachea

   Ⓑ its wingspan

   Ⓒ its beak

   Ⓓ its toes

2. Based on the third and the tenth crane facts on page 141, what can you tell about cranes?

   Ⓐ They need wetlands to survive.

   Ⓑ They can adapt to different habitats.

   Ⓒ They are extinct in Antarctica.

   Ⓓ They can survive anywhere.

3. How is the scope of "The Peace Crane" different from the scope of "What Is a Crane?"

   Ⓐ It covers cultural history.

   Ⓑ It is more specific.

   Ⓒ It covers several countries.

   Ⓓ It is on a different topic.

4. The first paragraph of "The Peace Crane" helps to establish the article's focus by

   Ⓐ calling cranes "a symbol of happiness"

   Ⓑ mentioning other symbols of good luck

   Ⓒ describing cranes' migration pattern

   Ⓓ naming several things cranes symbolize

5. Both "The Crane Maiden" and "The Peace Crane" mention

   Ⓐ the clacking sounds cranes make

   Ⓑ images of cranes being sewn into cloth

   Ⓒ folk songs about cranes

   Ⓓ folding paper cranes

6. If a friend wanted to learn some basic facts about real cranes, which selection would you recommend?

   Ⓐ "The Crane Maiden"

   Ⓑ "What Is a Crane?"

   Ⓒ "The Peace Crane"

   Ⓓ "Aunty Misery"

7. The word *vocalization* under "Long Trachea" on page 142 refers to

   Ⓐ sounds produced by voice

   Ⓑ a breast bone

   Ⓒ a long wind pipe

   Ⓓ the tubing in a trombone

8. An *elevated* hind toe under "Feet" on page 143 is

   Ⓐ harder than the others

   Ⓑ higher than the others

   Ⓒ taller than the others

   Ⓓ lighter than the others

Timed Writing Practice

BUDGET YOUR TIME

You have 45 minutes to complete this assignment. Decide how much time to spend on each step.

Analyze _____

Plan _____

Write _____

Review _____

45

PROMPT

Both (Aunty Misery) and (the old couple) in "The Crane Maiden" face a situation in which they must let something go. Write a compare-contrast essay in which you discuss how these two situations are alike and different.

Test-Taker's Toolkit

1. ANALYZE THE PROMPT

A. Read the prompt carefully Then reread it to make sure you understand exactly what it is asking you to do.

B. Circle key words The characters you will write about have been circled for you. Circle the parts of the prompt that tell what situations you will write about and what writing form you are to use.

C. Restate the prompt in your own words. You may use the lines on the right.

_____

_____

_____

_____

_____

2. PLAN YOUR RESPONSE

A. Make notes Find details about the situations in which each character lets something go.

B. Organize ideas The outline on the right will help you organize your notes into an essay.

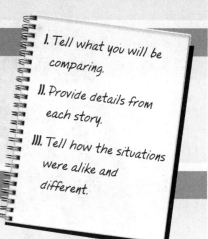

I. Tell what you will be comparing.

II. Provide details from each story.

III. Tell how the situations were alike and different.

3. WRITE AND REVIEW

A. Craft a beginning Try to capture your readers' interest with a question or an example. Write a draft of your opening below.

_____

_____

_____

B. Write out your full response Leave enough time to read through your essay. Make sure you have met all the requirements of the prompt.

from *The Story of My Life*
BY HELEN KELLER

RELATED NONFICTION

Biography of Helen Keller

How Do People Who Are Deaf-Blind Communicate?

Do we have to accept *our* LIMITS?

Sometimes the things that we most want to do are the hardest to accomplish. Fortunately, many obstacles can be overcome with creativity and determination. In the following excerpt from *The Story of My Life*, Helen Keller describes her first steps toward triumphing over her limitations. She begins to understand the world around her—despite being unable to see or hear.

CHART IT In the chart shown, write a few sentences about a person who has succeeded despite a major difficulty. Write about someone you know or someone from a book or movie. Then form a small group and share your examples. What common elements do you discover?

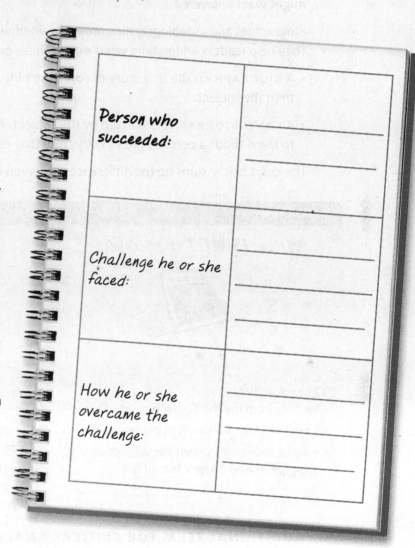

Person who succeeded:

Challenge he or she faced:

How he or she overcame the challenge:

ASSESSMENT GOALS

By the end of this lesson, you will be able to...

- understand the characteristics of biographies and autobiographies
- apply critical thinking skills to analyze text
- synthesize information in nonfiction text
- analyze a writing prompt and plan an autobiographical narrative

Biography and Autobiography

Most people are curious about the lives of fascinating individuals. Who or what inspired them? Where did they get their brilliant ideas? How did they find the courage to succeed against all odds? These are just a few of the questions people might want answered.

Biographies and autobiographies provide a window into the lives of amazing people. They help readers understand what makes these people who they are.

- A **BIOGRAPHY** is the true story of someone's life, written by someone other than the subject.

- An **AUTOBIOGRAPHY** is written by the subject. Autobiographies allow you to learn about a person's life directly from that person.

The chart below sums up the differences between biographies and autobiographies.

BIOGRAPHY	AUTOBIOGRAPHY
*Writer **IS NOT** the Subject*	*Writer **IS** the Subject*
Characteristics	**Characteristics**
• written from the third-person point of view	• written from the first-person point of view
• based on information from many sources	• based mostly on details from the subject's own memories
• may include quotes from the subject or from people who knew him or her	• may include information from other sources, such as the subject's friends and family

ADDITIONAL TERM FOR CRITICAL ANALYSIS

Knowing this additional term will help you discuss biographies and autobiographies more precisely.

An **AUTHOR'S PERSPECTIVE** is a unique combination of ideas, values, feelings, and beliefs that influences the way a writer looks at a topic. Tone, or attitude toward a topic, often reveals an author's perspective.

The Story of My Life

Helen Keller

MARK & ANALYZE
Read this selection once on your own, marking the text in any way that is helpful to you.

Then read the story a second time, using the questions in the margins to help you analyze the literature. When you see this pencil 🖉, you'll be asked to mark up the text.

BACKGROUND Before Helen Keller was two years old, she developed a severe fever that left her blind and deaf. The young girl was highly intelligent, but her parents did not know how to communicate with her. Anne Sullivan, a teacher from the Perkins Institution for the Blind, became Keller's tutor when Keller was six years old.

The most important day I remember in all my life is the one on which my teacher, Anne Mansfield Sullivan, came to me. I am filled with wonder when I consider the immeasurable contrasts between the two lives which it connects. It was the third of March, 1887, three months before I was seven years old. ▶

On the afternoon of that eventful day, I stood on the porch, dumb,[1] expectant. I guessed vaguely from my mother's signs and from the hurrying to and fro in the house that something
10 unusual was about to happen, so I went to the door and waited on the steps. The afternoon sun penetrated the mass of honeysuckle that covered the porch, and fell on my upturned face. My fingers lingered almost unconsciously on the familiar leaves and blossoms which had just come forth to greet the sweet southern spring. I did not know what the future held of marvel or surprise for me. Anger and bitterness

INTERPRET
What are the "two lives" Keller mentions in line 4?

_____

_____

_____

_____

---

1. **dumb:** unable to speak; mute.

TestSmart

How would the boxed
passage be different if it
were told by a biographer
instead of by Helen Keller
herself?

Ⓐ It would be told in the
   first person.

Ⓑ It would be told in the
   second person.

Ⓒ It would be told in the
   third person.

Ⓓ It would be more
   accurate.

TIP A question may
ask you to compare the
way a **biography** and an
autobiography treat a
subject. An autobiography
gives a firsthand account of
what the subject felt and
thought. A biography is
based on information from
various sources.

DRAW CONCLUSIONS

Consider what happens next
in this selection. In what way
does Anne Sullivan "reveal all
things" to Keller?

---

had preyed upon me continually for weeks and a deep languor
had succeeded[2] this passionate struggle.

> Have you ever been at sea in a dense fog, when it seemed
> as if a <u>tangible</u> white darkness shut you in, and the great ship,
> tense and anxious, groped her way toward the shore with
> plummet and sounding-line,[3] and you waited with beating
> heart for something to happen? I was like that ship before my
> education began, only I was without compass or sounding-
> line, and had no way of knowing how near the harbor was.
> "Light! Give me light!" was the wordless cry of my soul, and
> the light of love shone on me in that very hour. ◄

I felt approaching footsteps. I stretched out my hand as I
supposed to my mother. Someone took it, and I was caught up and
held close in the arms of her who had come to reveal all things to
me, and, more than all things else, to love me. ◄

The morning after my teacher came she led me into her
room and gave me a doll. The little blind children at the
Perkins Institution had sent it and Laura Bridgman[4] had
dressed it; but I did not know this until afterward. When I
had played with it a little while, Miss Sullivan slowly spelled
into my hand the word "d-o-l-l." I was at once interested
in this finger play and tried to imitate it. When I finally
succeeded in making the letters correctly I was flushed with
childish pleasure and pride. Running downstairs to my
mother I held up my hand and made the letters for *doll.* I
did not know that I was spelling a word or even that words
existed; I was simply making my fingers go in monkey-like
imitation. In the days that followed I learned to spell in this

---

2. **deep languor had succeeded:** a complete lack of energy had followed.

3. **plummet and sounding-line:** a weighted rope used to measure the depth of
   water.

4. **Perkins Institution . . . Laura Bridgman:** The Perkins Institution was a school
   for the blind, located in Massachusetts. Laura Bridgman (1829–1889), a student
   at the Perkins Institution, was the first deaf and blind child to be successfully
   educated. Like Keller, Bridgman became quite famous for her accomplishments.

uncomprehending way a great many words, among them *pin, hat, cup* and a few verbs like *sit, stand* and *walk.* But my teacher had been with me several weeks before I understood that everything has a name.

One day, while I was playing with my new doll, Miss
50 Sullivan put my big rag doll into my lap also, spelled "d-o-l-l" and tried to make me understand that "d-o-l-l" applied to both. Earlier in the day we had had a tussle over the words "m-u-g" and "w-a-t-e-r." Miss Sullivan had tried to impress it upon me that "m-u-g" is *mug* and that "w-a-t-e-r" is *water,* but I persisted in confounding the two. In despair she had dropped the subject for the time, only to renew it at the first opportunity. I became impatient at her repeated attempts and, seizing the new doll, I dashed[5] it upon the floor. I was keenly delighted when I felt the fragments of the broken doll
60 at my feet. Neither sorrow nor regret followed my passionate outburst. I had not loved the doll. In the still, dark world in which I lived there was no strong sentiment or tenderness. I felt my teacher sweep the fragments to one side of the hearth, and I had a sense of satisfaction that the cause of my discomfort was removed. She brought me my hat, and I knew I was going out into the warm sunshine. This thought, if a wordless **sensation** may be called a thought, made me hop and skip with pleasure. ▶

We walked down the path to the well-house, attracted by
70 the fragrance of the honeysuckle with which it was covered. Someone was drawing water and my teacher placed my hand under the spout. As the cool stream gushed over one hand she spelled into the other the word *water,* first slowly, then rapidly. I stood still, my whole attention fixed upon the motions of her fingers. Suddenly I felt a misty **consciousness** as of something forgotten—a thrill of returning thought; and somehow the mystery of language was revealed to me. I knew then that "w-a-t-e-r" meant the wonderful cool something

---

uncomprehending
(ŭn'kŏm-prǐ-hěn'dǐng) *adj.*
not understanding

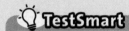

VOCABULARY
The word *sentiment* in line 62 most likely means

- (A) reason
- (B) emotion
- (C) friend
- (D) enemy

TIP If a test question asks the likely meaning of a word, reread the sentence in which the word appears and **use context clues** to figure out the meaning. Then substitute the word with each answer choice and identify the one that makes sense.

sensation (sĕn-sā'shən) *n.* a feeling

consciousness (kŏn'shəs-nĭs) *n.* awareness of one's own thoughts

---

5. **dashed:** threw or knocked with sudden violence.

_____

_____

_____

_____

Underline details in the text that support your answer.

repentance (rĭ-pĕn'təns) *n.* sorrow or regret

Big Question ?

Reread the Big Question on page 149. How do you think Anne Sullivan and Helen Keller would answer it? MAKE INFERENCES

Sullivan: _____

_____

Keller: _____

_____

80 that was flowing over my hand. That living word awakened my soul, gave it light, hope, joy, set it free! There were barriers still, it is true, but barriers that could in time be swept away.

I left the well-house eager to learn. Everything had a name, and each name gave birth to a new thought. As we returned to the house every object which I touched seemed to quiver with life. That was because I saw everything with the strange, new sight that had come to me. On entering the door I remembered the doll I had broken. I felt my way to the hearth and picked up the pieces. I tried vainly to put them together. Then my eyes filled with tears; for I realized what I had done,
90 and for the first time I felt **repentance** and sorrow. ◄

I learned a great many new words that day. I do not remember what they all were; but I do know that *mother, father, sister, teacher* were among them—words that were to make the world blossom for me, "like Aaron's rod, with flowers."[6] It would have been difficult to find a happier child than I was as I lay in my crib at the close of that eventful day and lived over the joys it had brought me, and for the first time longed for a new day to come. ◄

---

6. **like Aaron's rod, with flowers:** a reference to a story in the Bible in which a wooden staff suddenly sprouts flowers.

Reading Comprehension

DIRECTIONS *Answer these questions about the excerpt from* The Story of My Life *by filling in the correct ovals.*

1. According to the autobiography, what changed Helen Keller's life?

   (A) looking forward to a new day

   (B) hugging Anne Sullivan

   (C) understanding that every object has a name

   (D) getting a new doll

2. Which event would be most effectively described by Helen Keller?

   (A) the walk to the well-house

   (B) sweeping up the broken doll

   (C) Keller's joy at discovering language

   (D) Sullivan's arrival at the house

3. When the author says "I saw everything with the strange new sight that had come to me," she reveals that her approach to the world has

   (A) narrowed in focus

   (B) changed in a positive way

   (C) restored her vision

   (D) stayed the same

4. Which sentence is *not* an example of the author's perspective on her life before Anne Sullivan arrived?

   (A) Have you ever been at sea in a dense fog . . . ?

   (B) I did not know what the future held.

   (C) I was flushed with childish pleasure.

   (D) Anger and bitterness had preyed upon me.

5. Which phrase could be spoken only by a first-person narrator?

   (A) It was the third of March

   (B) Someone was drawing water

   (C) The Perkins Institution had sent it

   (D) Suddenly I felt a misty consciousness

6. What is Sullivan trying to teach Keller in lines 49–55?

   (A) how to spell *water*

   (B) the difference between a mug and the water inside it

   (C) how to spell *doll*

   (D) the difference between two dolls

7. In the context of line 55, the word *confounding* means

   (A) repeating   (C) naming

   (B) forgetting   (D) confusing

8. Reread this sentence from line 88:

   > I tried vainly to put them together.

   In this context, *vainly* means

   (A) in a conceited way

   (B) without success

   (C) proudly

   (D) in a successful way

GO ON ➡

For help, use
the **Test-Taker's
Toolkit** below.

Responding in Writing

9. Short Response Write a paragraph sharing your personal response to the excerpt
from *The Story of My Life.*

_____

_____

_____

_____

_____

Test-Taker's Toolkit

ACADEMIC VOCABULARY Sharing a **personal response** to literature is different from
retelling a story. When you are asked to write a personal response, you are being asked
to express how a selection affected you, what you thought of the topic, and how the
selection relates to your life.

GRAPHIC ORGANIZER Use the graphic organizer below to develop your response.

Title: _____ Author: _____

What the selection is about: _____

_____

What I liked best about it: _____

_____

I felt:		I thought about:

**Personal
Response**

It relates to my life because:

What's the Connection?

In *The Story of My Life*, Helen Keller describes the moment when she finally understands the mystery of language. The online article "Biography of Helen Keller" summarizes Keller's life. The pamphlet "How Do People Who Are Deaf-Blind Communicate?" discusses the different ways in which deaf-blind people find out about the world and communicate with others.

DISCUSS COMMUNICATION Discuss each question in the chart below with a partner. Write your ideas in the blank spaces provided.

Related Nonfiction

- *Biography of Helen Keller*
  ONLINE ARTICLE
- *How Do People Who Are Deaf-Blind Communicate?*
  PAMPHLET

Use with The Story of My Life, *p. 148*

Communicating and Learning	With Sight and Hearing	Without Sight and Hearing
How do people learn about the world?		
How do people communicate their needs?		
How do people share their ideas?		

LEARN THE SKILL: SYNTHESIZE INFORMATION

You can learn about a topic from many different sources. When you **synthesize information** in nonfiction text, you take individual pieces of information and combine them with facts, as well as with your knowledge and experiences. Synthesizing information is an important skill to learn. It can help you to

- gain a better understanding of a subject
- generate new ideas based on existing ones
- draw from a variety of sources when you write about a topic

For more on synthesizing information, see *Nonfiction Handbook* page R21.

http://www.helenkeller.org

HOME **BIOGRAPHY** ORGANIZATIONS BOOKS MOVIES

1 | 2 ▶

Biography of Helen Keller

The story of Helen Keller is the story of a normal child who, at the age of 18 months, was suddenly shut off from the world. Against overwhelming odds, she waged a slow, hard but successful battle to re-enter that same world. The child grew into a highly intelligent

10 and sensitive woman who wrote, spoke, and labored endlessly to help others. ◀

Helen was born in Tuscumbia, Alabama, on June 27, 1880. However, her real life began one day in March 1887, when she was almost seven years old. She was always to call that "the most important day I can remember in my life." It was the day when Annie Sullivan, a 20-year-old graduate of the Perkins School for the Blind, came to be Helen's teacher. They were inseparable until Annie's death in 1936.

20 Even as a little girl, Helen expressed a desire to go to college. In 1900, she entered Radcliffe College and graduated from

there in 1904 with honors. She thus became the first deaf-blind person to graduate from college. Throughout these years, Annie Sullivan spelled books and lectures into her student's hand. ▶

While still at Radcliffe, Helen Keller began the writing career, which was to continue for 50 years. In addition to *The Story of My Life*, she wrote 11 other books and numerous articles on blindness, deafness, social issues, and women's rights.

30 Despite the broad range of her interests, Helen Keller never lost sight of the needs of others who were blind and deaf-blind. She was a personal friend of Dr. Peter J. Salmon, Executive Director of Helen Keller Services for the Blind (then known as the Industrial Home for the Blind). She was a visitor to a number of facilities and programs operated by IHB. She also lent her support to the establishment of what has become known as the Helen Keller National Center for the Deaf-Blind Youths and Adults.

In 1936, Helen Keller moved to
40 Westport, Connecticut, where she lived until her death on June 1, 1968, at the age of 87. In his eulogy at her funeral, Senator Lister Hill said of her, "She will live on, one of the few, immortal names not born to die. Her spirit will endure as long as man can read and stories can be
50 told of the woman who showed the world there are no boundaries to courage and faith." ▶

SYNTHESIZE

Underline the details on this page that refer to Anne Sullivan. 👤

Then recall what you learned about Sullivan in Keller's **autobiography.** Synthesize these two sources to complete the items below.

Keller's age when Sullivan entered her life: _____

How Sullivan changed Keller's life: _____

_____

How Sullivan helped Keller in college: _____

_____

💡 TestSmart

What does the biography of Helen Keller reveal that her autobiography does not?

Ⓐ what others said about Helen Keller

Ⓑ Helen Keller's desire for knowledge

Ⓒ information about Anne Sullivan

Ⓓ the challenges Helen Keller faced

TIP A test may ask you to compare **biographies** with **autobiographies.** To answer this kind of question, **review the characteristics of each** (see page 150). Think about what each type of source can do that the other cannot do.

How Do People Who Are Deaf-Blind Communicate?

People who are deaf-blind have a significant impairment of both their hearing and vision. Some are totally blind and deaf, but others have some remaining use of one or both senses. . . . Some people are born with impaired vision and hearing, while others acquire their dual sensory impairment later in life.

About 95% of what we learn about ourselves and the world comes through our sight and hearing. People who are deaf-blind face enormous challenges, especially in learning to communicate, accessing information, and finding out about the world around them.

What are the challenges?

People who are deaf-blind may use, or be encouraged to use, different communication methods throughout their lives. It is likely that some people will always use more than one method of communication.

The communication challenges facing people who are born with impaired vision and hearing will be very different from people who have had some experience

Sign Language

Aa Bb Cc Dd Ee Ff Gg

Hh Ii Jj Kk Ll Mm

Nn Oo Pp Qq Rr Ss

Tt Uu Vv Ww Xx Yy Zz

Sign language can be used to spell out words for people who are deaf.

EVALUATE

How do you think communication challenges are different for the two groups of people listed below?

deaf-blind people who could once see and hear:

_____

_____

_____

_____

deaf-blind people who were born without sight and hearing:

_____

_____

_____

_____

20 of vision and hearing in their early years. It is important to stress that deaf-blind people have a great range of communication needs, which may change over time. Also some deaf-blind people may use two or more methods of communication to express themselves, but receive information by other methods. ▶

For example:
- a child who has some sight, is profoundly deaf, and has physical disabilities may learn to understand sign language, but may need to find another means of expressing him or herself
30
- an older person may have always used speech and hearing to communicate, but may need to learn to use hearing aids and low vision aids as his or her vision and hearing change over time

Total communication

It is important to be flexible when helping a person who is deaf-blind to communicate, and it may be helpful to use a range of communication methods together. This is often called the total communication approach.

40   Methods that can be used within the total communication approach might include:

- the use of speech
- writing words down
- finger spelling
- different types of sign language
- body language
- facial expression and gesture
50
- pictures
- significant objects of reference
- models
- symbols
- line drawings
- tape
- Braille ◀

CLASSIFY

Decide which sense each communication method listed in lines 42–57 appeals to. Then write *H* (hearing), *S* (sight), or *T* (touch) next to each method. Some methods may appeal to more than one sense.

MAKE JUDGMENTS

Based on your responses to the question above, which methods would be appropriate to use with a person who cannot hear or see?

_____

_____

_____

_____

Using body language

Some people, especially those born deaf-blind, may have
60 no apparent means of communication. In these cases it is
important to observe the person over a period of time to
look for subtle movements of their face or body.

   Over time, it is possible to set up a communication
method which will allow the person to understand
that their subtle body language movements are being
understood. It is vital to be sensitive to the range of ways
which may be used by someone who is deaf-blind to
communicate, such as body language and gestures. . . . ▶

Use of technology

70 Increasingly, deaf-blind people are making use of new
technology to communicate. The types of technology
that will be suitable will depend on the type and degree of
visual and/or hearing impairment. Deaf-blind people may
use computers, for example, to communicate in a large
variety of ways. Examples include:

- text can be printed in large sizes for people with
  partial sight
- text can be printed in braille for braille readers
- text can be read out by a voice synthesizer for people
80 with partial hearing
- people with multiple disabilities may be able to use
  computers for learning opportunities

Other examples of technological advances include:

- an amplifier on a telephone
- textphones—which are like telephones with a text
  display ▶

This is only a very brief summary of some of the uses
of technology. There are many more technological
adaptations, and more are being developed all the time.

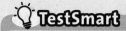

TestSmart

In order to be effective, a
communication system
must be

(A) set up by an expert

(B) legal

(C) understood by both
     parties

(D) changed frequently

TIP Some test questions
ask you a question that is
not directly answered in the
text. To answer questions
such as this, you need to
infer, or combine text clues
with what you know. Reread
lines 60–68. Then consider
what you know about
how people communicate.
What must be true of a
communication system in
order for it to work?

SYNTHESIZE

Which method of
communicating is mentioned
in all three selections in this
lesson? Circle it.

amplifier   *braille*

finger spelling

Reading Comprehension

DIRECTIONS *Answer these questions about the three selections in this lesson by filling in the correct ovals.*

1. When the biographer says that Helen Keller was "suddenly shut off from the world" (lines 4–5), it means that she

   Ⓐ was isolated at home

   Ⓑ became blind and deaf

   Ⓒ got very sick

   Ⓓ died at age 87

2. After Anne Sullivan died, Helen Keller

   Ⓐ attended Radcliffe College

   Ⓑ founded the IHB

   Ⓒ began her writing career

   Ⓓ moved to Connecticut

3. The author of "How Do People Who Are Deaf-Blind Communicate?" explains that deaf-blind people

   Ⓐ all have the same needs

   Ⓑ vary in the degree of their challenges

   Ⓒ usually rely on one method of communication

   Ⓓ cannot learn about the world around them

4. The first three devices listed under the heading "Use of technology" are appropriate for people who have

   Ⓐ some hearing or some sight

   Ⓑ no hearing but some sight

   Ⓒ no sight but some hearing

   Ⓓ no hearing and no sight

5. Synthesizing all three selections could help you write a report about

   Ⓐ how deaf-blind people use technology

   Ⓑ how braille works

   Ⓒ how Keller learned to communicate

   Ⓓ whom Keller met during her life

6. Through synthesizing details from *The Story of My Life* and "Biography of Helen Keller," you can infer that the *most* important person in Helen's life was

   Ⓐ Anne Sullivan

   Ⓑ Helen's mother

   Ⓒ Dr. Peter J. Salmon

   Ⓓ Laura Bridgman

7. Based on its use in line 43 of "Biography of Helen Keller," a *eulogy* is

   Ⓐ an immortal name not born to die

   Ⓑ a funeral for someone famous

   Ⓒ a book about someone who has died

   Ⓓ a speech about someone who has died

8. In the first sentence of "How Do People Who Are Deaf-Blind Communicate," an *impairment* is

   Ⓐ something damaged or weak

   Ⓑ a repair job

   Ⓒ something that works well

   Ⓓ an improvement in something

Timed Writing Practice

PROMPT

Write an (autobiographical narrative) about the positive effect a person has had on your life. Tell who the person is, how you met him or her, and what the positive effect has been.

BUDGET YOUR TIME

You have 30 minutes to complete this assignment. Decide how much time to spend on each step.

Analyze _____

Plan _____

Write _____

Review _____

30

Test-Taker's Toolkit

1. ANALYZE THE PROMPT

A. **Read the prompt** carefully.

B. **Circle key words** in each sentence. One has been done for you.

C. **Restate the prompt** to make sure you understand it.

2. PLAN YOUR RESPONSE

A. An **autobiographical narrative** is a story about an event or experience in your life. It should be organized by sequence of events and told from the first-person point of view. A flow chart can help you plan your response.

Introduction: Who the person is; how I met the person

↓

My first impressions

↓

How our relationship developed

↓

How the person has affected me

↓

Conclusion: What the person means to me now

3. WRITE AND REVIEW

A. **Focus on transitions** As you write the body, or main part, of your narrative, try to make the transitions from one place or time to another clear for your readers. Using specific words for time and place will help. Here is an example:

vague: After some time, Maria coached me on the field.

clear: Within two months, Maria started to meet me after school at Edgewood Ballpark to coach me.

B. **Write out your full response** Leave enough time to read through it and make sure you have used spelling and punctuation correctly.

UNIT 8

INFORMATION, ARGUMENT, AND PERSUASION

LESSON 8A

SuperCroc
BY PETER WINKLER

RELATED NONFICTION

An Interview with Dino Hunter Paul Sereno

"Godzilla" Fossil Reveals Real-Life Sea Monster

Are *MONSTERS* real?

Monsters have always existed in the world of the imagination. Yet fierce, deadly creatures that could be considered monsters exist in reality as well. In fact, scientists have discovered a prehistoric creature so terrifying that even dinosaurs may have feared it.

CHART IT Complete the chart shown to share your favorite monsters. In the first column, list imaginary monsters from stories or movies. In the second column, list some frightening and dangerous creatures from the real world that you have learned about. Two have been listed for you. Share your completed chart with a group of classmates. Which list is more frightening?

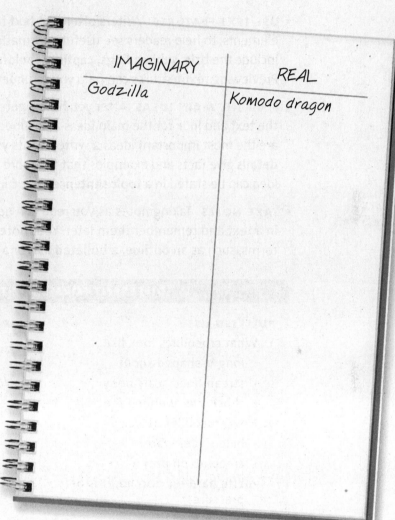

IMAGINARY

Godzilla

REAL

Komodo dragon

ASSESSMENT GOALS

By the end of this lesson, you will be able to...

• use text features to identify main ideas and details in nonfiction

• apply critical thinking skills to analyze text

• evaluate the accuracy of information in sources

• analyze a writing prompt and plan an explanatory essay

Reading for Information

Truth is sometimes stranger than fiction. Nonfiction text can be fascinating to read. But have you ever felt overwhelmed by a magazine article or Web site that was packed with information? The tips below can help you get the most out of nonfiction text.

- **USE TEXT FEATURES** Writers often use **text features,** or special design elements, to help readers see useful information at a glance. Text features include the **title, subheadings, captions, boldfaced terms,** and **sidebars.** Previewing text features can help you to understand the "big picture."

- **FIND THE MAIN IDEAS** After you have figured out the "big picture," read the text and look for the main ideas and supporting details. The **main ideas** are the most important ideas a writer wants you to understand. **Supporting details** give facts and examples that tell more about the main ideas. A main idea can be stated in a **topic sentence,** or it can be **implied.**

- **TAKE NOTES** Taking notes as you read can help you track the main ideas in a text and remember them later. Your notes can take any number of forms, such as an **outline,** a **bulleted list,** or a **graphic organizer.**

DIFFERENT FORMS FOR TAKING NOTES

BULLETED LIST

1. What crocodiles look like
   - long V-shaped snout
   - streamlined scaly body
   - short legs, webbed feet
2. How crocodiles attack
   - hide under water
   - creep up on prey
   - bite hard—3,000 pounds of pressure

GRAPHIC ORGANIZER

Nile crocodile · West African dwarf crocodile · TYPES OF CROCODILES · saltwater crocodile

---

ADDITIONAL TERMS FOR CRITICAL ANALYSIS

In "SuperCroc," the author includes quotes and opinions from an expert.

An **EXPERT-SUPPORTED INFERENCE** is an educated guess; it is not a **FACT.** However, an expert uses available factual evidence plus knowledge and experience to make the inference.

SUPERCROC

PETER WINKLER

MARK & ANALYZE

Read this selection once on your own, marking the text in any way that is helpful to you.

Then read the selection a second time, using the questions in the margins to help you analyze the text. When you see this pencil (✐), you'll be asked to mark up the text.

Out of Africa comes a giant reptile that lived with dinosaurs—and ate them.

"We're stuck again!" Scientist Paul Sereno and his team said those words many times as they drove into a rugged part of Africa. Desert sand kept stopping their vehicles. It took 10 hours to go just 87 miles.

That long crawl ended at Gadoufaoua,[1] a dry region in the country of Niger.[2] To most
10 eyes, the place looked empty. There was sand. There was wind. There was nothing else. Or so it seemed.

But Sereno saw much more. He saw a chance to find dinosaurs. Sereno, a

The country of Niger is in West Africa.

🔆 TestSmart

The map helps to define Niger as a

Ⓐ rugged, sandy place

Ⓑ windy, dry region

Ⓒ country in West Africa

Ⓓ capital city

TIP A test may ask you to interpret information in a **graphic aid,** such as a map. To answer, read all the text in the graphic aid. Make sure you understand what all of the symbols mean.

1. **Gadoufaoua** (gə-dōō′fä′wŏh).
2. **Niger** (nī′jər).

fossil (fŏs'əl) *n.* the remains of a living thing, preserved in soil or rock

paleontologist, knew that the region contains countless <u>fossils</u> from ancient dinosaurs. Gadoufaoua is one of Africa's richest sources of dino fossils.

20   Sereno found some fossils there in 1997. He came back in 2000 to seek more. The team spent four months in the desert. Crew members woke at 6:00 each morning, then explored the sand dunes for about 12 hours. They worked even when the temperature hit 125°F.

    And they found fossils. By the end of the expedition, Sereno and his team had collected 20 tons of bones. Most of the fossils came from dinosaurs, including types never seen before. Others came from turtles, fish, and crocodiles. ◄

    One of those crocodiles was *Sarcosuchus imperator*,[3] a
30 name that means "flesh crocodile emperor." Sereno's team nicknamed it "SuperCroc."

INFER

Based on what you find out about Gadoufaoua later in this article, explain why Sereno found fish fossils in the desert.

_____

_____

_____

What Makes This Croc So Super?

In a word, size. The skull alone was six feet long. Sereno says it's "about the biggest I've ever seen."

    Naturally, Sereno wondered how big SuperCroc was overall. The team found only part of its skeleton, so Sereno had to make an estimate. To do that, he looked at crocodiles that live today. He and other <u>experts</u> compared the animals' skull and body sizes.

40   Based on his research, Sereno concluded that an adult SuperCroc could grow to be 40 feet long and probably weighed as much as 10 tons. That's heavier than an African elephant.

    Those measurements make SuperCroc one of the largest crocodiles ever to walk Earth. Today's biggest crocs grow to about 20 feet. ◄

expert (ĕk'spûrt') *n.* one who is skilled in or knowledgeable about a particular thing

EVALUATE

Underline the sentences that explain how Paul Sereno used evidence from modern times to help him estimate SuperCroc's length.

Is SuperCroc's length a **fact**, or is it an **expert-supported inference**?

_____

3. **Sarcosuchus imperator** (sär'kō-soo'kĭs ĭm-pîr'ā-tôr).

A Different-Looking Beast

SuperCroc's long head is wider in front than in the middle.
That shape is unique. No other croc—living or __extinct__—has
50 a snout quite like it.

At the front of SuperCroc's head is a big hole. That's
where the nose would be. That empty space may have given
the ancient __predator__ a keen sense of smell. Or perhaps it
helped SuperCroc make noise to communicate with other
members of its __species__.

SuperCroc wore serious armor. Huge plates of bone,
called scutes, covered the animal's back. Hundreds of them
lay just below the skin. A single scute from the back could
be a foot long! ▶

When Did SuperCroc Live?

60 Estimating a fossil's age is a challenge. Sereno and his team
looked carefully at the group of fossils they had found. They
compared the fossils to others whose ages the scientists
did know. Based on those comparisons, Sereno believes
SuperCroc lived
about 110 million
years ago.

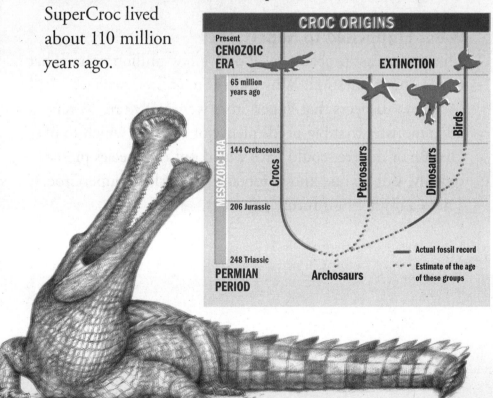

CROC ORIGINS

Present
CENOZOIC ERA

EXTINCTION

65 million years ago

MESOZOIC ERA

144 Cretaceous

Crocs

Pterosaurs

Dinosaurs

Birds

206 Jurassic

248 Triassic

PERMIAN PERIOD

Archosaurs

— Actual fossil record
···· Estimate of the age of these groups

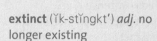

extinct (ĭk-stĭngkt′) *adj.* no longer existing

predator (prĕd′ə-tər) *n.* an animal that feeds on other animals

species (spē′shēz) *n.* a variety or type of something

CLASSIFY

Take notes about SuperCroc's physical features using the **graphic organizer** below.

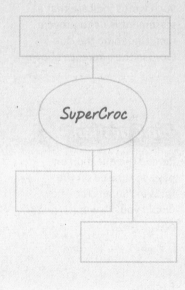

SuperCroc

INTERPRET

Which parts of the graph present **expert-supported inferences?** Circle them.

How do you know?

_____

_____

Which sentence is an expert-supported inference, *not* a fact?

A SuperCroc's jaws held about 130 teeth.

B SuperCroc likely spent most of its life in rivers.

C SuperCroc's teeth were short but strong.

D No other croc has had a snout like SuperCroc's.

TIP A test question may ask you to decide if a statement is a **fact** or an **inference**. To answer this kind of question, look for clue words such as *probably*, *might*, *likely*, or *unlikely*. Such words indicate that a statement is not a proven fact. Underline the clue word in the inference above.

Gadoufaoua looked a bit different in those days. What is now a desert was a land of winding rivers. Plenty of trees grew
70 along the banks. Huge fish swam the rivers, while various dinosaurs lived in the forests.

Five or more crocodile species lurked in the rivers. SuperCroc, Sereno says, was "the monster of them all."

What Did SuperCroc Eat?

"Anything it wanted," Sereno says. SuperCroc's narrow jaws held about 130 teeth. The teeth were short but incredibly strong. SuperCroc's mouth was "designed for grabbing prey[4]— fish, turtles, and dinosaurs that strayed too close."

SuperCroc likely spent most of its life in the river. Water
80 hid the creature's huge body. Only its eyes and nostrils poked above the surface.

After spotting a meal, the giant hunter moved quietly toward the animal. Then—*wham!* That huge mouth locked onto its prey. SuperCroc dragged the stunned creature into the water. There the animal drowned. Then it became food. ◄

What Happened to SuperCroc?

The giant beast probably lived only a few million years. That raises a huge question: Why didn't SuperCroc survive?

Sereno suspects that SuperCrocs were fairly rare. After
90 all, a monster that big needs plenty of room in which to live. Disease or disaster could have wiped out the species pretty quickly. But no one knows for sure what killed SuperCroc. That's a mystery for future scientists. ◄

---

4. **prey:** animals that become the food of another animal.

Reading Comprehension

DIRECTIONS *Answer these questions about "SuperCroc" by filling in the correct ovals.*

1. The details in lines 20–24 of "SuperCroc" support which implied main idea?

   (A) Sereno returned to Africa in 2000.

   (B) Crew members worked for 12 hours a day.

   (C) Hunting for fossils can be hard work.

   (D) Some fossils were found in 1997.

2. The implied main idea under the subheading "A Different-Looking Beast" is that

   (A) SuperCroc's head had a big hole in it

   (B) SuperCroc had a keen sense of smell

   (C) SuperCroc had an unusual appearance

   (D) bony plates covered SuperCroc's back

3. When SuperCroc lived, Gadoufaoua was

   (A) green and lush

   (B) full of fossils

   (C) empty of animals

   (D) dry and dusty

4. Which detail under the subheading "What Did SuperCroc Eat?" supports the idea that SuperCroc's mouth was designed for grabbing prey?

   (A) The jaw was narrow.

   (B) Water hid SuperCroc's body.

   (C) Eyes poked above the surface.

   (D) The teeth were short but strong.

5. Which sentence is an expert-supported inference, not a fact?

   (A) SuperCroc had a big hole in its head.

   (B) SuperCroc may have had a keen sense of smell.

   (C) A single scute was one foot long.

   (D) SuperCroc's head was wider in front than in the middle.

6. Which sentence is a fact, not an expert-supported inference?

   (A) SuperCrocs probably lived only a few million years.

   (B) Disease could have wiped out the species quickly.

   (C) No one knows what killed SuperCroc.

   (D) SuperCrocs may have been fairly rare.

7. The graph on page 171 tells you that the words *Permian*, *Mesozoic*, and *Cenozoic* all name

   (A) time periods   (C) pterosaurs

   (B) dinosaurs   (D) fossil groups

8. The graph on page 171 tells you that *pterosaurs* are

   (A) the birds of today

   (B) flying dinosaurs

   (C) ancestors of archosaurs

   (D) extinct creatures

GO ON ➡

Responding in Writing

9. Short Response Write a summary of "SuperCroc." Retell each main idea in your own words. Include one or two interesting details to support each main idea.

_____

_____

_____

_____

_____

_____

Test-Taker's Toolkit

GRAPHIC ORGANIZER Use the chart below to help you plan your response. In your own words, write the main idea of each section in the second column. In the third column, write one or two details that support that main idea.

SECTION	MAIN IDEA	DETAILS
Introduction		
What Makes This Croc So Super?		
A Different-Looking Beast		
When Did SuperCroc Live?		
What Did SuperCroc Eat?		
What Happened to SuperCroc?		

For help, use the **Test-Taker's Toolkit** below.

What's the Connection?

"SuperCroc" is about dinosaur hunter Paul Sereno's discovery of a huge, ancient crocodile fossil. In "An Interview with Paul Sereno," Michelle Laliberte asks the paleontologist questions about his work as a fossil hunter. The online article "'Godzilla' Fossil Reveals Real-Life Sea Monster" describes a fearsome ancient crocodile whose fossil has been found in Argentina.

ASK A FOSSIL HUNTER In the chart, you will find some questions that you might want to ask a fossil hunter. Guess the answer for each question now, then fill in the real fossil hunter's answers as you read.

QUESTION	MY GUESS	SERENO'S ANSWER
Did all the dinosaurs become extinct because of an asteroid?		
Where in the world do you go to find fossils?		
Can you find fossils without digging underground?		

Related Nonfiction

- *An Interview with Dino Hunter Paul Sereno*
  INTERVIEW

- *"Godzilla" Fossil Reveals Real-Life Sea Monster*
  ONLINE ARTICLE

Use with "SuperCroc," p. 166

LEARN THE SKILL: EVALUATE SOURCES

Imagine that you are doing a report about fossils. The Internet and print media may contain hundreds of thousands of articles, books, and other documents about this topic. Which **sources** of information will be useful to you? When you do choose an article to use, how do you know that the **facts** in it are correct? As you read a nonfiction source, ask these questions to evaluate its usefulness:

- Is the information **current?** Information that is out of date is not very useful.

- Is the information **accurate?** If the information was written or prepared by an **expert,** it should be accurate.

For more on evaluating sources, see *Nonfiction Handbook,* page R11.

An Interview with

DINO HUNTER
Paul Sereno

by Michelle Laliberte

💡 **TestSmart**

What helps you trust the accuracy of the information in this interview?

- (A) Michelle Laliberte is the interviewer.
- (B) The interview is about a science topic.
- (C) The person being interviewed is a dinosaur expert.
- (D) The information in an interview is always accurate.

TIP A test question may ask you to **evaluate the accuracy** of a text. To answer a question like this, ask yourself: Was an **expert** involved in preparing the text? What are the expert's qualifications? How much experience does the expert have? Have you heard of the expert before? Underline the sentences that describe Paul Sereno's qualifications as a dinosaur expert. 👆

Paul Sereno could be called the "Indiana Jones" of paleontology. The University of Chicago paleontologist and professor admits to enjoying high adventure, but he says his ultimate thrill comes from unearthing the bones of dinosaurs that walked the Earth and stalked their prey millions of years ago. Sereno's expeditions have . . . made a significant contribution to the understanding of the dinosaur family tree. ◀

Q: What do you think is the biggest misconception that people have about dinosaurs?

10 **A:** Well, most people think that all the dinosaurs lasted for the entire Mesozoic Era and got snuffed out by an asteroid. That couldn't be further from the truth. Your average species lasted only a few million years, and new species arose all the time. It was a conveyer belt of species! . . .

Q: What has been the most thrilling discovery of your career?

A: When we found skeletons of *Herrerasaurus*—a little-known flesh-eating theropod—against the odds, in Patagonia, Argentina. It was my first team—six young people joined me, and we found the earliest dinosaur on record, dating back to the middle Triassic Period, some 228 million years ago. Everyone said we couldn't do it. So, after three weeks of searching, walking up to the skeleton—the way it was exposed with part of the skull and neck just visible on the surface of a rocky ledge—was the thrill of a lifetime! ▶

Q: What is the most dangerous expedition that you've been on?

A: The 1993 expedition to Niger [Africa] when we crossed the Sahara Desert twice, excavated six tons of dinosaur bone, and got it all back—as well as us—at the same time. That was a very exciting expedition!

Q: How do you actually search for dinosaur fossils?

A: With legs, brains, and action. You need energy—lots of it; you need good legs. I like to go to places with good exposure—where there are dinosaur beds and outcroppings on the surface. You don't dig blindly. When you get into the area, you make appropriate strategic decisions based on fragments of fossils that you find. So first you have to find a bone, and that's where the team comes into play. Why does our team find fossils every time? Well, we take a very young crew that can walk incredible distances! ▶

Q: What advice can you give to readers who are fascinated by dinosaurs and would love to have a career in paleontology?

A: Well, I think you can be whatever you want to be as long as you give yourself a chance. Find the talents that are locked inside you just under your skin. You can begin to do that by volunteering in labs and museums or by joining a group that is going into the field. In school, take lots of science—from math to biology—and also take art. ▶

MAKE JUDGMENTS

Name two personal qualities the interview reveals about Paul Sereno.

1. _____

2. _____

Underline examples in the text that support your answers.

SYNTHESIZE

What do you think would be the best and worst things about hunting for dinosaur fossils? To answer, synthesize information from this interview and from "SuperCroc."

best: _____

_____

worst: _____

_____

DRAW CONCLUSIONS

Why do you think taking art classes is important for a paleontologist?

_____

_____

_____

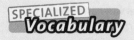

http://news.nationalgeographic.com/kids/

KIDS HOME | KIDS NEWS | KIDS TV | KIDS GAMES | KIDS SHOP

1 | 2 ▶

"Godzilla" Fossil Reveals Real-Life Sea Monster

by Stefan Lovgren

Scientists have discovered the fossil skull of a 135-million-year-old "sea monster." They nicknamed it Godzilla.

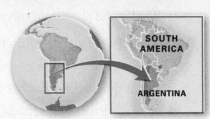

SOUTH AMERICA

ARGENTINA

The large skull was found in southern Argentina in an area that was once part of the Pacific Ocean.

The creature, named *Dakosaurus andiniensi*, is an entirely new kind of ancient crocodile. Scientists believe that the giant animal belongs to ◀

The fossil skull of "Godzilla" was found in Argentina. Photo and drawing courtesy of Diego Pol, Ohio State University.

the crocodyliforms (crock-oh-DILL-uh-forms), a group of animals that

10 includes today's crocodiles and their extinct relatives.

Unlike today's crocodiles, "Godzilla" lived entirely in the water. It measured 13 feet from nose to tail. Instead of legs, it had four paddle-like limbs. These were used mostly to keep it stable. A fish-like tail propelled the beast through the water.

What made Godzilla especially unusual was its snout and teeth. Until now, every known marine crocodilian (crock-oh-DILL-yin) had a head of one basic type, with a long snout

20 and many sharp, identical teeth. But Godzilla had a short, high snout and teeth that were large and jagged, like a land reptile's.

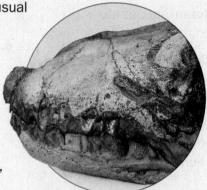

View of left side of *Dakosaurus andiniensi* skull. Photo courtesy of Diego Pol, Ohio State University.

The animal's unusual features suggest that it had completely different feeding habits from its relatives. While other marine crocs fed on small fish, Godzilla hunted for marine reptiles and other large sea creatures. It used its jagged teeth to bite and cut its prey.

30 "Presumably it moved its head mainly up and down rather than sweeping it from side to side, like fish-eating crocodilians," said James Clark, a dinosaur expert at George Washington University in Washington, D.C. ▶

"It is more like a meat-eating dinosaur than like a marine crocodilian," Clark said.

EVALUATE SOURCES

Reread lines 30–35. Which word signals that this idea is an **expert-supported inference,** not a **fact?**

Reading Comprehension

DIRECTIONS *Answer these questions about the three selections in this lesson by filling in the correct ovals.*

1. According Paul Sereno, which belief is *not* correct?

   (A) Dinosaurs lived during the Mesozoic Era.

   (B) The average dinosaur lived for a few million years.

   (C) New dinosaur species arose all the time.

   (D) All the dinosaurs lived and died out at the same time.

2. The fossil hunt that is described in both "SuperCroc" and the interview with Paul Sereno is the hunt that took place in

   (A) China

   (B) Niger

   (C) Patagonia

   (D) Mongolia

3. The ancient crocodilians in both "SuperCroc" and "Godzilla" had

   (A) unusual tail structures

   (B) ancestors in Argentina

   (C) paddle-like limbs

   (D) unique snouts and feeding habits

4. Both SuperCroc and Godzilla

   (A) had a big hole in the snout

   (B) ate large animals

   (C) were found in Niger

   (D) had 130 teeth

5. All three selections you have read describe scientists who study

   (A) oceans

   (B) fossils

   (C) SuperCrocs

   (D) Niger

6. What helps you trust the accuracy of the information in "'Godzilla' Fossil Reveals Real-Life Sea Monster"?

   (A) It was written by Stefan Lovgren.

   (B) It describes a scientific discovery.

   (C) It includes illustrations and a map.

   (D) Dinosaur expert James Clark is quoted in it.

7. Which scientific word contains a word part often seen in dinosaur names?

   (A) *imperator*

   (B) *andiniensi*

   (C) *Herrerasaurus*

   (D) *crocodyliform*

8. Which word part is found in the words *crocodile*, *crocodyliform*, and *crocodilian*?

   (A) lian

   (B) cr

   (C) croco

   (D) dile

Timed Writing Practice

BUDGET YOUR TIME

You have 45 minutes to complete this assignment. Decide how much time to spend on each step.

Analyze _____

Plan _____

Write _____

Review _____

45

PROMPT

Write an (explanatory essay) about unusual "monsters" from the animal world. Include at least one example from the ancient world and one from modern times.

Test-Taker's Toolkit

1. ANALYZE THE PROMPT

A. **Read the prompt** carefully.

B. **Circle key words** in each sentence. One has been done for you. These words tell you what you must include to get a good score.

C. **Restate the prompt** in your own words to make sure you understand it. You may use the lines on the right.

2. PLAN YOUR RESPONSE

A. **Identify your examples** Before you begin writing, you need to identify the examples you will discuss in your essay.

B. **Organize your information** You may want to organize your ideas this way: First introduce the two animals that you will discuss in your essay. Then describe the animal from history and the modern animal. Sum up your essay in a concluding paragraph.

Example of animal from the ancient world
- Its "monstrous" features
- Why it was unique

Example of animal from the modern world
- Its "monstrous" features
- Why it is unique

3. WRITE AND REVIEW

A. **Write the body of your essay** Each paragraph in the body of the essay should state the main idea in a **topic sentence.** The other sentences should give **supporting details.** Sometimes you can state the main idea first and follow with the supporting details. Other times you can state the main idea at the end of the paragraph.

B. **Add the introduction and the conclusion** to the body of your essay. Be sure to leave time to revise your full response and check your spelling and grammar.

UNIT 8

INFORMATION,
ARGUMENT, AND
PERSUASION

LESSON 8B

What Video Games Can Teach Us

The Violent Side of Video Games

BY EMILY SOHN

RELATED NONFICTION

P.E. Classes Turn to Video Game That Works Legs

Playing for a Living

Can a GAME play YOU?

Are video games helpful or harmful? Do they teach people any important skills, or are they a waste of time? The following activity will help you find out how your classmates would answer these questions.

SURVEY Ask three classmates to complete the survey shown. Then meet in a group and compare the surveys. Do your classmates feel generally positive or generally negative about video games?

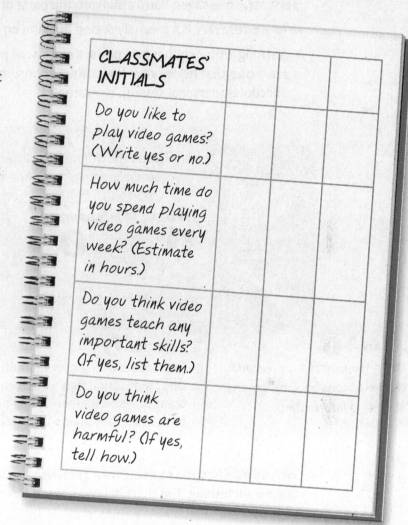

CLASSMATES' INITIALS			
Do you like to play video games? (Write yes or no.)			
How much time do you spend playing video games every week? (Estimate in hours.)			
Do you think video games teach any important skills? (If yes, list them.)			
Do you think video games are harmful? (If yes, tell how.)			

ASSESSMENT GOALS

By the end of this lesson, you will be able to...

- analyze argument and persuasion in nonfiction
- apply critical thinking skills to analyze text
- recognize bias in nonfiction texts
- analyze a writing prompt and plan a persuasive essay

Argument and Persuasion

Think of the decisions you make, big and small. Which persuasive messages might be influencing your decisions? In this unit you'll learn how to analyze text for persuasive messages. You'll also learn the parts of a strong argument.

- An **ARGUMENT** is a carefully stated position on an issue.

- A strong argument has two parts: a **CLAIM**, or position on an issue; and **SUPPORT** that helps prove the claim. Support may include statistics, anecdotes (personal stories), or examples.

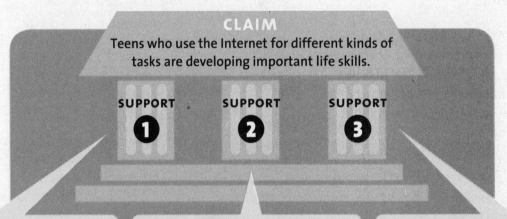

CLAIM
Teens who use the Internet for different kinds of tasks are developing important life skills.

SUPPORT 1

SUPPORT 2

SUPPORT 3

SUPPORT 1
Using the Internet for research can help teens become experts at finding information.

SUPPORT 2
Teens are learning how to multi-task. One study found that 30 percent of teens do more than one thing at a time when they are on the Internet.

SUPPORT 3
The immediate responses required by e-mails and instant messages can help teens learn to type faster and to process information quickly.

Writers may also use **PERSUASIVE TECHNIQUES** to convince their readers to do or believe something. The chart below shows different kinds of persuasive techniques.

APPEALS BY ASSOCIATION	EMOTIONAL APPEALS	LOADED LANGUAGE
"sell" something by linking it with a positive thing	use strong feelings rather than evidence to persuade	use words with positive or negative associations

ADDITIONAL TERMS FOR CRITICAL ANALYSIS

- A **COUNTERARGUMENT** is an argument made to oppose another argument. A strong argument anticipates opposing viewpoints and provides counterarguments to disprove them.

- An **OVERGENERALIZATION** is a statement that is too broad to be accurate. You can often recognize overgeneralizations by the appearance of words and phrases such as *all, everyone,* or *no one.*

What Video Games Can Teach Us

Emily Sohn

MARK & ANALYZE
Read these two selections once on your own, marking the text in any way that is helpful to you. Then read the selections a second time, using the questions in the margins to help you analyze the text. When you see this pencil, you'll be asked to mark up the text.

Here's some news for you to share with your parents and teachers: video games might actually be good for you. ▶

Whenever a wave of teenage violence strikes, movies, TV, or video games often take the heat. Some adults assume that movies, TV, and video games are a bad influence on kids, and they blame these media[1] for causing various problems. A variety of studies appear to support the link between media violence and bad behavior among kids.

10 But media don't necessarily *cause* violence, says James Gee. Gee is an education professor at the University of Wisconsin, Madison. "You get a group of teenage boys who shoot up a school—of course they've played video games," Gee says. "Everyone does. It's like blaming food because we have obese people." ▶

CONTRAST
Contrast the **claims** made in these two selections.

_____
_____
_____
_____

ANALYZE
What **argument** does the author anticipate in lines 4–9?

_____
_____
_____

Put a box around the **counterargument.**

---

1. **media:** a general term that includes television, films, magazines, newspapers, and video games.

Video games are innocent of most of the charges against them, Gee says. The games might actually do a lot of good. Gee has written a book titled *What Video Games Have to Teach Us About Learning and Literacy.*

20　A growing number of researchers agree with Gee. If used in the right way, video and computer games have the potential to inspire learning. And they can help players improve coordination[2] and visual skills. ◄

Attention-Getting Games

A good video game is challenging, entertaining, and **complicated**, Gee says. It usually takes 50 to 60 hours of intense concentration to finish one. Even kids who can't sit still in school can spend hours trying to solve a video or computer game. . . .

30　The **captivating** power of video games might lie in their interactive nature. Players don't just sit and watch. They get to participate in the action and solve problems. Some games even allow players to make changes in the game, allowing new possibilities.

And kids who play computer games often end up knowing more about computers than their parents do. "Kids today are natives in a culture in which their parents are immigrants," Gee says.

In his 2 to 3 years of studying the social influences of video

40　games, Gee has seen a number of young gamers become computer science majors in college. One kid even ended up as a teaching assistant during his freshman year because the school's computer courses were too easy for him. ◄

Screen Reading

Video games can enhance reading skills too. In the game *Animal Crossing,* for instance, players become characters who live in a town full of animals. Over the course of the

---

2. **coordination:** the ability to make multiple muscle groups work smoothly together.

ANALYZE

Underline two reasons the author gives in lines 20–23 to **support** her **claim**. Label them *Reason #1* and *Reason #2.*

complicate (kŏm′plĭ-kāt′) *v.* to make difficult or complex

captivate (kăp′tə-vāt′) *v.* to attract and hold interest

EVALUATE

Complete the graphic organizer below. Put a plus sign next to **support** that seems strong. Put a minus sign next to support that seems weak.

Claim (from lines 1–3)

Reason #1 (from lines 21–22)

Evidence to Support Reason (from lines 24–43)

game, you can buy a house, travel from town to town, go to museums, and do other ordinary things. All the while, you're writing notes to other players and talking to the animals. Because <u>kids are interested in the game</u>, they often end up reading at a level well above their grade, even if they say they don't like to read.

Games can inspire new interests. After playing a game called *Age of Mythology,* Gee says, kids (like his 8-year-old son) often start checking out mythology books from the library or join Internet chat groups about mythological characters. History can come alive to a player participating in the game. . . . ▶

Improved Skills

Video games might also help improve visual skills. That was what researchers from the University of Rochester in New York recently found.

In the study, frequent game players between the ages of 18 and 23 were better at monitoring what was happening around them than those who didn't play as often or didn't play at all. They could keep track of more objects at a time. And they were faster at picking out objects from a cluttered environment.

"Above and beyond the fact that action video games can be beneficial," says Rochester neuroscientist Daphne Bavelier, "our findings are surprising because they show that the learning induced by video game playing occurs quite fast and generalizes outside the gaming experience." ▶

The research might lead to better ways to train soldiers or treat people with attention problems, the researchers say, though they caution against taking that point too far.

Says Bavelier, "We certainly don't mean to convey the message that kids can play video games instead of doing their homework!"

ANALYZE

The underlined phrase is an example of an **overgeneralization.** Underline another overgeneralization in lines 54–59.

What makes these statements overgeneralizations?

_____

_____

_____

_____

EVALUATE

Complete the graphic organizer below. Put a plus sign next to **support** that seems strong. Put a minus sign next to support that seems weak.

Claim (from line 61)

Reason (from lines 61–63)

Evidence to Support Reason (from lines 64–74)

simulate (sĭm′yə-lāt′) v. to
imitate

EVALUATE

Which of the points the
author makes seems *most*
persuasive? Which point
seems *least* persuasive?

most persuasive:

_____

_____

least persuasive:

_____

_____

EXAMINE PERSPECTIVES

What opposite perspectives
does the author present in the
last sentence?

1. _____

_____

2. _____

_____

Do you think it is possible for
video games to either save or
destroy society? Explain.

_____

_____

_____

_____

_____

If Gee gets his way, though, teachers might some day
start incorporating computer games into their assignments.
Already, scientists and the military use computer games to
help <u>simulate</u> certain situations for research or training, he
says. Why shouldn't schools do the same thing? . . .

Researchers at the Massachusetts Institute of Technology
have started a project they describe as the "Education
Arcade." The project brings together researchers, scholars,[3]
game designers and others interested in developing and using
90 computer games in the classroom. . . .

Looking at the bright side of video and computer games
could also help bring kids and adults closer together.
Playing games can be a social activity, during which kids
and adults learn from one another. By opening up lines of
communication and understanding, maybe one day we'll
praise video games for saving society, not blame them for
destroying it. ◄

---

3. **scholars:** people who study a particular subject.

The Violent Side of Video Games

Emily Sohn

WHEN I WAS A KID, I WAS OBSESSED WITH VIDEO GAMES. ▶

I saved my allowance to buy new games every month. I read Nintendo magazines for tips about solving the Super Mario Brothers adventures. I played so many hours of *Tetris* that I used to dream about little blocks falling perfectly into place.

There were physical effects too. My thumbs turned into machines, quick and **precise**. During especially difficult
10 levels of play, my palms would sweat. My heart would race. I'd have knots in my stomach from anxiety. It was the same feeling I'd sometimes get from watching scary movies or suspenseful TV shows.

After a while, I started to think that looking at screens and playing games all the time might be affecting me in ways I didn't even suspect. It turns out that I was probably right. ▶

Scientists are discovering that playing video and computer games and watching TV and movies can change the way we

act, think, and feel. Whether these changes are good or bad
20 has become a subject of intense debate.

Concerns About Violence

Violence is one of the biggest concerns, especially as computer
graphics and special effects become more realistic. Some
parents and teachers blame . . . aggressive behavior on media
violence—as seen in TV programs, movies, and video games.

"If you've ever watched young children watching
kickboxing," says child psychologist[1] John Murray, "within
a few minutes they start popping up and pushing and
shoving and imitating the actions." Murray is at Kansas State
30 University in Manhattan, Kansas.

There's also evidence that people become less sensitive to
violence after a while, Murray says. In other words, you get
so used to seeing it that you eventually think it's not such a
big deal.

Then there's the "mean world syndrome."[2] If you watch lots
of violence, you may start to think the world is a bad place. I
still sometimes have trouble falling asleep if I watch the news
on TV or read the newspaper right before going to bed.

Still, it's hard to prove that violence on TV leads to
40 violence in real life. It might be possible, for example, that
people who are already aggressive for other reasons are more
drawn to violent games and TV shows. . . . ◄

Video Power

Most of the research has focused on TV and movie violence,
mainly because TV and movies have been around much
longer than video games, says psychologist Craig Anderson
of Iowa State University in Ames, Iowa. Anderson has a Web

---

1. **child psychologist** (sī-kŏl′ə-jĭst): a person trained to study thought and behavior patterns in children.

2. **syndrome** (sĭn′drōm′): a group or pattern of symptoms that make up a disease or condition.

site dedicated to looking at the link between video games and violence.

50 In his own research and in analyses[3] of research by others, Anderson says that he has detected a connection between violent video games and violent behavior. He has found that people who repeatedly play violent games have aggressive thoughts and become less helpful and sociable. Physically, their heart rates accelerate. ▶

Video games might have an even more powerful effect on the brain than TV does, Murray says. Players actively participate in the violence. . . .

Next time you play a violent video game, Murray suggests, 60 check your pulse just before and after each round as one way to see how the game affects you.

"Ninety-nine percent of the time, I'll bet your heart rate will have increased rather dramatically while playing one," Murray says. "This indicates that . . . you are being affected." ▶

Three teenagers from Puerto Rico have data to back up that observation. With the help of a school nurse, the high school seniors found that people of all ages showed a rise in blood pressure and heart rate after playing a superviolent game. Playing an active, nonviolent game did not have the 70 same effect. ▶

3. **analyses** (ə-năl′ĭ-sēz′): examinations of different information or experimental results.

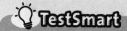

TestSmart

VOCABULARY

In line 54, the word *sociable* means

(A) against society

(B) outside of society

(C) able to leave society behind

(D) able to interact socially

TIP If a test question asks you about an unfamiliar word, **look for a familiar base word, prefix, or suffix.** The base word of *sociable* is *social*. The suffix *-able* means "the ability to." Which answer choice combines the meanings of these word parts?

EVALUATE

Reread the boxed text. Do you think the evidence in this section provides strong **support** for the **claim**? Why or why not?

_____

_____

_____

_____

Big Question

Review the results of the survey on page 183. Which of your classmates' responses are supported by one or both of these selections?

_____

_____

_____

Reading Comprehension

DIRECTIONS *Answer these questions about "What Video Games Can Teach Us" and "The Violent Side of Video Games" by filling in the correct ovals.*

1. Which statement is a claim?

    (A) *Super Mario Brothers* is a video game.

    (B) Video games are harmful to kids.

    (C) Many kids play video games.

    (D) *Tetris* is a puzzle game.

2. According to "What Video Games Can Teach Us," the military is using computer games for training because they can

    (A) improve visual skills

    (B) demonstrate aggressive moves

    (C) teach soldiers to multi-task

    (D) interest soldiers in other topics

3. Which statement is an overgeneralization?

    (A) There may be a connection between violent games and violent behavior.

    (B) Some people experience increased pulse rate when playing video games.

    (C) Video games might have an effect on the brain.

    (D) People who play violent video games are less helpful and less sociable.

4. According to "The Violent Side of Video Games," the "mean world syndrome" causes kids to

    (A) commit crimes

    (B) believe the world is evil

    (C) learn multi-tasking

    (D) behave meanly

5. Read the following sentence from "The Violent Side of Video Games":

    > It might be possible . . . that people who are already aggressive for other reasons are more drawn to violent video games.

    This sentence is an example of

    (A) overgeneralization

    (B) counterargument

    (C) evidence

    (D) support

6. The description of rising blood pressure (lines 56–70 of "The Violent Side . . .") supports the idea that video games can

    (A) make kids less social

    (B) make kids less able to focus

    (C) cause loss of sleep

    (D) affect a player's brain

7. In line 71 of "What Video Games Can Teach Us," the word *neuroscientist* means

    (A) a scientist who studies the nervous system

    (B) a scientific study of neuros

    (C) a scientist's nerves and brain

    (D) the science of the nervous system

8. In line 74 of "What Video Games Can Teach Us," the word *generalizes* means

    (A) becomes a general

    (B) becomes specialized

    (C) extends to general life

    (D) exists across generations

Responding in Writing

9. Short Response Do you think video games are harmful or helpful? Write a paragraph explaining which argument you agree with and why. Give one reason from the articles in this lesson and one reason from your own experience to support your argument.

_____

_____

_____

_____

_____

Test-Taker's Toolkit

GRAPHIC ORGANIZER Use the graphic organizer below to help you plan your response.

My Position	Supporting Reason from the Articles	Supporting Reason from My Experience

- **P.E. Classes Turn to Video Game That Works Legs**
  NEWSPAPER ARTICLE

- **Playing for a Living: Video Game Careers**
  ONLINE ARTICLE

Use with "What Video Games Can Teach Us" and "The Violent Side of Video Games," p. 182

What's the Connection?

"What Video Games Can Teach Us" and "The Violent Side of Video Games" present two different arguments about how video games affect players. The newspaper article "P.E. Classes Turn to Video Game That Works Legs" describes how some P.E. teachers use video games to inspire physical activity. The online article "Playing for a Living: Video Game Careers" describes several ways video game lovers can turn that interest into a career.

DISCUSS With a group of classmates, discuss the questions below. Record the group's responses on the lines.

1. How can a video game help kids stay fit?

_____

_____

_____

2. What kinds of jobs are available in the video game industry?

_____

_____

_____

LEARN THE SKILL: RECOGNIZE BIAS

In a piece of writing, the writer's **bias** is the side of an issue that he or she favors. **Loaded language** often reveals a writer's bias. For example

- Our state leaders have failed to deal with the number-one health problem of today, obesity. *(a biased statement)*
- Our state ranks among the nation's leaders in obesity. *(an unbiased statement)*

As you read the next articles, pay attention to how each writer seems to feel about the issue.

For more on recognizing bias, see *Nonfiction Handbook* page R3.

P.E. Classes Turn to Video Game That Works Legs

by Seth Schiesel
from *The New York Times*

SET A PURPOSE
My purpose for reading is

MORGANTOWN, W.VA.
Children don't often yell in excitement when they are let into class. But as the doors opened to the gym at South Middle School one recent Monday, the waiting students let out a chorus of shrieks.

In they rushed, past the table tennis, the balance beams, and the wrestling mats stacked unused. They sprinted past the ghosts of Gym Class Past toward two TV sets looming over square plastic mats on the floor. In less than a minute a dozen seventh graders were dancing in union to the thumps of a techno song. ▶

Bill Hines, a physical education teacher at the school for 27 years, shook his head a little, smiled and said, "I'll tell you one thing: they don't run in here like that for basketball."

It is a scene being repeated across the country as schools use the blood-pumping video game *Dance Dance Revolution* as the latest weapon in the nation's battle against childhood obesity. While traditional video games are often criticized for contributing to the expanding waistlines of the nation's children, hundreds of schools in at least 10 states are now using *Dance Dance Revolution,* or D.D.R., as a regular part of their physical education curriculum. ▶

Born nine years ago in the arcades of Japan, D.D.R. has become a small craze. It is popular among a generation of young Americans who appear less interested in traditional team sports than their parents were and more interested in modern technology.

Using D.D.R. in gym class is part of a general shift in physical education. School districts are de-emphasizing traditional sports in favor of less competitive activities.

MAKE INFERENCES

How do the students seem to feel about going to gym class?

Underline details in the text that suggest this.

RECOGNIZE BIAS

Reread the underlined text. Notice the use of the **loaded language** *weapon* and *battle*. What does it suggest about the author's attitude toward childhood obesity?

Lacy Campbell (center), age 11, waits to try *Dance Dance Revolution* at South Middle School in Morgantown, West Virginia.

CONNECT

Which kind of physical activity do you prefer—traditional sports and games or alternative activities such as dancing? Why?

_____

_____

_____

_____

SYNTHESIZE

How might the author of "What Video Games Can Teach Us" have used D.D.R. to support her argument that video games can be good for kids?

_____

_____

_____

_____

"Traditionally, physical education was about team sports and was very skills oriented," said Chad Fenwick, who oversees physical education for the Los Angeles Unified School District, where about 40 schools now use *Dance Dance Revolution*. "What you're seeing is a move toward activities where you don't need to be so great at catching and throwing and things like that, so we can appeal to a wider range of kids." ◀

A basic D.D.R. system, including a television and game console, can be had for less than $500. But most schools that use the game choose to spend from $70 to $800 each for stronger mats, rather than rip apart the relatively flimsy versions meant for home use.

In a study last year, researchers from the Mayo Clinic in Rochester, Minn., found that children playing *Dance Dance Revolution* expended significantly more energy than children watching television and playing traditional video games. West Virginia, which ranks among the nation's leaders in obesity, diabetes, and hypertension, has sponsored its own study. It has taken the lead in using the game, which requires players to dance in ever more difficult patterns in time with electronic dance music. ◀

As a song plays, arrows pointing one of four directions—forward, back, left, right—scroll up the screen in various sequences and combinations. The player steps on corresponding arrows on a mat on the floor. Players can dance by themselves, with a partner, or in competition.

As a result of a partnership among West Virginia's Department of Education, its Public Employees Insurance Agency, and West Virginia University, the state has committed to installing the game in all 765 of its public schools by next year. Almost all of its 185 middle schools already use it.

The mastermind behind the project is Linda M. Carson, distinguished professor at West Virginia University's School of Physical Education and director of the state's Motor Development Center. ▶

"I was in a mall walking by the arcade and I saw these kids playing D.D.R., and I was just stunned," she said. "There were all these kids dancing and sweating and actually standing in line and paying money to be physically active. And they were drinking water, not soda. It was a physical educator's dream."

In February, Ms. Carson and her main collaborator, Emily Murphy, a doctoral candidate at the university's School of Medicine, announced the results of a multiyear study. They found significant health benefits for overweight children who played the game regularly, including improved blood pressure and overall fitness scores.

None of that would come as a surprise to Maureen Byrne, mother of two boys in Chesterfield, Mo. She introduced the game to her local school district after seeing its impact on one of her sons.

"My oldest son, Sean, used to have love handles. He was kind of pudgy, and I'll be honest: we were worried about it," she said. "We had heard of D.D.R., and I got it for him for his birthday. We put limits on the other video games he plays, but we told him he could play D.D.R. as much as he wanted. And now it's like he's a different kid. He's playing sports and running, and we see D.D.R. as like his bridge to a more active lifestyle."

Ms. Byrne and her family demonstrated the game for the local parent-teacher organization in the hope of convincing it to underwrite a test at school.

💡 TestSmart

What bias in the author's thinking is revealed in the boxed text?

(A) West Virginia University is an excellent school.

(B) The Motor Development Center is useless.

(C) Linda Carson is a professor.

(D) Linda Carson is very intelligent.

TIP A test question may ask you about an author's **bias**. To answer, look for **loaded language**. For example, the word *mastermind* describes a very smart person who thinks up a complex plan, and *distinguished* means "highly respected." These words show that the author has a positive opinion of Linda Carson.

"I remember going to the P.T.O. meeting and getting in front of all of them without my shoes on and doing the moves, and that was kind of funny," said Sean, now a 12-year-old sixth grader.

Today, eight schools in the Parkway School District, based in Chesterfield, have their own D.D.R. systems. And three other game systems circulate among various schools in the district, said Ron Ramspott, the district coordinator of health and physical education.

"Our teachers are really buying into D.D.R. as a way to promote both physical health and learning," he said. "When you're playing the game you really have to process the information and then also do the moves physically. So we think it can help with brain development as well."

As Leighton Nakamoto, a physical education teacher at Kalama Intermediate School in Makawao, Hawaii, put it: "The new physical education is moving away from competitive team sports and is more about encouraging lifetime fitness, and D.D.R. is a part of that. They can do it on their own,

and they don't have to compete with anyone else."

Mr. Nakamoto said that he had used the game in class for four years and that his school had also installed the game in its "Active Lifestyle" room, where students are encouraged to play in their free time.

Dave Randall, the educational specialist for coordinated school health for the Hawaii Department of Education, said Hawaii was trying to put together a program like West Virginia's. They hope to get the game into all of the state's 265 public schools over the next three years.

Back in West Virginia, Anna Potter, 12, and Mikayla Leombruno, 13, were not concerned about all of the academic theories as they shimmied and bounced to the beat in Mr. Hines's gym class.

"I like that you get to listen to music and you don't have to be on a team or go anywhere special to play," Anna said after their song. "If you do baseball or basketball, people get really competitive about it."

Mikayla chimed in, "And you don't have to be good at it to get a good workout." ◀

180

190

200

210

220

230

240

CLASSIFY

Next to each characteristic below, write whether it applies to traditional sports (label as *TS*) or *D.D.R.*

_____ individual activity

_____ team activity

_____ competitive

_____ noncompetitive

_____ requires skill

_____ no skill required

◀ ▶ ✕ ⟳   SEARCH 🔍

HOME | I WANT TO LEARN | WHAT'S NEW

Playing for a Living: Video Game Careers

1 | 2 | 3 ▶

Imagine that you attend video game school. Your homework might involve playing video games, dreaming up new games, and creating cool characters. Sounds like a dream come true, right? For some students, it's all in a day's work.

At universities across the country, video games are moving out of the dorm rooms and into the classrooms. College programs now offer video game degrees to prepare students for careers in the video game industry.

Plus, the skills gained from a degree in game development can apply to other career fields. Recent video game school graduates have found
10 jobs creating <u>3-D</u> models for surgeons, flight training programs for pilots, and simulation software for satellite repair. ▶

Now, why would you choose to sit at a desk pushing paper when you could sit at a computer creating animated worlds? Here are a few of the exciting careers available:

GAME DESIGNER

Game designers decide what games make it into your living room. The designer's job is to <u>map out the game</u>—from the initial idea to every game-play element. Their only requirement is to <u>make it fun</u>. This can be more difficult than it sounds. Games must be challenging enough
20 to keep advanced gamers interested but not so difficult that they frustrate the average player.

SKILLS: Game designers are creative directors as well as project managers. Directing a team of writers, programmers, animators, and sound designers requires (strong leadership and communication skills.) Designers may major in video game development, computer science, film studies, or liberal arts. ▶

SPECIALIZED **Vocabulary**

The abbreviation 3-D stands for *three-dimensional.* Some terms that have to do with computers and video games may be unfamiliar to you. Use a dictionary whenever you are unsure of a word's meaning. *WORD ANALYSIS*

ANALYZE

As you read "Playing for a Living," underline the sentence or sentences that tell what each job involves. Circle the skill requirements for each job. The first job, *GAME DESIGNER,* has been done for you. ⟳

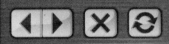

WRITER

Writers are responsible for producing a game's script. These can be simple, with little to no dialogue, or involve detailed plots with many
30 character interactions. Video game scriptwriters work closely with a designer to determine what each scene should include. Many scriptwriters also write game manuals and hint books. Other options are to work as a staff writer or editor for a gaming magazine or Web site.

SKILLS: As you'd expect, writers must be skilled in written communication. It also helps to be able to handle criticism. A script often goes through many changes, and the entire team may suggest edits. A degree in English, theater, creative writing, or journalism is ideal for this position.

ARTIST AND ANIMATOR

40 Artists are responsible for everything you see in a game. They create all the graphics, whether the game involves medieval castles, basketball courts, or outer space. The work of an artist often starts with a simple sketch. Animators translate these drawings into 3-D computer images. The animation process brings the images to life within the game environment.

SKILLS: Artists and animators must have superior artistic skills. Those working in 3-D also need to have knowledge of human and animal anatomy, because characters' movements need to look realistic. Most game artists have a degree in art, animation, or industrial design.

50 ## AUDIO DESIGNER

The audio designer composes the game's sounds. Early games had nothing but bleeps and beeps, while today's games feature complex soundtracks. ◀

Audio designers have to keep in mind the mood and pacing of the game. Quick action sequences call for fast, upbeat music. Scary scenes might feature slow, creepy music. The audio team also produces sound effects such as creaking stairs, growling monsters, or squealing car tires.

RECOGNIZE BIAS

What bias about today's video games is revealed in lines 51–52?

_____

_____

_____

SKILLS: A strong music background is the most important qualification for an audio designer. Many audio designers have a
60 background in audio engineering or editing, as well as having studied music theory, music composition, sound engineering, or film scoring.

PROGRAMMER

Programmers make up about 50% of a video game development team. They write the code or mathematical equations that drive the game. This code controls everything on the screen: where objects are placed, when characters appear, and what the player is able to do. Programmers also control the speed and pacing of the game.

SKILLS: Programming is the most technical of the video gaming careers. Strong math and computer skills are required. Many
70 companies look for programmers with a degree in computer science or electrical engineering. ▶

GAME TESTER

By far the coolest job available is video game tester. Yes, this job is exactly what it sounds like: Game testers play games for a living! Their job is to find errors in the game before it's released to the public. They go through every level of a game to make sure characters don't walk through walls or through other characters. They also make sure a sidewalk doesn't suddenly drop off and a knight's sword doesn't disappear in the middle of a scene. Game testers also check whether
80 a game is too easy or too hard, too fast or too slow.

SKILLS: Game testers need strong communication skills. Testers have to clearly explain every problem they find, so the design team can go back and fix it. Other necessary skills are attention to detail and good eye-hand coordination.

For many video gamers, it's a dream come true to be able to make a living doing what they love. So get gaming! You're not just playing a game—you're studying to be a video game professional. ▶

CONTRAST

What is the difference between a video game programmer and a video game designer?

_____

_____

_____

_____

CONNECT

Which job would be the best fit for you? Why?

_____

_____

_____

_____

Reading Comprehension

DIRECTIONS *Answer these questions about the four selections in this lesson by filling in the correct ovals.*

1. *Dance Dance Revolution* (D.D.R.) offers P.E. teachers an opportunity to combine

   (A) sports and fitness

   (B) TV and computers

   (C) fun and physical activity

   (D) P.E. and sports

2. Students who are using D.D.R. move in response to

   (A) music and scrolling arrows

   (B) commands from P.E. teachers

   (C) written directions on screen

   (D) numbers on a mat

3. According to "P.E. Classes Turn to Video Game That Works Legs," P.E. classes are beginning to promote

   (A) sports that emphasize teamwork

   (B) noncompetitive activities that encourage fitness

   (C) required dance classes and activities

   (D) formal games in addition to informal ones

4. According to "Playing for a Living," half of a video game development team is made up of

   (A) designers

   (B) writers

   (C) animators

   (D) programmers

5. Which of the following items contains bias?

   (A) Why would you choose to sit at a desk pushing paper

   (B) designers decide what games make it into your living room

   (C) animators must have superior artistic skills

   (D) this code controls everything on the screen

6. Which statement would all three authors of the selections agree with?

   (A) Video games have great potential to help people.

   (B) Violent games are harmful to users.

   (C) Video games cause numerous physical reactions.

   (D) Video games are a popular pastime with young people.

7. The word *collaborator* (line 137 of "P.E. Classes Turn to Video Game That Works Legs") means

   (A) co-creator

   (B) doctoral candidate

   (C) physical educator

   (D) coordinator

8. The word *composes* (line 51 of "Playing for a Living") means

   (A) orders   (C) settles

   (B) creates   (D) softens

Timed Writing Practice

PROMPT

Write a (persuasive essay) stating whether young people should be allowed to play video games as a classroom exercise. Support your argument using examples from at least three of the four articles you have read.

BUDGET YOUR TIME

You have 45 minutes to complete this assignment. Decide how much time to spend on each step.

Analyze _____

Plan _____

Write _____

Review _____

45

Test-Taker's Toolkit

1. ANALYZE THE PROMPT

A. **Read the prompt** carefully.

B. **Circle key words** and phrases in each sentence. One has been done for you. The prompt tells you what you must include to get a good score.

C. **Restate the prompt** in your own words to make sure you understand it. You may use the lines on the right.

2. PLAN YOUR RESPONSE

A. **Organize ideas** Before you begin to write, organize your essay. Write your claim. Then go back to the selections and find reasons that support your claim. The graphic organizer at the right will help you.

B. **Plan the essay** You might begin by stating your claim. Then devote one paragraph to each reason and its supporting evidence. Conclude by restating your claim.

3. WRITE AND REVIEW

A. **Craft a powerful ending** End your essay with a memorable statement. You might try appealing to readers' emotions. Restate this ending in a more powerful way:

Before you give up on video games, consider their possible benefits.

_____

_____

B. **Write out your full response** Leave enough time to read through your essay to check your grammar and spelling.

MY CLAIM: _____

_____

REASON I. _____
Support: A. _____
B. _____

REASON II. _____
Support: A. _____
B. _____

REASON III. _____
Support: A. _____
B. _____

Student Handbooks

Nonfiction Skills Handbook

Test-Taking Handbook

Author's Credibility or Bias

ACADEMIC VOCABULARY

author: the person who wrote a book or an article or who created a Web page; some texts do not name an individual but only an organization

bias: an inclination for or against a particular person, group, topic, or issue

credibility: the knowledge and trustworthiness of an author

loaded words: words that show bias because of their intensely positive or negative associations

STEP 1 **Look for the name of the author or authors.** Get in the habit of asking who wrote a piece. If there is no name—individual or organization, credited for the work, then no one is responsible, or accountable for factual, truthful content. It may not be credible. Look in the following places for a name:

- **Book:** on the cover or title page
- **Article** or **periodical:** at the beginning or end of the text
- **Web site:** on the home page or "contact" page

STEP 2 **Examine the author's credibility.** To examine **credibility** means to determine if the author has enough **knowledge** to write factually and accurately, and whether the author has **balance** or **bias,** is truthful and fair, or leans toward one belief or interest.

- **Background:** First, look for information about the author (for example, "Director, Excelsior University Museum of Art"). If you don't see any information given with the author's name, try a reference book, such as *Current Biography*, or try a search engine.

- **Knowledge:** As you read about an author, ask yourself: Does the author have direct experience with the topic? What are the author's credentials— recognition and achievement such as, education, training, experiences, job title, and publishing record?

- **Bias:** As you read an author's work, ask yourself: Does the author make direct statements or give hints about opinions, beliefs and interests? Is the author well-regarded? Does the author work for a group that advocates a certain position? Does the author use loaded words?

  EXAMPLE

  "The electoral college has served us well."

STEP 3 **Evaluate the usefulness and importance of the work.** In light of the author's credibility, ask yourself whether you should discount the piece, rely on it as a source, or get the viewpoint of another author.

Author's Perspective

ACADEMIC VOCABULARY

background: facts about an author's experience and knowledge

bias: an author's preference or slant on a particular topic

perspective: the way an author looks at a topic

selective details: information an author includes—and decides not to include—in a text

word choice: the words an author uses to create a specific effect on readers

STEP 1 **Identify the author.** Look for the author's name and any additional information about the person. This usually can be found at the beginning or end of a text, sometimes set off as a separate feature. Ask the following questions for clues about the author's experiences, values, and beliefs:

- What does the author's name suggest about the person's sex and possibly nationality?
- What is the author's education? Did he or she earn degrees from a respected institution?
- What do the author's activities, responsibilities, and publications say about his or her reliability?

STEP 2 **Examine the text for clues to the author's point of view.** Carefully read the text, looking for indications of the author's point of view. Focus on:

- **word choice**—words with strong positive or negative emotional associations, or connotations
- **selective details**—facts and opinions that support a specific point of view
- **biased language**—statements that reveal a one-sided belief
- **direct statements**—clear admissions of point of view, often beginning with the words "I believe" or "In my opinion"

Then record specific instances of these elements in a chart like the one below:

TYPE OF EVIDENCE	SPECIFIC INSTANCE
word choice selective details biased language direct statements	

STEP 3 **Identify the author's perspective.** Review the evidence you entered in your chart and ask yourself, "What does this information tell me about the author's point of view on the topic?" Then write a sentence describing that point of view. Finally, read through the text again, keeping the author's perspective in mind. Write down questions, comments, or counterevidence that occurs to you as you read. Take this information into account as you evaluate the reliability or usefulness of the text.

Author's Purpose

ACADEMIC VOCABULARY

author's purpose: the reason(s) an author has for writing a particular work

STEP 1   **Learn common purposes.** Keep the four common author purposes in mind as you read: to explain or inform, to persuade, to entertain, and to express emotion and ideas.

STEP 2   **Identify clues to author's purpose.** As you read a text, look for clues in the work's title, subject, and tone; the choice of details and words; the context, or intended audience; the effects on you as a reader; and the pattern of organization or structure. There are some common match-ups between text structure and purpose, but beware that there are no firm rules.

EXAMPLE

Sequence, cause-effect, or **main idea and details** are often used to explain or to inform.

Problem-solution, proposition-support, or **compare-contrast** order may signal that the author's purpose is to persuade.

Chronological order is often used in dramatic histories or storytelling and may signal that the purpose is to entertain.

Order of degree or **spatial order** may be used to express emotion.

STEP 3   **Infer the author's main purpose.** Review the clues and recall the common purposes. Decide what is *most likely* the main purpose the author has for the writing. Check your answer by ruling out the other purposes.

STEP 4   **Use purpose to evaluate the work.** Evaluate the piece in light of the author's purpose: How well did the passage achieve the goal? How well were you entertained, informed, persuaded, or instructed?

Cause-and-Effect Order

ACADEMIC VOCABULARY

cause-and-effect order: a method of organizing ideas and information in an essay that shows causal relationships

cause: why something happens

effect: a result; what happened as an outcome of the cause

STEP 1 Look for effects. Ask: "What was the outcome?" Check for multiple effects.

EXAMPLE
Because Harry left the cage open, the canary escaped and flew around the room.

STEP 2 Look for causes. Ask: "Why did it happen?" Check for multiple causes.

EXAMPLE
Because Harry left the cage open and never noticed, the canary escaped.

STEP 3 Check for cause-effect chains. A cause can lead to an effect that then causes another effect, and so on. A series of such linked events is a cause-effect chain.

EXAMPLE
Harry left the cage open, allowing the canary to escape. As a result, Harry chased the bird around the room for an hour.

STEP 4 Find signal words. Signal words and phrases for cause and effect include: *because, since, as a result, therefore,* and *due to.*

EXAMPLE
I forgot to study, and as a result, I didn't do very well on the quiz.

STEP 5 Use a Graphic Organizer. Arrange ideas in a cause-and-effect diagram or chain.

EXAMPLE

Cause: Angel oversleeps. → Effect: Angel misses bus.

STEP 6 Check your logic. The cause must spark, or set in motion the result. They do not have to be presented in sequence. In many sentences, the effect appears first.

EXAMPLE
Angel missed the bus due to oversleeping.

Charts and Other Graphic Aids

ACADEMIC VOCABULARY

bar graph: a coordinate grid with shaded bars, used to compare amounts or levels in various categories

chart: a table, displaying information in rows and columns or in boxes

diagram: a sketch or plan designed to explain how something works or to show the relationship of parts to the whole

illustration: usually a drawing designed to explain a concept or to show relationships of parts to the whole

map: a drawing of a region of the earth, showing the location of places

pie chart/circle graph: a circle divided into sliced sections, measured to represent percentages of a whole

STEP 1 Read the title. Ask yourself: What information does the graphic aid display? Does the title include time periods, locations, ages, or other details about the subject?

STEP 2 Study the data. Read all the headings, labels, and captions. Make sure you understand any symbols or abbreviations. Look at the lines, bars, slices, row and column heads, and other labels. Try comparing just two bars, points, rows, or slices to be sure you understand the information in a chart or graph. Ask yourself: what question might be answered from this display?

STEP 3 Draw conclusions. Decide why the information in the graphic aid is useful and how it could be used. Ask yourself:

- What can I conclude from the information in the graphic aid?
- Which data allow me to make that conclusion?
- What further information would be helpful?
- What new questions arise from learning this data?

Classification Order

STEP 1 **Look for words and phrases that signal groups.** Words and phrases
writers use to indicate a subject's class include *group, category, kind, set, type, class,
classification, division, divided into,* and *common characteristics*. Notice how many
groups there are.

STEP 2 **Look for how classes or groups are defined.** What do each of these
objects, ideas, or facts have in common? What qualities or attributes unite the items
in each group?

STEP 3 **Look for subgroups.** Under each of your major groups or classes, are there
other items that share common attributes with each other?

STEP 4 **Write categories and subcategories in a graphic organizer.** A
classification organizer like the one shown can help you keep track of the major
groups and subgroups mentioned in the text. Recognizing classification order can
help you understand the relationships between ideas and details and help you
remember important information.

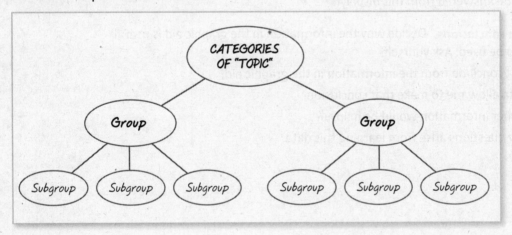

Compare-and-Contrast Order

ACADEMIC VOCABULARY

compare-and-contrast order: organization of writing to show the similarities and differences between two or more subjects.

feature-by-feature: a text pattern in which a writer compares and contrasts two subjects one feature or characteristic at a time.

subject-by-subject: a text pattern in which a writer presents the features of one subject first, then moves on to features of a second subject, showing how they are alike and different.

STEP 1 Look for signal words and phrases:

- **Similarities:** To **compare** subjects, writers use words and phrases such as *like, likewise, both, similarly, are similar* and *neither.*
- **Differences:** To **contrast** subjects, writers use words and phrases such as *unlike, in contrast, different from,* and *on the other hand.*

STEP 2 Identify the subjects being compared or contrasted. Usually the subjects have similar characteristics. They may be works in one genre or items in one category.

STEP 3 Identify the pattern. Does the text use feature-by-feature or subject-by-subject order?

Subject-by-subject	Feature-by-feature
Subject A	**Feature 1**
Feature 1	Subject A
Feature 2	Subject B
Subject B	**Feature 2**
Feature 1	Subject A
Feature 2	Subject B

STEP 4 Organize similarities and differences in a graphic. Use a Venn diagram or other graphic to take notes on the similarities and differences described in the text.

Electronic Texts

ACADEMIC VOCABULARY

credits and sponsor: information about the creator of an electronic text

home page: opening or main page of an electronic text that gives introductory information and links to other features included in the text

icons: pictures that you can click on to perform a function or access information in the text

menus and hyperlinks: drop-down lists or highlighted or underlined words in an electronic text that you can click on to move to another page of related information

URL: Universal Resource Locator, address of an electronic text on the World Wide Web

STEP 1 Analyze the features of the Website. Before gathering information from an electronic text, or Website, familiarize yourself with its features. Identify and ask yourself questions about the following elements:

- **URL**—Look at the address of the Website in the locator box on your search engine. What clues does the address give you about the sponsor and purpose of the site? Websites whose addresses end in .*gov* or .*edu* usually publish reliable information.

- **Credits and sponsor**—At the top of the home page, find the name and any supporting details about the individual or organization that is responsible for the text. What does this information suggest about the point of view of the site?

- **Menus**—Click on any menu tabs along the top or sides of the home page. What options do these features offer?

- **Hyperlinks**—Locate words in the text that are highlighted or underlined and click on two or three. Do these links take you to other pages within the same Website, to other Websites, or to both?

STEP 2 Analyze the purpose of the Website. What do you learn from the features you have identified as well as from the title, headings, and subheadings of the text?

- Is the purpose of the site primarily to convey information, to persuade, or to entertain?

- What point of view does the text support?

STEP 3 Evaluate the purpose and usefulness of the site. Based on your answers to the questions in Step 2, identify the purpose of the Website. Compare this purpose with your need for information. For example, if you want to learn many points of view about a topic and the Website focuses only on one side of a topic or issue, you should look for other sites that present different approaches to the topic.

Evaluate Support

ACADEMIC VOCABULARY

evaluate evidence: determine the strength and quality of the facts, statistics, reasons, examples, and sources that support a position or claim

evidence: a reason, fact, statistic, example, or expert opinion that supports a proposition or claim

objective: not influenced by emotions or personal prejudices; factual

proposition or claim: the writer's position on an issue or problem

subjective: personal to a given person; existing only in the mind

STEP 1 **Look for opinions to be sure they are supported.** No one can check whether an opinion is true or false. So a writer must support any claims, positions, or personal opinions with examples, facts, and reasons. For any expert opinions, be sure that sources are clearly identified. Don't accept vague language, such as "experts agree."

STEP 2 **Look for facts-statistics, examples, and expert opinions.** Part of a writer's job is to present enough facts to support each claim. Facts include quotations from experts, anecdotes and examples, and definitions, as well as **statistics** (mathematical data). Decide whether there is enough evidence. Decide if the evidence is up to date. If there are no data to back up the ideas, don't accept the claim.

STEP 3 **Look for ways in which sources are documented.** Writers should name the source of their facts. Look for sources that are **objective** and **credible,** like an encyclopedia, rather than **subjective** and **biased** like a personal blog. Good documentation includes the *who, where,* and *when* of each source, so readers can check it.

STEP 4 **Weigh the evidence.** After evaluating the support, the hard data, and the documentation, a reader can decide whether to accept or agree with the writer's position or not. You can also weigh how reasonable, valuable, or useful the writer's ideas are to you.

Evaluate Usefulness

ACADEMIC VOCABULARY

accuracy: correctness of statements and facts

author credibility: author's education and background

evaluation: rating the strength of a source

incomplete information: missing facts or explanations

realistic suggestions: plans of action that make sense and are possible to carry out

solid information: facts that are complete, well-supported, and reliable

STEP 1 Make a checklist. To help you decide whether or not you should use the information in a source, create a checklist of questions to ask about it. Copy the form below or use it as an example to create your own:

Yes	No	
☐	☐	Is the author an expert in the field?
☐	☐	Is he/she affiliated with a respected institution?
☐	☐	Does the information seem solid and accurate?
☐	☐	Are statements supported by facts that can be verified?
☐	☐	Do you need more information after reading?
☐	☐	Are the author's suggestions realistic?

STEP 2 Evaluate the text. Read through the text with the questions on your checklist in mind. Pay special attention to the following text features:

- the author's byline and biographical information
- boldfaced statements
- charts and graphs

STEP 3 Determine the usefulness of the source. Tally the "yes" and "no" marks on your checklist.

- If you answered "no" to any question about the author or the reliability of the information, DO NOT use the source.
- If you answered "yes" to the question about needing more information after reading, you may be able to use the source and look for the missing information in other sources.

Forms of Nonfiction Texts

ACADEMIC VOCABULARY

accuracy: correctness of statements and facts

bias: a person's particular ideas about and approach to a topic

feature articles: in-depth coverage of human-interest or lifestyle topics found in newspapers or magazines

instructions: information on how to do something, often including diagrams and numbered steps, found in manuals and product inserts

interviews: conversations between two people in which one person asks questions and the other person responds, often presented with text features such as subheads that help readers follow the conversation

thoroughness: complete coverage of all aspects of a topic from several perspectives

STEP 1 Identify the author's purpose. Look at the title, subheads, and graphics and skim the article for clues to the subject, tone, and intended audience. Does the author intend to

- describe?
- inform?
- persuade?
- entertain?

STEP 2 Identify the form. Look for the features that characterize three main forms of nonfiction texts:

- **feature articles**—front-page or main articles including subheadings, graphics, illustrations, and often multiple pages
- **instructions**—numbered steps, illustrations or diagrams, and short paragraphs
- **interviews**—alternating statements by the interviewer and person being interviewed sometimes introduced by the name or initials and a colon

STEP 3 Evaluate for effectiveness. Ask yourself these questions about the text:

- **How thorough is it?** Look for complete explanations of all steps in a process or complete background information on a topic.
- **How accurate is it?** Find facts from reliable sources that support statements.
- **What is the author's bias?** Identify how the author's beliefs about the topic affect the ideas presented.

Main Ideas and Supporting Details

ACADEMIC VOCABULARY

main idea: the most important idea about a topic. It can be the central idea of an entire work or of just a paragraph.

supporting details: words, phrases, or sentences that tell more about the main idea or topic sentence. Types of supporting details include:

    examples: specific instances that explain or support a point

    sensory details: details that appeal to one or more of the five senses

    reasons: details that tell why an opinion is valid or why something occurs

    facts: statements that can be proved

    statistics: facts expressed in numbers

topic: what a piece of nonfiction writing is about; its subject matter

topic sentence: a sentence that states the main idea of a paragraph

STEP 1 **Identify the topic.** Ask yourself: What is this passage or paragraph about?

STEP 2 **Think about the main idea.** Ask yourself: What idea does the writer express?

STEP 3 **Look for a topic sentence.** The topic sentence is usually either the first or last sentence in a paragraph, although it can occur anywhere. In some paragraphs, the main idea is not stated directly, but is implied by the supporting details.

STEP 4 **Identify the supporting details.** Writers use different types of details to support different purposes and main ideas. Sensory details describe, examples illustrate, reasons persuade, and facts and statistics explain.

STEP 5 **Use a graphic organizer.** A chart can help you take notes on the main idea and supporting details in a paragraph. List a main idea, then note all the details that support it.

Patterns of Organization

ACADEMIC VOCABULARY

cause-and-effect order: shows the relationship between events and their results

chronological order: shows the sequence of events in time

classification: assigns people, places, things, or events to groups based on specific characteristics

comparison-contrast order: presents the similarities and differences between people, places, things, or events

problem-solution: explains a problem and offers a solution

spatial order: presents things or events according to their arrangement in space

STEP 1. Get a general sense of the organization. To form an initial impression of how a text is organized, skim it quickly, asking yourself, "Am I learning about:

- time sequence?"
- relation in space?"
- relative ranking?"
- membership in a category?"
- causes and effects?"
- similarities and differences?"
- the solution to a problem?"

STEP 2 Look for clues to the organization. Each organizational pattern uses a variety of signal words and structural patterns.

Cause-and-Effect Order

- Look for signal words like *because, therefore, since, as a result, the effect of, consequently.*
- Look for answers to the question, "What happens next?"
- Study the text for clues to implied causes and effects.

Chronological Order

- Look for signal words like *first, next, then, afterward, before.*
- Study the text for times, dates, or numbers that show order.

Classification

- Look for words or phrases that signal groups: *group, category, kind, set, type, class, classification, division, divided into, common characteristics.*
- Look for definitions of the groups used in the text. What do each of these objects, ideas, or facts have in common?
- Look for subgroups under the major groups.

Comparison-Contrast Order

- Signal words for this pattern are *similarly, also, both, like, neither, unlike, instead, in contrast.*
- Identify the subjects being compared or contrasted. The subjects usually have similar characteristics.
- Look for the pattern. Does the text compare each subject in turn, or does it compare each subject feature by feature?

Problem-Solution Order

- Look for words like *problem, solution, pros, cons,* and *recommendation.*
- Examine the text for a clear statement of the problem, an analysis of the problem, and a proposed solution.
- Look for a discussion of the causes and effects of the problem.

Spatial Order

- Look for signal words such as *in front of, behind, under, above, left, right, top, bottom.*
- Identify the specific way in which the spatial details are organized. A writer usually arranges spatial details in a certain order such as front to back, near to far, low to high, and so on.

STEP 3 Determine the most important ideas and supporting details. Once you have determined how the text is organized, focus on the main ideas the author is presenting and the support that he/she provides. Making an informal outline like the one below can help you understand how he organizational pattern helps convey author's message.

Organizational pattern _____

 I. Main idea
    A. Supporting detail
    B. Supporting detail
 II. Main idea related to first idea by _____
    A. Supporting detail
    B. Supporting detail
 III. Main idea related to first and second ideas by _____
    A. Supporting detail
    B. Supporting detail

Problem-Solution Order

ACADEMIC VOCABULARY

problem-solution order: presents a problem, explores various solutions, and identifies a solution, or outcome

STEP 1 **Identify the problems or problems.** To signal a **problem,** writers may use words and phrases like *problem, difficulty, issue, conflict,* and *need for change.*

STEP 2 **Look for solutions.** Signal words and phrases can help you.

- **solutions**—words like *solution, answer, approach, method, way, option, remedy, alternative*
- **outcomes**—words and phrases like *but, however, can lead to, would result in, most likely, might also, on the other hand*
- **preferred solution**—words and phrases like *best, most effective, useful, helpful, valuable*

STEP 3 **Use a graphic organizer** to keep track of the problem, solutions, and possible outcomes.

State Problem	

Solution 1	Pros
	•
	•
	•
	Cons
	•
	•
	•
Solution 2	Pros
	•
	•
	•
	Cons
	•
	•
	•

Decision	

Rhetorical Devices

STEP 1 Scan the text for rhetorical devices. Read quickly through the text looking for clues to the following rhetorical devices:

- **analogies**—the phrases *is like* and *is to the* _____ *as* _____ *is to the* _____
- **parallelism**—repeated grammatical structures, such as similar parts of speech, phrases, or sentence types
- **repetition**—words or phrases that appear several times

STEP 2 Determine how each rhetorical device contributes to the text. Ask the following questions about each rhetorical device you identified:

Analogies
- What two things are being compared?
- How are they similar?
- How are they different?
- What idea is the author trying to convey?

Parallelism
- What do the ideas being expressed have in common?
- Why might the author want to stress these ideas?

Repetition
- Why is this word or phrase especially important?
- What is the effect of repeating it?

STEP 3 Determine the key ideas in the text. Review your answers to the questions in Step 2. Then examine the entire text closely. As you read, keep the ideas conveyed by the rhetorical devices in mind. Integrate them with additional ideas that you learn.

Sequence and Chronological Order

ACADEMIC VOCABULARY

chronological order: organization in order of occurrence, forward in time, usually used to tell stories, to report events, or to record histories.

sequence order: the order in which events should, may, or usually occur; sequence order is used to give directions or to show steps or events in a process.

STEP 1 **Look for times, dates, or numbers that show order.** Clue words such as *first, second,* and so on indicate sequence of information. Numerals (*1, 2, 3, . . .*) or dates and times may give order of events.

STEP 2 **Organize information in a graphic.** Based on any time-order clue words, place the events in a graphic organizer. The organizer can be a numbered list. Or you can create a left-to-right series of boxes and arrows to track information.

STEP 3 **Look for words and phrases that show duration or sequence.** Certain signal words and phrases help structure both chronological and sequential texts: *then, next, before, after, during, finally,* and so on.

STEP 4 **Infer the author's purpose.** The author may want to explain how to carry out a task or report a story about how events unfolded in time. Ask yourself: Why does the author arrange details in this way? What is he or she trying to achieve?

Spatial Order

STEP 1 Look for **signal words or phrases** that show physical position or location—words such as *top, bottom above, below,* phrases, such as *away from, close to, in front of*.

EXAMPLE

What words signal a spatial position or location in the following sentences? The kitten curled up *beneath* the rocking chair *beside* the stove. The tea kettle simmered slowly, its steam blowing *past* the open door. *Just to the right,* the clock ticked toward noon, hanging *above* the sink, whose dripping faucet drummed.

STEP 2 Identify the **specific way in which the spatial details are organized.** Usually a writer arranges spatial details in a certain order, such as near to far, front to back, low to high, and so on.

EXAMPLE

In the passage that follows, how has the writer organized the information?

At the bottom of the totem pole, there was a fish. In the middle, a man's hard face stared out. A sun with rays crowned the top of the totem pole, as though the sun were shining down on the face.

STEP 3 **Take notes.** Once you have identified how the details are organized, you can take notes, by listing details, such as people, objects, or actions, in order. You can also create a drawing or map that helps you see clearly see whatever is being described. If the text is a guide or instruction, your graphic may help you use the information.

STEP 4 **Infer author's purpose.** An author may use spatial order to create effects such as a tense or tranquil mood, a confused or orderly character, a or other effects in a literary work. Other writers organize factual information or directions spatially to make them clear and easy to follow.

EXAMPLE

What is the writer's purpose in the following sentence? "Turn *left* after the library, and *in front of* you there will be a small yellow building. Your class is *inside* the yellow building."

Synthesize

ACADEMIC VOCABULARY

synthesize: to combine individual ideas, influences, or materials to create a
new product or idea

synthesizing information: drawing from a variety of research materials,
combining new ideas with prior knowledge, and applying the information to
some new work or creation

STEP 1 **Determine the message in each source.** Decide what is most memorable
or important about each work you are using. Then look for details the writers use to
support these main ideas.

STEP 2 **Paraphrase the main ideas.** You will find the main ideas easier to work
with after you have rephrased them in your own words. You should also paraphrase
difficult concepts and wording in each selection to improve your understanding.

STEP 3 **Compare sources in light of author's purpose and audience.** Determine
whether each selection was written to explain, inform, express an opinion, persuade,
tell a story, or express emotion. You may interpret information in different ways
depending on its purpose and audience.

STEP 4 **Ask questions about your sources.** The right questions will help you view
your subject from different perspectives. Ask questions starting with *who, what,
where, when, why, how,* and even *what if.* For example:

- How do the sources differ?
- What approach has the author of each work taken?
- Whose perspective is, or is *not*, represented?
- Who is the intended audience?
- Why is the message important to the author? To me?
- When and where is the writing set? When and where was it created?

STEP 5 **Connect to other sources, or your own experiences.** Look for ways that
key ideas relate to other works on the same subject, or to your prior knowledge of the
subject. Use your imagination to find connections that may not seem obvious at first.
Ask yourself:

- How does the information confirm or refute other material?
- How does the information relate to my life or to world affairs?

STEP 6 **Synthesize.** After reviewing your sources as a group, piece the
information together to create something new—an essay, story, poem, research
paper, map, poster or other work. Be sure to offer your own original insights about
the topic.

Text Features

ACADEMIC VOCABULARY

text features: design elements that highlight the organization and especially important information in a text

boldface type: thicker, darker type, often used for key terms

bulleted list: each listed item is signaled with a dot or "bullet"

caption: written information about an illustration, photograph, or graphic

graphic aid: visual tool (a photograph, table, graph, or other illustration)

head or heading: title that identifies the topic of the content that follows it

key word: important term, may be italicized, boldfaced, or highlighted

sidebar: additional information set in a box or apart from the main text

subhead or subheading: signals the beginning of a new topic or section under a more general heading

title: name given to a book, chapter, play, film, or poem

STEP 1 Before you read, identify the text features. Knowing the kinds of features that a text contains can help you find information.

STEP 2 Preview the text features. As you preview, follow these steps:

- Read the heads and subheads to get an overview of the material and to determine which details go with which main ideas.
- Scan for boldfaced terms, other key words, and lists to get a sense of the important details you will encounter in this text.
- Glance at the graphic aids (and corresponding captions) to see what kind of data the text offers besides words.
- Familiarize yourself with the kind of material that is covered in the sidebars, but don't read them yet.

STEP 3 Now read the text and organize information. As you read, paragraph by paragraph, work in the graphic aids and sidebars as convenient. Use the text features to help your note taking, outlining, summarizing, and questioning.

Textbooks

ACADEMIC VOCABULARY

bulleted or numbered lists: each of these brief items of information or explanation is preceded by a dot or "bullet" or by a number

captions: information about photographs, illustrations, or other graphics

footnotes: numbered notes placed at the bottom of a page that provide additional or source information

graphic aids: information presented visually, such as graphs, charts, maps, photographs, and diagrams, to help clarify ideas in the text

headings/subheadings: boldfaced text titles that indicate the start of a new section of text and identify its main idea

review questions: a way for readers to focus or assess their understanding

side bars: focused information set apart from the main text that relates to or contrasts with the topic

specialized vocabulary: boldfaced words with definitions in the text or in a separate list that help readers understand the topic

timeline: graphic showing dates or periods of time along with captions

STEP 1 Scan text features to help identify the overall topic and purpose of the text. To get a good idea of what an instructional text is about, follow these steps:

- **Read the title, headings and subheadings.** What do they tell you about the topic?
- **Read any opening questions or boldfaced text.** Often a textbook chapter will open with signals about the key ideas.

STEP 2 Analyze the text features. Focus carefully on the text features you've identified.

- **Note the main ideas** you have identified from the heads and subheads.
- **Examine the photographs**, illustrations, maps, charts, and graphs in detail. These graphic aids help explain the concepts discussed in the text.
- **Read the review questions** to identify the concepts you are expected to learn.

STEP 3 Identify key ideas. Finally, read the full text. Make a list of important details. Then examine all your notes, looking for main ideas that they support. It is these ideas that the author wants you to remember.

Transitions and Other Text Clues

ACADEMIC VOCABULARY

demonstrative pronouns: words like *this, these,* and *those* that refer to people, places, and things and clarify relationships between ideas

synonyms: words with similar meanings that help define and elaborate on ideas

transitions: signal words that indicate how ideas relate to each other, such as *but* and *however* for contrast; *like* and *similarly* for comparison; and *first, then,* and *next* for sequence

STEP 1 Scan the text for an overall impression. As you skim the title, subheads, graphics, and first few paragraphs, ask yourself:

- What is this text about?
- What is the author's purpose?
- Who is the intended audience?
- What is the author's tone?

STEP 2 Preview the text clues. Look for words that signal relationships between the ideas and list them in a three-column chart like this one.

Demonstrative Pronouns	Synonyms	Transitions

Then add the following information for each entry:

- **demonstrative pronouns**—the word each refers to
- **synonyms**—the meaning (using a dictionary if necessary)
- **transitions**—the type of relationship each transition word signals— comparison, contrast, sequence, or some other connection

STEP 3 Analyze the flow of ideas. Then read the text carefully, using your chart to help you understand the main ideas and how they relate to each other. Make an informal outline as you read or summarize the information afterward to make sure you understand the author's point.

Treatment, Organization, and Scope of Ideas

> **ACADEMIC VOCABULARY**
>
> **organization:** a particular arrangement, or pattern, of ideas in text
>
> **scope:** the focus of a text, the depth and breadth of detail included
>
> **tone:** the writer's attitude toward his or her subject
>
> **treatment:** the way a topic is handled; includes the form a writer uses, the writer's purpose, and tone

STEP 1 Identify and compare treatment. Look for differences and similarities in form, purpose, and tone between two works. Ask yourself:

- **What is the form, or genre, or each text?** Examples of forms include news reports, summaries, editorials, interviews, and reviews.
- **What is the writer's purpose?** Is it to inform, persuade, instruct, advise, warn, critique, promote, amuse, or inspire readers?
- **What is the tone of the writing?** Is it serious? Comical? Angry? Fearful?

STEP 2 Identify and compare organization. Some common patterns of organization include:

- **Chronological order** arranges events from earliest to latest in time. Reverse chronological order starts with recent events.
- **Deductive order** begins with a general statement, followed by facts and evidence, building toward a specific conclusion.
- **Main idea and supporting details** begins with the main idea, followed by reasons, facts, and examples that strengthen the reader's understanding of it.
- **Cause-effect organization** shows that a certain event, idea, or trend causes a change. The writing may begin with the cause or begin with the effects.

STEP 3 Identify and compare scope. Two texts about one subject may each have a different focus, such as an overview versus a close-up look. Ask:

- **What is the topic?** This may appear in the title or first sentence.
- **What aspects of the topic are covered?** Scan headings or topic sentences throughout the work to see what the focus is.
- **How much and what sort of details are used?** In articles with wide scope, facts and statistics are given and background is provided. A narrow piece covers personal anecdotes and minor incidents.

Successful Test Taking

You can prepare for tests in several ways. First, study and understand the content that will be on the test. Second, learn as many test-taking techniques as you can. These techniques will help you better understand the questions and how to answer them. Following are some general suggestions for preparing for and taking tests. Starting on page R30, you'll find more detailed suggestions and test-taking practice.

 ## Study Content Throughout the Year

1. **Master the content of your language arts class.** The best way to study for tests is to read, understand, and review the content of your language arts class. Read your daily assignments carefully. Study the notes that you have taken in class. Participate in class discussions. Work with classmates in small groups to help one another learn. You might trade writing assignments and comment on your classmates' work.

2. **Use your textbook for practice.** Your textbook includes many different types of questions. Some may ask you to talk about a story you just read. Others may ask you to figure out what's wrong with a sentence or how to make a paragraph sound better. Try answering these questions out loud and in writing. This type of practice can make taking a test much easier.

3. **Learn how to understand the information in charts, maps, and graphic organizers.** One type of test question may ask you to look at a graphic organizer, such as a spider map, and explain something about the information you see there. Another type of question may ask you to look at a map to find a particular place, such as the Sahara Desert setting of the story "Nadia the Willful." You'll find charts, maps, and graphic organizers to study in your literature textbooks. You'll also find charts, maps and graphs in your science, mathematics, and social studies textbook. When you look at these, ask yourself, What information is being presented and why is it important?

4. **Practice taking tests.** Use copies of tests you have taken in the past or in other classes for practice. Every test has a time limit, so set a timer for 15 or 20 minutes and then begin your practice. Try to finish the test in the time you've given yourself.

5. **Talk about test-taking experiences.** After you've taken a classroom test or quiz, talk about it with your teacher and classmates. Which types of questions were the hardest to understand? What made them difficult? Which questions seemed easiest, and why? When you share test-taking techniques with your classmates, everyone can become a successful test taker.

Use Strategies During the Test

1. **Read the directions carefully.** You can't be a successful test taker unless you know exactly what you are expected to do. Look for key words and phrases, such as *circle the best answer, write a paragraph,* or *choose the word that best completes each sentence.*

2. **Learn how to read test questions.** Test questions can sometimes be difficult to figure out. They may include unfamiliar language or be written in an unfamiliar way. Try rephrasing the question in a simpler way using words you understand. Always ask yourself, What type of information does this question want me to provide?

3. **Pay special attention when using a separate answer sheet.** If you accidentally skip a line on an answer sheet, all the rest of your answers may be wrong! Try one or more of the following techniques:

   - Use a ruler on the answer sheet to make sure you are placing your answers on the correct line.

   - After every five answers, check to make sure you're on the right line.

   - Each time you turn a page of the test booklet, check to make sure the number of the question is the same as the number of the answer line on the answer sheet.

   - If the answer sheet has circles, fill them in neatly. A stray pencil mark might cause the scoring machine to count the answer as incorrect.

4. **If you're not sure of the answer, make your best guess.** Unless you've been told that there is a penalty for guessing, choose the answer that you think is likeliest to be correct.

5. **Keep track of the time.** Answering all the questions on a test usually results in a better score. That's why finishing the test is important. Keep track of the time you have left. At the beginning of the test, figure out how many questions you will have to answer by the halfway point in order to finish in the time given.

Understand Types of Test Questions

Most tests include two types of questions: multiple choice and open-ended. Specific strategies will help you understand and correctly answer each type of question.

A **multiple-choice question** has two parts. The first part is the question itself, called the stem. The second part is a series of possible answers. Usually four possible answers are provided, and only one of them is correct. Your task is to choose the correct answer. Here are some strategies to help you do just that.

1. Read and think about each question carefully before looking at the possible answers.

2. Pay close attention to key words in the question. For example, look for the word *not,* as in "Which of the following is *not* a cause of the conflict in this story?"

3. Read and think about all of the possible answers before making your choice.

4. Reduce the number of choices by eliminating any answers you know are incorrect. Then, think about why some of the remaining choices might also be incorrect.

   • If two of the choices are pretty much the same, both are probably wrong.

   • Answers that contain any of the following words are usually incorrect: *always, never, none, all,* and *only.*

5. If you're still unsure about an answer, see if any of the following applies:

   • When one choice is longer and more detailed than the others, it is often the correct answer.

   • When a choice repeats a word that is in the question, it may be the correct answer.

   • When two choices are direct opposites, one of them is likely the correct answer.

   • When one choice includes one or more of the other choices, it is often the correct answer.

   • When a choice includes the word *some* or *often,* it may be the correct answer.

   • If one of the choices is *All of the above,* make sure that at least two of the other choices seem correct.

   • If one of the choices is *None of the above,* make sure that none of the other choices seems correct.

An **open-ended test item** can take many forms. It might ask you to write a word or phrase to complete a sentence. You might be asked to create a chart, draw a map, or fill in a graphic organizer. Sometimes, you will be asked to write one or more paragraphs in response to a writing prompt. Use the following strategies when reading and answering open-ended items:

1. If the item includes directions, read them carefully. Take note of any steps required.

2. Look for key words and phrases in the item as you plan how you will respond. Does the item ask you to identify a cause-and-effect relationship or to compare and contrast two or more things? Are you supposed to provide a sequence of events or make a generalization? Does the item ask you to write an essay in which you state your point of view and then try to persuade others that your view is correct?

3. If you're going to be writing a paragraph or more, plan your answer. Jot down notes and a brief outline of what you want to say before you begin writing.

4. Focus your answer. Don't include everything you can think of, but be sure to include everything the item asks for.

5. If you're creating a chart or drawing a map, make sure your work is as clear as possible.

Functional Reading Test

DIRECTIONS *Study the following warranty information for a binocular. Then answer the questions that follow.*

READING STRATEGIES FOR ASSESSMENT

Identify significant details. Read the first paragraph carefully. Underline the conditions under which the warranty is valid. Circle what someone must do to have a defective instrument repaired or replaced.

Find the main idea. Underline the conditions that make the warranty invalid.

Notice exceptions and exclusions. If you own a Behold Extendable Binocular, what does the last line tell you?

ANSWER STRATEGIES

The key words in this question are *would be repaired*. Eliminate choices that the second paragraph says would make the warranty invalid or that are excluded from the protection of the warranty.

Check each choice against the conditions in the first paragraph. Which answer does not fall within the warranty's restrictions?

Read the choices carefully. If three of them express similar ideas, then look at the fourth or different answer more closely. In this case, three describe the company's willingness to repair or replace the binocular without question. What does the fourth choice suggest that the company will do?

Binocular Limited Warranty

Behold Binoculars*

This binocular is warranted to be free of defects in materials and workmanship for a period of **10 Years.** This warranty is for the benefit of the original retail purchaser only. During this warranty period Behold Binoculars and Optical Instruments will repair or replace, at Behold's option, any warranted instrument that proves to be defective provided it is returned postage-paid to Behold Warranty Repair, 21 Panorama, Vista Village, MN 21777. If your product is not registered, proof of purchase (such as a copy of the original invoice) is required.

This warranty does not apply if, in Behold's judgment, the instrument has been abused, mishandled, self-repaired, or modified, nor does it apply to normal wear and tear. This warranty gives you specific legal rights, and you may also have other rights, which vary from state to state. For further warranty service information, contact Customer Service, Behold Binoculars and Optical Instruments, P.O. Box 1815, Starlight, CA 92220; phone 800–555–1234.

* Behold Extendable Binoculars excluded.

---

1. Which of the following types of damage would be repaired under this warranty?
   - (A) the shattering of the lenses as a result of dropping the binocular
   - (B) the inability to focus the binocular after taking it apart and putting it back together again
   - (C) a crack in the central focusing wheel noticed soon after purchase
   - (D) a scratched lens on a Behold Extendable Binocular

2. Which of the following conditions would make the warranty invalid?
   - (E) the passage of eight years from date of purchase
   - (F) a different owner from the purchaser of the binocular
   - (G) prepaid shipment of the binocular to the repair center
   - (H) damage resulting from improper workmanship

3. What does the phrase at *Behold's option* mean?
   - (A) The company will replace or repair anything defective without questions.
   - (B) The company will automatically send a new binocular to replace the old.
   - (C) The company will decide whether to repair or replace the damaged parts.
   - (D) The company will give the customer the choice of having the binocular repaired or replaced.

Answers:
1.C, 2.F, 3.C

Functional Reading Test

DIRECTIONS *Study the prescription medicine label below. Circle the information that you think is the most important. Answer the multiple-choice questions that follow.*

Davis Pharmacy
1700 West Wilson
Chicago, IL 60640
800-555-1234

Dr. JUNE SUMMERS   05/11/08
RX: 576-00598
ROBERT HANSEN

PLAQUENIL 200 MG TABLETS
QTY: 90
Mfg: Watson
TAKE ONE TABLET BY MOUTH THREE TIMES DAILY
No Refills   Dr. Authorization Needed
KEEP OUT OF REACH OF CHILDREN
TAKE WITH FOOD OR MILK

---

1. How many milligrams of Plaquenil must Robert take daily?
   - (A) 200 mg
   - (B) 400 mg
   - (C) 600 mg
   - (D) 900 mg

2. How many days will this prescription last?
   - (E) 90 days
   - (F) 270 days
   - (G) 15 days
   - (H) 30 days

3. In order to follow the directions on the prescription, what should Robert do if he normally doesn't eat lunch?
   - (A) take two tablets at once either at breakfast or dinner
   - (B) take one tablet in the middle of the day with a glass of milk
   - (C) take only two tablets a day for a greater number of days
   - (D) take one tablet in the middle of the day with a glass of water

Revising-and-Editing Test

DIRECTIONS *Read the following paragraph carefully. Then answer the multiple-choice questions that follow. After answering the questions, read the material in the side columns to check your answer strategies.*

¹ There are many differences between the book and the movie version of *Father, Dancing*. ² The book has stronger characters, who's personalities are fully developed. ³ The director of the movie must of thought that having big-name actors would make up for weak characters. ⁴ The plot of the book is also more better than the movie's, because some scenes they leave out are important. ⁵ On the other hand, the movie has flashy special effects however, effects have less meaning than plot. ⁶ In my opinion, the book is more interesting than the movie, even though the movie was the most expensive production in the history of Hollywood.

ANSWER STRATEGIES

Possessive Pronouns A possessive pronoun is needed in sentence 2. Possessive pronouns are not spelled with apostrophes.

1. Which of the following is the correct spelling of *who's* in sentence 2?
   - (A) whos'
   - (B) whose
   - (C) whose'
   - (D) who's

Verb Tenses The word *of* is a preposition and does not belong in a verb phrase. It is sometimes used incorrectly to replace *have*.

2. What is the correct verb phrase in sentence 3?
   - (E) must think
   - (F) must of been thinking
   - (G) must have thought
   - (H) must thought

Comparative Adjectives *Good* is an irregular adjective. The comparative form is *better*, and the superlative is *best*.

3. In sentence 4, which of the following is the correct form of the comparative adjective?
   - (A) more better
   - (B) most better
   - (C) best
   - (D) better

Pronoun References Avoid unclear and inaccurate pronoun references by repeating the noun when necessary. Does the movie or the book leave out scenes?

4. What is the best way to rewrite the second part of sentence 4?
   - (E) because some scenes the movie leaves out are important
   - (F) because some scenes the book leaves out are important
   - (G) because some left-out scenes are important
   - (H) because some scenes are important that are left out

5. In sentence 5, what does the transitional phrase *On the other hand* suggest about sentences 4 and 5?

  (A) that their messages are similar

  (B) that their messages are different

  (C) that their messages are related as cause and effect

  (D) that their messages are related as main idea and supporting details

6. Which sentence in the paragraph is a run-on sentence?

  (E) sentence 3

  (F) sentence 4

  (G) sentence 5

  (H) sentence 6

Transitions Transitions show relationships between ideas. *On the other hand* signals a contrast or change.

Run-on Sentences A run-on is two or more complete thoughts joined without correct punctuation. Often the word *however* in the middle of a sentence without a preceding semicolon is a clue that the sentence is a run-on.

Revising-and-Editing Test

DIRECTIONS *Read the following paragraph carefully. As you read, circle each error that you find and identify the error in the side column—for example, write* misspelled word *or* not a complete sentence. *When you have finished, fill in the letter of the correct choice for each question that follows.*

¹ The gods odin in norse mythology and zeus in Greek mythology are very different from each other. ² Odin don't eat with the other gods and goddesses. ³ He sits quietly, and thinks about the advice of his two ravens, whose names are Thought and Memory. ⁴ Furthermore, Odin is willing to pursue wisdom even if he has to suffer. ⁵ When Odin learns that he will have to sacrifice one of his eyes to gain the knowledge he seeks, he makes it. ⁶ In your opinion, do you think that wisdom is worth such a price? ⁷ Zeus certainly wouldn't think so.

1. What is the correct capitalization in sentence 1?
   - (A) The Gods odin in Norse mythology and zeus in Greek mythology
   - (B) The gods Odin in norse mythology and Zeus in Greek mythology
   - (C) The gods Odin in Norse Mythology and Zeus in Greek Mythology
   - (D) The gods Odin in Norse mythology and Zeus in Greek mythology

2. What is the correct verb phrase in sentence 2?
   - (E) do not eat
   - (F) don't eats
   - (G) doesn't eat
   - (H) doesn't eats

3. What change, if any, should be made in sentence 3?
   - (A) change *Thought* and *Memory* to *thought* and *memory*
   - (B) change *quietly, and* to *quietly and*
   - (C) change *the advice of his two ravens* to *the advise of his two Ravens*
   - (D) no change

4. Which sentence in this paragraph is *not* a declarative sentence?
   - (E) sentence 2
   - (F) sentence 3
   - (G) sentence 4
   - (H) sentence 6

5. What is the best replacement for *it* in sentence 5?
   - (A) his goal
   - (B) the knowledge he seeks
   - (C) the sacrifice
   - (D) one of his eyes

6. What is the best way to rewrite sentence 6?

(E) In your opinion, do you believe wisdom is worth such a price?

(F) Do you, in your opinion, think that wisdom is worth such a price?

(G) Do you think that wisdom is worth such a price?

(H) Do you think, in your opinion, that wisdom is worth such a price?

7. On the basis of this paragraph's first and last sentences and main topic, what would you expect the main topic of the next paragraph to be?

(A) the knowledge Odin gains

(B) the Greek god Zeus

(C) Odin's lost eye

(D) all the gods of Greek mythology

Acknowledgments

UNIT 1

Random House, Inc.: "The School Play" by Gary Soto, from *Funny You Should Ask,* edited by David Gale. Copyright © 1992 by Gary Soto. Used by permission of Dell Publishing, a division of Random House, Inc.

Carus Publishing Company: "Through Children's Eyes" by Sandra Weber, adapted from *Cobblestone*, November 2002 issue "The California Trail." Copyright © 2002 by Carus Publishing Company. Published by Cobblestone Publishing, 30 Grove Street, Suite C, Peterborough, New Hampshire 03458. All rights reserved. Used by permission of Carus Publishing Company.

National Oregon/California Trail Center: "Trail Basics," from www.oregontrailcenter.org. Copyright © 2006 by the National Oregon/California Trail Center in Montpelier, Idaho. Reprinted by permission.

UNIT 2

Barry N. Malzberg: "Ghost of the Lagoon" by Armstrong Sperry, from *Children's Stories to Read or Tell.* Copyright © 1961 by Armstrong Sperry. Copyright © 1989 by the Estate of Armstrong Sperry. Reprinted by permission of Barry N. Malzberg.

National Geographic Society: Excerpt from "Great White Shark Attacks: Defanging the Myths" by Jennifer Hile, from www.NationalGeographic.com, January 23, 2004. Copyright © 2004 by National Geographic. Reprinted by permission of National Geographic Society.

UNIT 3

Curtis Brown, Ltd.: *Nadia the Willful* by Sue Alexander, first published by Alfred A. Knopf. Copyright © 1983 by Sue Alexander. Reprinted by permission of Curtis Brown, Ltd.

Thirteen/WNET New York: Excerpt from "Sahara," from *Africa, a Special Presentation of Nature* (2002), from www.pbs.org. Copyright © 2002 by the Educational Broadcasting Corporation. Reprinted courtesy of Thirteen/WNET New York.

Carus Publishing Company: "Meeting the Blue People of the Desert" by Lesley Reed, adapted from *Appleseeds*, April 2002 issue Exploring the Sahara. Copyright © 2002 by Cobblestone Publishing, 30 Grove Street, Suite C, Peterborough, New Hampshire 03458. All rights reserved. Used by permission of Carus Publishing Company.

UNIT 4

Ruth Cohen, Inc.: "The All-American Slurp" by Lensey Namioka, from *Visions: Nineteen Short Stories by Outstanding Writers for Young Adults,* edited by Donald R. Gallo. Copyright © 1987 by Lensey Namioka. Reprinted by permission of Lensey Namioka. All rights reserved.

San Francisco Chronicle: "Potstickers" by Bill Daley, from the *San Francisco Chronicle*, from http://sfgate.com, November 5, 2003. Copyright © 2003 by the San Francisco Chronicle. Reprinted by permission of the San Francisco Chronicle.

UNIT 5A

Carus Publishing Company: "Life Fore and Aft on a Sailing Ship" by Lucie Germer, adapted from *Cobblestone*, April 1988 issue The Seafaring Life. Copyright © 1988 by Cobblestone Publishing, 30 Grove Street, Suite C, Peterborough, New Hampshire 03458. All rights reserved. Used by permission of Carus Publishing Company.

UNIT 5B

Scott Treimel NY: "People" from *All That Sunlight* by Charlotte Zolotow. Copyright © 1967 by Charlotte Zolotow, copyright renewed 1995. Used by permission of Scott Treimel NY.

Random House, Inc.: Excerpt from "April Rain Song," from *The Collected Poems of Langston Hughes* by Langston Hughes, edited by Arnold Rampersad with David Roessel, Associate Editor. Copyright © 1994 by the Estate of Langston Hughes. Used by permission of Alfred A. Knopf, a division of Random House, Inc.

Simon & Schuster: "Something Told the Wild Geese" from *Poems* by Rachel Field. Copyright © 1934 by Macmillan Publishing Company; copyright renewed 1962 by Arthur S. Pederson. Reprinted with the permission of Atheneum Books for Young Readers, an imprint of Simon & Schuster Children's Publishing Division.

Scott Treimel NY: "Change" from *River Winding* by Charlotte Zolotow. Copyright © 1970 by Charlotte Zolotow. Used by permission of Scott Treimel NY.

Friends of the Great Plains Nature Center: Excerpt from "Canada Goose" by Jim Mason, from www.gnpc.org. Copyright © by Friends of the Great Plains Nature Center. Reprinted by permission of the Great Plains Nature Center.

UNIT 6

Penguin Group (USA) Inc.: "The Crane Maiden," from *Mysterious Tales of Japan* by Rafe Martin. Text copyright © 1996 by Rafe Martin. Used by permission of G. P. Putnam's Sons, a Division of Penguin Young Readers Group, a Member of Penguin Group (USA) Inc., 345 Hudson Street, New York, NY 10014. All rights reserved.

Judith Ortiz Cofer: "Aunty Misery" retold by Judith Ortiz Cofer, from *Third World: Pig Iron No. 15*. Copyright © Judith Ortiz Cofer. Reprinted by permission of Judith Ortiz Cofer (www.english.uga.edu/~jcofer).

UNIT 7

Helen Keller Services for the Blind: Excerpt from "Biography of Helen Keller," from www.helenkeller.org. Copyright © Helen Keller Services for the Blind. Reprinted by permission of Helen Keller Services for the Blind.

Sense: Excerpt from "How do people who are deafblind communicate?" from www.sense.org. Copyright © Sense.org. Reprinted by permission of Sense, the National Deafblind and Rubella Association.

UNIT 8A

National Geographic Society: Excerpt from "SuperCroc" by Peter Winkler, from *National Geographic for Kids,* March 2002. Copyright © 2002 by National Geographic. Reprinted by permission of National Geographic Society.

Carus Publishing Company: "Tracking the Dinosauria Family Tree: An Interview with Dino Hunter Paul Sereno" by Michelle Laliberte, adapted from *Odyssey,* September 2000 issue "What is a Dinosaur?" Copyright © 2000 by Cobblestone Publishing, 30 Grove Street, Suite C, Peterborough, New Hampshire 03458. All rights reserved. Used by permission of Carus Publishing Company.

National Geographic Society: Excerpt from "'Godzilla' Fossils Reveals Real-Life Sea Monster" by Stefan Lovgren, from *National Geographic Kids News,* November 22, 2005. Copyright © 2005 by National Geographic. Reprinted by permission of National Geographic Society.

UNIT 8B

Science News For Kids: Excerpts from "The Violent Side of Video Games" and "What Video Games Can Teach Us" by Emily Sohn, from *Science News* for Kids (www.sciencenewsforkids.org). Copyright © 2004 by *Science News* for Kids. Reprinted by permission of *Science News* for Kids.

New York Times: Excerpt from "P.E. Classes Turn to Video Game That Works Legs" by Seth Schiesel, from the *New York Times,* National Section, 4/30/2007 Issue, page A-1. Copyright © 2007 by the New York Times. Reprinted by permission of the New York Times.

FRONT PAGES

ix Tree Goddess (1994), Jerry N. Uelsmann. © Jerry N. Uelsmann; **x** © Insy Shah/Gulfimages/Getty Images; **xiii** © Gary Godby/ShutterStock; **xiii–xvi** © Damien Dewitte/ShutterStock; **xix** © Insy Shah/Gulfimages/Getty Images; **xx** © David Kay/ShutterStock; **xx–xxi** © Damien Dewitte/ShutterStock; **xxi** © Vladimir Korostyshevskiy/ShutterStock; **xxii** © Govert Nieuwland/ShutterStock.

UNIT 1

2 © Adam Taylor/Getty Images; **3** © Jacob/ShutterStock; **5** © AudreyTTL/ShutterStock; **6–11** © Zimmytws/ShutterStock; **14** © Adam Taylor/Getty Images; **15, 17** Library of Congress, Prints and Photographs Division.

UNIT 2

24 © Steve Mason/Digital Vision/Alamy Ltd.; **27** © BioWorkZ/ShutterStock; **28–35** © Jupiterimages Corporation; **38** © Steve Mason/Digital Vision/Alamy Ltd.; **39** © iLexx/ShutterStock; **40–41** *background* © Kato Inowe/ShutterStock; *center* © Stephen Sweet/ShutterStock; **40** © Hemera Technologies/Jupiterimages Corporation; **42** © Digital Vision/PunchStock; **43** *top* © Petr Masek/ShutterStock; *bottom* © Jupiterimages Corporation; **44** NOAA.

UNIT 3

48 © Insy Shah/Gulfimages/Getty Images; **51** *top* © Damien Dewitte/ShutterStock; *bottom* © Gary Godby/ShutterStock; **52–57** © Damien Dewitte/ShutterStock; **59** © Insy Shah/Gulfimages/Getty Images; **60** © David Kay/ShutterStock; **60–61** © Damien Dewitte/ShutterStock; **61** © Vladimir Korostyshevskiy/ShutterStock; **62–63** © Govert Nieuwland/ShutterStock; **63** © Nola Rin/ShutterStock; **64** *top* © Christopher Gannon/Alamy Ltd.; *bottom* © Dainis Derics/ShutterStock; **65** © Egmont Strigl /imagebroker/Alamy Ltd.

UNIT 4

68 © Steve Hamblin/Alamy Ltd.; **71** © Jupiterimages Corporation; **84** © Steve Hamblin/Alamy Ltd.; **86** © Amihays/ShutterStock; **89** © Yang Xiaofeng/ShutterStock.

UNIT 5A

94 © Ryan McVay/Digital Vision/Getty Images; **98–99** © Anna Dickie/ShutterStock; **102** © Ryan McVay/Digital Vision/Getty Images; **103** Library of Congress, Prints and Photographs Division; © Jupiterimages Corporation; **105** © Stephen Coburn/ShutterStock; **106** Library of Congress, Prints and Photographs Division; **107** © Albert Michael Cutri/ShutterStock.

UNIT 5B

110 © Photodisc/PunchStock; **114** © John Farrall/Getty Images; **117** © Photodisc/PunchStock; **118** © Purestock/Getty Images; **119** © John Czenke/ShutterStock; **120** *top left* © Jupiterimages Corporation; *top right* © Bruce MacQueen/ShutterStock; *bottom* © Darryl Brooks/ShutterStock; **123** *top* © Jon Sturgeon/ShutterStock; *bottom* © Alan Schein/Alamy.